D0801735

THE OXFORD LIBRARY OF FRENCH CLASSICS

General Editor: Robert Baldick

VICTOR HUGO

THINGS SEEN

VICTOR HUGO

THINGS SEEN

Selected, Translated, and Edited
by
DAVID KIMBER

Introduced by
JOANNA RICHARDSON

London
OXFORD UNIVERSITY PRESS
NEW YORK   TORONTO
1964

Oxford University Press, Amen House, London E.C.4.

GLASGOW NEW YORK TORONTO MELBOURNE WELLINGTON
BOMBAY CALCUTTA MADRAS KARACHI LAHORE DACCA
CAPE TOWN SALISBURY NAIROBI IBADAN ACCRA
KUALA LUMPUR HONG KONG

Printed in Great Britain
by Richard Clay and Company Ltd.,
Bungay, Suffolk

84
H87
WTh

CONTENTS

62792

INTRODUCTION

VICTOR HUGO died on 22 May 1885, just after he had entered his eighty-fourth year. His funeral was an apotheosis; the works he left were awesome in quantity. The standard edition of his *Complete Works* was published over nearly half a century, from 1904 to 1952; it filled forty-five massive volumes. The year 1913 saw the publication of two volumes of *Things Seen*: Hugo's scattered notes on men and events.

Paul Meurice, one of Hugo's satellites and editors, had published a first selection of *Things Seen* only two years after the poet's death, and from the countless manuscripts he had chosen fragments covering the years 1838 to 1875. The sequel had appeared in 1900, but even so there remained enough unpublished material for a third volume. The 1913 edition included the published work and a certain amount of new material, all arranged in chronological order. Hugo's comment on Talleyrand's *hôtel* might now have been applied to his own work: 'In this palace, like a spider in its web, he had attracted and caught in turn . . . all the gilded and glittering flies which buzzed through the history of the last forty years.'

Things Seen is indeed an extraordinary close-up of history; and few others would have had the opportunities, let alone the skill, to write it. But, as a peer of France, an exile, a Deputy, a Senator, Hugo entered many political doors in his lifetime; and as the pre-eminent and most versatile poet of his age, he was intimate with the world of the arts. He was not only a poet and dramatist, he sometimes turned his hand to drawing and water-colour painting; his eye was trained to take in the vivid, essential dramatic detail. The man and the opportunities met. This is the result.

Here, to begin with, as Hugo heard it from an eye-witness as late as 1840, is an account of the execution of Louis XVI. How vividly Hugo records the scene: the executioners wearing three-cornered hats with enormous tricolour cockades, and Sanson even keeping on his *tricorne* as he displays the King's head to the mob. Two priests are laughing aloud at the sight of the fat and headless body; and there, pushing his way through the crowd, seeking oblivion, is the Abbé Edgeworth, who had been moved on the scaffold to bid the King a classic farewell: 'Son of St. Louis, ascend to Heaven!'

Hugo's father was one of Napoleon's generals and Hugo worshipped the Emperor all his life; his hero bulks large in these pages. We follow Hugo into the busy workshop where Napoleon's coffin is being made, we stand beside him on the day that the Emperor's remains are brought home to Paris; and, jostled by the gaping crowds and the itinerant tobacco-sellers peddling their wares, we see the funeral carriage in all its extravagant detail.

Hugo not only hears the last echoes of the great Revolution of 1789. He follows all the French revolutions of the nineteenth century. There is the revolution of 1830, which puts an end to the Bourbon restoration, and brings the abdication of Charles X and the proclamation of Louis-Philippe. There is the revolution of 1848, when Louis-Philippe, in his turn, is overthrown, and Louis-Napoleon, the Emperor's nephew, becomes Prince-President of the Republic. Four years later, in 1852, comes the Second Empire. In 1870 the Empire falls.

It is all reflected in *Things Seen*: in a meeting with Louis-Philippe, who gives his candid comments on William IV; in a meeting with Louis-Napoleon, who will shortly force the poet to flee the country, and who will be pilloried in *Napoléon le Petit*. Hugo reported few *Things Seen* in the nineteen years of his exile; but on 5 September 1870, the second day of the Third Republic, he returned to Paris; and we have the laconic notes he made during the Siege. The price of elephant meat, he tells us, rose to 40 francs a pound on 13 January 1871; a sack of onions cost 800 francs. Here are the details that make history real.

Hugo reminds us constantly, if we need reminding, that he has an unerring eye for dramatic detail. His picture of

Balzac, purple-faced, on his death-bed in the Avenue Fortunée, is likely to remain in the memory. So is his recollection of the shrunken, dead Chateaubriand in an untidy room in the Rue du Bac, in the summer of 1848, with the forty-eight notebooks of his memoirs in a wooden case at his feet. It is a pathetic final likeness of the father of Romanticism.

Things Seen is nothing if not a Romantic work. It shows a vivid interest in the exotic; it shows a certain sympathy for the humble (like the maid imprisoned for stealing six pairs of stockings). It is also dark with Gothic horror and Gothic gloom. Hugo indulges to the full in his love of the macabre: in the graphic details of Balzac's decomposition, of the blade which killed Louis XVI. He is fascinated by the torture-chamber at the Conciergerie, the equipment of the condemned cell, the anecdotes of Sanson, the executioner; and captivated by the thought that when Talleyrand's body was sealed in its coffin, his valet found his brains left on a table, and promptly dropped them in the nearest gutter.

Yet perhaps it would be unfair to say that Hugo revels in the gruesome for its own sake. The thought of Talleyrand's valet leads him to reflect on the humiliation of the great, and on death the leveller. It recalls Hamlet in the churchyard at Elsinore: 'Alexander died, Alexander was buried, Alexander returneth into dust . . . and why of that loam whereto he was converted might they not stop a beer-barrel?' Art, as Shake-speare knew, must reflect the whole of existence; and Hugo had long ago professed, in his literary creed, the *Préface de Cromwell*, his belief that the grotesque, like the sublime, was essential to modern art. Rubens understood the need for the grotesque when he introduced the figure of a Court dwarf in his paintings of pomp and circumstance. Hugo created the Hunchback of Notre Dame. For him, and for his followers, the grotesque existed as much as the sublime. No novel could be devised, no drama could be written, which did not take them both into account.

Things Seen reflects more than Hugo's own acceptance of the grotesque. We see his sense of the visual in his graphic account of Court functions in the days of Louis-Philippe. We catch the glitter of the red and green fairy-lights at the Duc de Montpensier's fête, the glow of the Chinese lanterns, the glint of the illuminations on the suits of armour hung for decoration on the trees. Turning to the theatre, Hugo offers us a report on Mademoiselle Mars's funeral and a pathetic portrait of Mademoiselle George, once Napoleon's mistress, massive and unemployed in her old age. And we are given thumbnail sketches of Dumas, Sainte-Beuve, Vigny, and Musset at a dinner-party. The whole book, in fact, is a vivid panorama of the celebrities of the nineteenth century.

And among these celebrities, by implication, moves Hugo: handsome, successful, worshipped, humourless and—one need hardly add—quite intolerably conceited. Even in these notes, which he may not have meant for publication, he shows his inordinate admiration of himself. And nothing, alas, is more characteristically Hugolian than the notes he writes on the death of his wife.

How could he show any egotism at that moment? With Hugo, we can ask the question. He carves his initials, VH, on the lead coffin over her head: assuming that this alone is glorification. Adèle Hugo died during the exile; and as Hugo steps from the train that is taking her coffin to the French frontier, he does not record his grief: he records instead the crowd of sympathizers who greet him on the platform. He stays at a private house that night, and finds an illustrated copy of *Les Misérables* in his room; he cannot resist the temptation to autograph it: 'I wrote my name and the date in it, leaving my host this memento.' Victor Hugo, as Cocteau said, was a madman who thought he was Victor Hugo.

Hugo passed through many vicissitudes in his political life; but his patriotism (if over-dramatized) remained sincere and intense. And just as his contemporary, Tennyson, dreamed of 'the parliament of man, the federation of the world', so Hugo looked beyond patriotism to a wider international order. In *La Légende des Siècles*, at the end of *Plein Ciel*, he sees the miraculous airborne vessel rising from earth to heaven, symbolizing human progress, and symbolizing too the unity of the nations, the divine inspiration and freedom of man. In one of the final entries in his diary, written down on 25 February 1884, a year before his death, he dreamed he was addressing the Senate; and the words he spoke in his dream, and duly recorded, were a prose version of those verses in *Plein Ciel*: 'A free France wants the nations to be free. What France wants, what she demands, she will obtain. And from the union of freedoms, the brotherhood of people, will be born the sympathy of minds, the germ of that boundless future in which universal life will begin for the human race.'

When the early volumes of *Things Seen* appeared, they were greeted ecstatically. Édouard Thierry wrote in the *Moniteur universel*: 'He does not seek colour as much as lucidity. He is sincere. He enlarges the theme, when the theme is large; but he is never excessive, never exaggerates. The poet is faithful to his family traditions and to the enthusiasm of his youth.' One critic declared: 'Victor Hugo is Saint-Simon with a heart.' Another called him 'a reporter of genius'. And another wrote: 'He comes and goes, he stops and lingers, hovers round, and muses; suddenly he goes up to a window and opens it. Do you think it looks on to a garden? It looks on to infinity.'

The style of *Things Seen* is certainly simple, graphic, direct, as befits a journalist. There are no stylistic tricks, except the antithesis which is not so much a trick of speech as part of Hugo's philosophy. Good and evil, light and darkness, strong and weak, grotesque and beautiful: the dramatization of contrasts is fundamental to Hugo's work. But, as Édouard Thierry observed, in general, in *Things Seen*, Hugo is seeking clarity. There is a refreshing lack of bombast and affectation. And he does write with the sharp touch of Saint-Simon (but more heart than Saint-Simon) when he describes injustice and indignity.

Is Hugo 'a reporter of genius'? Do we merely share the uncritical adulation of contemporaries if we apply the word to these erratic notes? Hugo imposed no rules on himself when he jotted down these impressions. He wrote a good many of them before he went into exile, he wrote very few in the nineteen years he was away from France, and he did not plan them as a balanced whole. He did not try to charm or infuriate, but simply wrote as and when he felt inclined.

And this naturalness is one of the chief distinctions of the book. When a great poet is a witness of great men and events, he may give us a true and vivid reflection of history; when he jots down his observations without thought of publication, he is likely to tell us a good deal about himself. We may relate random passages in *Things Seen* to finished poems; we may, for example, compare Hugo's comments on the Emperor's reburial with *Le Retour des Cendres de Napoléon*. It is always instructive to compare the casual jotting with the final version.

But perhaps *Things Seen* is best considered as a web into which Hugo has drawn 'all the gilded and glittering flies' of contemporary history. It is a far slighter work than the Goncourt *Journal*; it lacks the Goncourts' malice and wit, and it cannot for a moment compete with the *Journal* as a record of the social and intellectual scene. But for all its limitations, and whether or not it opens a window on to infinity, *Things Seen* remains one of the few examples in French literature of sporadic observations that are literary works in their own right. These random jottings have become a classic.

JOANNA RICHARDSON

AT REIMS

1825–1838

It was at Reims that I heard the name of Shakespeare for the first time. It was uttered by Charles Nodier. That was in 1825, during the coronation of Charles X.

Nobody at that time spoke of Shakespeare really seriously. Voltaire's ridicule of him was law. Madame de Staël, that noble mind, had adopted Germany, the great land of Kant, Schiller, and Beethoven. Ducis was at the height of his triumph; he and Delille sat side by side in academic glory, which is something not unlike theatrical glory. Ducis had succeeded in doing something with Shakespeare; he had made him possible; he had extracted 'some tragedies' from him; Ducis gave the impression of being a man who could chisel an Apollo out of Moloch. It was the time when Iago was called Pézare; Horatio, Norceste; and Desdemona, Hédelmone. A charming and very witty woman, the Duchesse de Duras, said: 'Desdemona? What an ugly name!' Talma, Prince of Denmark, in a lilac satin tunic trimmed with fur, used to exclaim: 'Avaunt, dread spectre!' The poor ghost, in fact, was only tolerated in the wings. If it had ventured to put in the slightest appearance Monsieur Évariste Dumoulin would have given it a severe scolding. Some Genin or other would have hurled at it the first tag he could lay his hand on— a line from Boileau: *L'esprit n'est point ému de ce qu'il ne croit pas.* It was replaced on the stage by an 'urn' which Talma carried under his arm. A ghost is ridiculous; 'ashes' are all right. Do we not talk about the 'ashes' of Napoleon nowadays? Is not the translation of the coffin from St. Helena to the Invalides referred to as 'the return of the ashes'? As for the witches of *Macbeth*, they were rigorously barred. The porter at the Théâtre-Français had his orders. They would have been received with their own brooms.

I am mistaken, however, in saying that I did not know Shakespeare. I knew him as everybody else did, not having read him, and treating him with ridicule. My childhood began, as everybody's childhood begins, with prejudices. Man finds prejudices beside his cradle, puts them from him a little in the course of his life, and often, alas, takes to them again in his old age.

During this journey in 1825 Charles Nodier and I spent our time telling each other the Gothic tales and romances which have taken root in Reims. Our memories, and sometimes our imaginations, combined. Each of us contributed his own legend. Reims is one of the most improbable towns in the geography of story. Pagan lords have lived there, one of whom gave his daughter as a dowry the strips of land in Borysthenes called the 'race-courses of Achilles'. The Duc de Guyenne, in the fabliaux, passes through Reims on his way to besiege Babylon; Babylon moreover, which is very worthy of Reims, is the capital of Admiral Gaudissius. It is at Reims that the deputation sent by the Locri Ozolae to Apollonius of Tyana, 'high priest of Bellona', 'disembarks'. In connexion with this disembarkation we had an argument about the Locri Ozolae. These people, according to Nodier, were called the Fetidae because they were half monkeys; according to myself, because they inhabited the marshes of Phocis. We reconstructed on the spot the tradition of St. Remigius and his adventures with the fairy Mazelane. The Champagne country is rich in tales. Nearly all the old Gallic fables originated there. Reims is the land of Chimeras. It is perhaps for that reason that kings were crowned there.

Legends are so natural to this place, find such good soil there, that they promptly started to germinate on the very coronation of Charles X. The Duke of Northumberland, England's representative at the coronation, was reputed to be fabulously wealthy. Wealthy and English, how could he help being in fashion? The English, at that period, enjoyed in France all the popularity it is possible to have outside the common people. They were liked in certain drawing-rooms because of Waterloo, which was still fairly recent, and to Anglicize the French language was the done thing in the best circles. Lord Northumberland, therefore, long before his arrival, was popular and legendary at Reims.

A coronation was a godsend for Reims. A flood of rich people inundated the city. It was the Nile which was passing. Landlords rubbed their hands with glee.

There was at Reims in those days, and there probably still is today, at the corner of the street leading into the square, a fairly big house with a carriage entrance and a balcony, built of stone in the royal style of Louis XIV, and facing the cathedral. About this house and Lord Northumberland the following story was told:

In January 1825 the balcony of the house bore the notice 'House for Sale'. Suddenly the *Moniteur* announced that the coronation of Charles X would take place at Reims in the spring. There was tremendous rejoicing in the city. Notices of rooms to let were promptly posted up everywhere. The meanest room was destined to bring in at least sixty francs a day. One morning a man of irreproachable appearance, in a black coat with a white cravat, an Englishman speaking broken French, presented himself at the house for sale in the square. He asked to see the proprietor, who looked him up and down.

'You wish to sell your house?' asked the Englishman.

'Yes.'

'How much?'

'Ten thousand francs.'

'But I don't want to buy it.'

'Then what do you want?'

'Just to hire it.'

'That's different. For a year?'

'No.'

'For six months?'

'No. I should like to hire it for three days.'

'Ah!'

'How much will you charge?'

'Thirty thousand francs.'

The gentleman was Lord Northumberland's steward, who was looking for a lodging for his master during the coronation celebrations. The proprietor had scented the Englishman and guessed at the steward. The house was satisfactory, and the proprietor stood firm; faced with a Champenois the Englishman, being only a Norman, gave way; the duke paid the 30,000 francs, and spent three days in the house at the rate of 400 francs an hour.

Nodier and I were two hunters. When we travelled together, as we occasionally did, we went hunting, he in search of rare books, I in search of old buildings. He would go into ecstacies over a *Cymbalum Mundi* with margins, and I over a crude portal. We had attributed a devil to each other. He used to say to me: 'You are possessed of the demon Ogive.' 'And you,' I would say to him, 'of the demon Elzevir.'

At Soissons, while I was exploring Saint-Jean-des-Vignes, he had discovered, in a suburb, a ragpicker. The ragpicker's basket is the hyphen between rags and paper, and the ragpicker is the hyphen between the beggar and the philosopher. Nodier, who gave to the poor, and sometimes to philosophers, had entered the ragpicker's house. The ragpicker had turned out to be a tradesman. He sold books. Among these books Nodier noticed a fairly thick volume of six or eight hundred pages, printed in Spanish, two columns to a page, badly damaged by worms, and with nothing left of the binding except the spine. The ragpicker, asked what he wanted for it, replied, trembling in case the price should be refused: 'Five francs,' which Nodier paid, also trembling, but with joy. This book was the *Romancero* complete. There are only three copies of this complete edition now in existence. One of these was sold a few years ago for 7,500 francs. Moreover, the worms are vying with each other in eating up these three remaining copies. The peoples of this earth, with princes to support, have better things to do than spend their money to preserve for new editions the legacies of the human mind, and the *Romancero*, being merely an Iliad, has not been reprinted.

During the three days of the coronation there were great crowds in the streets of Reims, at the Archbishop's palace, and in the walks along the Vesdre, trying to catch a glimpse of Charles X. I said to Charles Nodier: 'Let us go and see His Majesty the Cathedral.'

Reims is a proverb in Gothic Christian art. One speaks of the nave of Amiens, the spires of Chartres, the façade of Reims. A month before the coronation of Charles X a swarm of masons, perched on ladders and clinging to knotted ropes, spent a whole week smashing with hammers every piece of sculpture on the façade which jutted out, for fear some stone might come away from one of these reliefs and fall on the King's head. The debris littered the pavement and was swept up. For a long time I had in my possession a head of Christ which fell in this way. It was stolen from me in 1851. This head was unfortunate; broken by a king, it was lost by an outlaw.

Nodier was an admirable antiquary, and we explored the cathedral from top to bottom, encumbered though it was with scaffolding, painted scenery, and stage scenery. The nave being only of stone, they had hidden it inside with an edifice of cardboard, doubtless because the latter bore a greater resemblance to the monarchy of that time. For the coronation of the King of France they had built a theatre inside the church; so that it has since been related, with perfect accuracy, that on arriving at the entrance I asked the bodyguard on duty: 'Where is my box?'

This cathedral of Reims is beautiful above all other cathedrals. On the façade are kings; on the apsis, people being tortured by executioners. Coronation of kings with an accompaniment of victims. The façade is one of the most magnificent

B

symphonies ever sung by that music which is architecture. You dream for a long time before this oratorio. Looking up from the square you see at a dizzy height, at the base of the two towers, a row of huge statues representing the kings of France. In their hands they hold the sceptre, the sword, the hand of justice, and the glove, and on their heads are the antique open crowns with broad fleurons. It is superb and awe-inspiring. You push open the bell-ringer's door, climb the spiral staircase, 'the screw of St. Giles', to the towers, to the lofty regions of prayer; you look down and the statues are below you. The row of kings is deep in the abyss. You hear the whispering of the enormous bells, which vibrate at the kiss of the gentle breezes of heaven.

One day I looked down from the top of the tower through an embrasure. The whole façade fell sheer below me. I noticed in the depths, not very far away, on top of a long stone upright support fastened to the wall, and whose shape I could not distinguish, foreshortened as it was by its position, a sort of round basin. Rain-water had collected in it and formed a narrow mirror at the bottom; a tuft of grass had grown there with some flowers, and a swallow had nested there. In a space only two feet in diameter there was a lake, a garden, and a dwelling—a birds' paradise. When I looked down, the swallow was giving water to her brood. Round the upper edge of the basin were what looked like crenellations, and betweeen these the swallow had built her nest. I examined these crenellations; they were in the form of fleurs-de-lis. The support was a statue. This happy little world was the stone crown of an old king.

And if God were asked: 'Of what use was this Lothario, this Philip, this Charles, this Louis, this emperor, this king?' God might reply: 'He had this statue made and lodged this swallow.'

The coronation was duly held. This is not the place to describe it. Besides, my recollections of that ceremony of 27

May 1825 have been recounted elsewhere by another, more ably than I could. Suffice it to say that it was a radiant day. God seemed to have given his assent to the fête. The long clear windows—for there are no longer any stained-glass windows at Reims—let dazzling daylight into the cathedral. All the light of May was in the church. The Archbishop was covered with gilding and the altar with rays. Marshal de Lauriston, Minister of the King's household, was delighted with the sunshine. He came and went, bustling around and talking in low tones with Lecointe and Hittorf, the architects. The fine morning provided an opportunity to say 'the sun of the coronation', as one used to say 'the sun of Austerlitz'. And in the resplendent light a profusion of lamps and tapers found means to glow.

There was one moment when Charles X, attired in a cherry-coloured satin simar striped with gold, lay down at full length at the Archbishop's feet. The peers of France on the right, embroidered with gold, beplumed in the Henri IV style, and clad in long cloaks of velvet and ermine, and the Deputies on the left, in dress-coats of blue cloth with silver fleurs-de-lis on the collars, looked on.

All the forms of chance were represented there to some extent: the Papal blessing by the cardinals, some of whom had witnessed the coronation of Napoleon; victory by the marshals; heredity by the dauphin, the Duc d'Angoulême; happiness by Monsieur de Talleyrand, lame but active; the rising and falling of stocks by Monsieur de Villèle; joy by the birds which were released and flew away; and the knaves in a pack of playing-cards by the four heralds at arms.

A vast carpet embroidered with fleurs-de-lis made expressly for this occasion, and called 'the coronation carpet', covered the old flagstones from one end of the cathedral to the other and concealed the tombstones in the pavement. A dense, luminous cloud of incense filled the nave. The birds which had been set at liberty flew frantically about in this cloud.

The King changed his costume six or seven times. The first prince of the blood, Louis-Philippe, Duc d'Orléans, helped him. The Duc de Bordeaux was five years old, and was in one of the galleries.

The pew in which Nodier and I were sitting adjoined those of the Deputies. In the middle of the ceremony, about the time the King prostrated himself at the feet of the Archbishop, a Deputy for the Doubs department, called Monsieur Hémonin, turned towards Nodier, who was close to him, and, putting his finger to his lips to indicate that he did not wish to disturb the Archbishop's orisons, slipped something into my friend's hand. This something was a book. Nodier took it and opened it.

'What is it?' I whispered.

'Nothing very valuable,' he replied. 'An old volume of Shakespeare, in the Glasgow edition.'

One of the tapestries from the treasurehouse of the cathedral, hanging exactly opposite us, represented a not very historic interview between John Lackland and Philip Augustus. Nodier glanced through the book for a few minutes, then pointed to the tapestry.

'You see that tapestry?'

'Yes.'

'Do you know what it represents?'

'No.'

'John Lackland.'

'Well, what of it?'

'John Lackland is in this book too.'

The volume, which was bound in sheepskin and worn at the corners, was in fact a copy of *King John*.

Monsieur Hémonin turned to Nodier and said: 'I paid six sous for it.'

In the evening of the coronation the Duke of Northumberland gave a ball. It was a fairylike spectacle. This Arabian Nights envoy brought one of those nights to Reims. Every woman found a diamond in her bouquet.

I could not dance. Nodier had not danced since he was sixteen, when an ecstatic great-aunt had congratulated him on his dancing in these terms: 'You are sweet. You dance like a darling!' We did not go to Lord Northumberland's ball.

'What shall we do tonight?' I asked Nodier.

He showed me his odd volume and said:

'Let us read this.'

We read.

That is to say, Nodier read. He knew English (without being able to speak it, I believe) well enough to make it out. He read aloud, and translated as he read. At intervals, while he rested, I took the other book wrested from the ragpicker of Soissons, and read passages from the *Romancero*. Like Nodier, I translated as I read. We compared the English book with the Castilian book; we confronted the dramatic with the epic. Nodier stood up for Shakespeare, whom he could read in English, and I for the *Romancero*, which I could read in Spanish. We brought face to face, he the bastard Faulconbridge, I the bastard Mudarra. And little by little, by contradicting each other, we convinced each other, and Nodier became filled with enthusiasm for the *Romancero*, and I with admiration for Shakespeare.

Meanwhile listeners had arrived. One passes the evening as best one can in a provincial town on a coronation day when one doesn't go to the ball. We ended up by forming quite a little club. There was an academician, Monsieur Roger; a man of letters, Monsieur d'Eckstein; Monsieur de Marcellus, a friend and country neighbour of my father's, who poked fun at his royalism and mine; the good old Marquis d'Herbouville, and Monsieur Hémonin, the donor of the book which had cost six sous.

'It isn't worth the money!' exclaimed Monsieur Roger.

The conversation turned into a debate. Judgement was passed on *King John*. Monsieur de Marcellus declared that the assassination of Arthur was improbable. It was pointed out to him that it was a historical fact. It was only with difficulty that he became reconciled to it. For kings to kill one another was impossible. To Monsieur de Marcellus's mind the murder-

ing of kings began on 21 January 1793. Regicide was synony-
mous with '93. To kill a king was an unheard-of thing of
which only the 'populace' were capable. No king except Louis
XVI had ever been violently put to death. However, he reluct-
antly admitted the case of Charles I. There too he saw the
hand of the populace. All the rest was demagogic falsehood
and calumny.

Although as good a royalist as he, I ventured to suggest that
the sixteenth century had existed, and that it was the period
when the Jesuits had clearly propounded the question of
'bleeding the basilic vein', that is to say of cases in which the
King ought to be killed, a question which, once brought forward, met with such success that it led to two kings, Henri III
and Henri IV, being stabbed, and a Jesuit, Father Guignard,
being hanged.

Then we went on to the details of the drama, the situations,
the scenes, and the characters. Nodier pointed out that Faulconbridge is the same person referred to by Mathieu Pâris as
Falcasius de Trente, bastard of Richard Coeur de Lion. Baron
d'Eckstein, in support of this, reminded his hearers that,
according to Holinshed, Faulconbridge, or Falcasius, killed the
Vicomte de Limoges to avenge his father Richard who had
been mortally wounded at the seige of Chaluz; and that this
castle of Chaluz being the property of the Vicomte de Limoges,
it was only right that the Vicomte, although absent, should
be made to answer with his head for the falling of an arrow or
a stone from the castle on the King. Monsieur Roger laughed
at the cry of 'Austria Limoges' in the play and at Shakespeare's
confusing the Vicomte de Limoges with the Duke of Austria.
Monsieur Roger obtained a great success and his laughter
settled the matter.

The discussion having taken this turn, I said nothing more.
This revelation of Shakespeare had moved me. I found him
impressive. *King John* is not a masterpiece, but certain scenes
are lofty and powerful, and in the motherhood of Constance
there are bursts of genius.

The two books, open and reversed, remained lying on the

table. The company stopped reading in order to laugh. Nodier
finally fell silent like myself. We were beaten. After a last
burst of laughter the gathering broke up. Nodier and I remained alone and pensive, thinking of the great works which
are unappreciated, and amazed that the intellectual education
of the civilized peoples, and even our own, his and mine,
had advanced no further than this.

At last Nodier broke the silence. I can remember his smile
to this day. He said:

'They know nothing about the *Romancero*!'

I replied:

'And they poke fun at Shakespeare!'

Thirteen years later chance took me back to Reims.

It was on 28 August 1838. It will be seen further on why this
date impressed itself on my memory.

I was returning from Vouziers. I saw the two towers of
Reims on the horizon and felt an urge to visit the cathedral
again. I therefore made for Reims.

On arriving in the cathedral square, I saw a gun drawn
up near the portal and beside it gunners with lighted fuses
in their hands. As I had seen artillery there on 27 May 1825,
I supposed it was customary to keep a cannon in the square
and paid scarcely any attention to it. I passed on and entered
the church.

A beadle in purple sleeves, a sort of priest, took me in charge
and showed me all round the church. It was deserted. The
stones were dark, the statues gloomy, the altar mysterious. No
lamps competed with the sun. The latter cast over the tombstones in the pavement the long white silhouettes of the windows, which in the melancholy obscurity of the rest of the
church looked like ghosts lying on these tombs. There was no
one else in the church. Not a whisper, not a footfall could be
heard.

This solitude saddened the heart and delighted the soul.
There were in it abandonment, neglect, oblivion, exile, and

sublimity. Gone the bustle of 1825. Not a single piece of finery, not a single vestment, nothing. It was bare and beautiful. The lofty vault no longer supported a canopy. Palace ceremonies are not suited to these severe places; a coronation ceremony is a favour; these noble ruins are not made to be courtiers; to rid it of the throne and remove the king from the presence of God increases the majesty of a temple. Louis XIV hides Jehovah from view.

Remove the priest as well, and having taken away everything that eclipsed it, you will see the light of day direct. Prayers, rites, bibles, formulas, refract and decompose the sacred light. A dogma is a dark chamber. Through a religion you see the solar spectrum of God, but not God. Age and decrepitude enhance the grandeur of a temple. As human religion retires from this mysterious and jealous edifice, divine religion enters it. Let solitude reign in it and you will feel heaven there. A sanctuary deserted and in ruins, like Jumièges, like Saint-Bertin, like Villers, like Holyrood, like Montrose Abbey, like the temple of Paestum, like the hypogeum of Thebes, becomes almost an element and possesses the virginal and religious grandeur of a savannah or of a forest. There is something of the real Presence there.

Such places are truly holy; man has meditated there. What they contained of truth has remained and become greater. Half-truths are no longer heard there. Extinct dogmas have not left their ashes; the prayer of the past has left its perfume. There is something of the absolute in prayer, and for that reason, that which was a synagogue, that which was a mosque, that which was a pagoda, is venerable. A stone on which that great anxiety which is called prayer has left its mark is never treated with ridicule by the thinker. The trace left by those who have knelt down before the infinite is always imposing. Who am I? What do I know?

Exploring the cathedral, I had climbed to the triforium, then under the arched buttresses, then to the top of the building. The timber-work under the pointed roof is chestnut-wood; admirable, but not as remarkable as the 'forest' of Amiens.

These cathedral attics are awe-inspiring. You could almost lose yourself in the labyrinths of rafters, squares, traverse beams, superposed joists, traves, architraves, girders, madriers, and tangled lines and curves; you might imagine yourself to be inside the skeleton of Babel. The place is as bare as a garret and as wild as a cave. The wind whistles mournfully. Rats are at home there. Spiders driven from the timber by the smell of chestnut take refuge in the stone of the basement where the church ends and the roof begins and, low down in the darkness, spin their webs in which you catch your face. You breathe in heaven knows what dust, and the centuries seem to mingle with your breath. The dust of churches is grimmer than the dust of houses; it suggests the tomb; it is composed of ashes.

The flooring of these colossal garrets has crevices in it through which you can look down into the church, into the abyss. In the corners into which you cannot penetrate there are pools of shadow, as it were. Birds of prey enter through one window and go out through the other. Lightning is also a frequent visitor; sometimes it comes too close, and then you have the burning of Rouen, of Chartres, or of St. Paul's in London.

My guide the beadle walked in front of me. He looked at the birds' droppings on the floor and shook his head. He recognized the bird by its dung and muttered between his teeth :

'This is a rook, this is a hawk, this is an owl.'

'You ought to study the human heart,' I said.

A frightened bat fluttered about in front of us.

Walking almost at random, following this bat, looking at this bird-dung, breathing this dust in the darkness, among these cobwebs and these scampering rats, we came to a dark corner in which, on a big wheelbarrow, I could just make out a long package tied with string and which looked like a piece of rolled-up material.

'What is that?' I asked the beadle.

'That,' he said, 'is Charles X's coronation carpet.'

I gazed at the thing. At that moment—I am not embroidering my story but giving a truthful account of what happened—there was a report under the roof which sounded like a thunder-clap, except that it came from below. It shook the timber-work and echoed again and again through the church. It was succeeded by a second roar, then a third, at regular intervals. I recognized the sound of gunfire, and remembered the cannon I had seen in the square.

I turned to my guide.

'What is that noise?'

'The telegraph has been at work and the cannon has been fired.'

'What does it mean?' I continued.

'It means,' said the beadle, 'that a grandson has just been born to Louis-Philippe.'

The cannon was in fact announcing the birth of the Comte de Paris.

These are my recollections of Reims.

TALLEYRAND

19 May 1838

In the Rue Saint-Florentin, there is a palace and a sewer.

The palace, which is of a rich, handsome, and gloomy style of architecture, was for a long time called: *Hôtel de l'Infantado*: nowadays the frontal of its principal doorway bears the words: *Hôtel Talleyrand*. During the forty years that he lived in this street, the last tenant of this palace may never have looked down at this sewer.

He was a strange, redoubtable, and important personage;

his name was Charles-Maurice de Périgord; he was of noble descent like Machiavelli, a priest like Gondi, unfrocked like Fouché, witty like Voltaire, and lame like the devil. It might be said that everything in him was lame like himself; the nobility which he had placed at the service of the Republic, the priesthood which he had dragged across the Champ-de-Mars and then thrown into the gutter, the marriage which he had broken with a score of scandals and a voluntary separation, the mind which he disgraced by acts of baseness.

This man, nevertheless, had grandeur; the splendours of the two régimes were united in him: he was Prince de Vaux in the kingdom of France, and a Prince of the French Empire.

For thirty years, from the interior of his palace, from the interior of his thoughts, he had almost controlled Europe. He had allowed the Revolution to speak to him in familiar terms and had smiled at it; ironically, it is true, but the Revolution had not noticed this. He had come in contact with, known, observed, penetrated, influenced, manipulated, fathomed, chaffed, inspired all the men of his time, and there had been moments in his life when, holding in his hand the four or five great threads which moved the civilized world, he had for his puppet Napoleon, Emperor of the French, King of Italy, Protector of the Confederation of the Rhine, Mediator of the Swiss Confederation. That is the game which was played by this man.

After the July Revolution, the old race, whose high chamberlain he was, having fallen, he found himself once more on his feet, and said to the people of 1830, seated bare-armed on a heap of paving stones: 'Make me your ambassador!'

He had heard Mirabeau's confession, and the first confidence of Thiers. He said of himself that he was a great poet, and that he had composed a trilogy in three dynasties:—Act I, The Empire of Bonaparte; Act II, The House of Bourbon; Act III, The House of Orleans.

He had done all this in his palace, and in this palace, like a spider in its web, he had attracted and caught in turn heroes, thinkers, great men, conquerors, kings, princes, emperors,

Bonaparte, Sieyès, Madame de Staël, Chateaubriand, Benjamin Constant, Alexander of Russia, William of Prussia, Francis of Austria, Louis XVIII, Louis-Philippe, all the gilded and glittering flies which buzz through the history of these last forty years. All this sparkling swarm, fascinated by the penetrating eye of this man, had passed in turn under that gloomy entrance bearing on the architrave the inscription: *Hôtel Talleyrand*.

Well, the day before yesterday, 17 May 1838, this man died. Doctors came and embalmed the body. To do this they, like the Egyptians, removed the bowels from the belly and the brain from the skull. The work done, after transforming the Prince de Talleyrand into a mummy, and nailing this mummy into a coffin lined with white satin, they withdrew, leaving on a table the brain—that brain which had thought so many things, inspired so many men, erected so many buildings, led two revolutions, duped twenty kings, contained the world. When the doctors had gone, a servant came in; he saw what they had left: 'Hullo! They have forgotten this.' What was to be done with it? He remembered that there was a sewer in the street; he went there and threw the brain into this sewer.

Finis rerum.

DIARY OF A PASSER-BY DURING THE RIOT OF 12 MAY

Sunday, 12 May 1839

MONSIEUR DE TOGORES has just left my house. We have been talking about Spain. To my mind, geographically since the formation of the continents, historically since the conquest of the Gauls, politically since the Duc d'Anjou, Spain has formed an integral part of France. *Jose primero* is the same fact as *Felipe Quinto*; Louis XIV's idea was continued by Napoleon. We cannot, therefore, without grave imprudence, neglect Spain. In illness, she weighs upon us; well and strong, she supports us. We drag her behind us, or we lean on her. Spain is one of our limbs; we cannot amputate it, it must be tended and cured. Civil war is a gangrene. Woe betide us if we let it grow worse, it will spread upon us. French blood is largely mixed with Spanish blood through Roussillon, Navarre, and Béarn. The Pyrenees are simply a ligature, which can be effective for only a while.

Monsieur de Togores shared my opinion. It was also, he said, the opinion of his uncle, the Duc de Frias, when he was President of the Council to Queen Christina.

We also spoke about Mademoiselle Rachel, whom he considered mediocre as Eriphila, and whom I had not yet seen.

At three o'clock, I return to my study.

My little daughter, in a state of excitement, opens my door and says: 'Papa, do you know what is going on? There is fighting at the Pont Saint-Michel.'

I do not believe a word of it. Fresh details. One of our cooks and the neighbouring wine-shop keeper have seen the occurrence. I ask the cook to come up. It seems that, passing along the Quai des Orfèvres, he saw a group of young men firing with muskets at the Prefecture of Police. A bullet struck the parapet near him. From there, the men ran to the Place du Châtelet and to the Hôtel-de-Ville, still firing. They had started out from the Morgue, which the good fellow calls the Morne.

Poor young fools! In less than twenty-four hours, a good many of those who set out from there will have returned there.

There is a sound of firing. The house is in a turmoil. Doors and casements open and shut noisily. The maidservants chat and laugh at the windows.

It is said that the insurrection has spread to the Porte Saint-Martin. I go out and follow the line of the boulevards. The weather is fine. There are crowds of strollers in their Sunday best. Drums beat to arms.

At the beginning of the Rue du Pont-aux-Choux there are some groups of people looking in the direction of the Rue de l'Oseille. There are a great crowd and a great din close to an old fountain which can be seen from the boulevard, and which forms the corner of an open space in the old Rue du Temple. In the midst of this hubbub, three or four little tricolour flags go by. The sight arouses comment. It is realized that these flags are simply decorating a hawker's barrow.

At the beginning of the Rue des Filles-du-Calvaire, groups of people are looking in the same direction. Some workmen in smocks pass close to me. I hear one of them say: 'What does that matter to me? I have neither wife, child, nor mistress.'

On the Boulevard du Temple the cafés are closing. The Cirque Olympique is also closing. The Gaîté stands firm, and will give a performance.

The crowd of strollers grows bigger at every step. There are a great many women and children. Three drummers of the National Guard—old soldiers, with solemn expressions—pass by, beating to arms. The fountain of the Château d'Eau suddenly throws up its grand holiday jets. Behind, in the low-lying street, the great railings and doorway of the Town Hall of the 5th Arrondissement are all closed. I notice in the door some little loopholes for muskets.

Nothing at the Porte Saint-Martin, but a large crowd peacefully moving about among regiments of infantry and cavalry stationed between the two gateways. The Porte Saint-Martin Theatre closes its box-office. The posters, on which I see the words *Marie Tudor*, are taken down. The omnibuses are running.

During the whole of this walk I have not heard any firing, but the crowd and vehicles make a great noise.

I return to the Marais. In the old Rue du Temple the women, in a state of great excitement, are gossiping in the doorways. Here are the details. The riot spread throughout the neighbourhood. About three o'clock two or three hundred

young men, poorly armed, suddenly broke into the Town Hall
of the 7th Arrondissement, disarmed the guard, and took their
muskets. From there they ran to the Hôtel-de-Ville and performed the same feat. As they entered the guardroom they
gaily embraced the officer. After taking the Hôtel-de-Ville,
what could they do with it? They went away and left it. If
they had the whole of France, would they be less embarrassed
with it than they were with the Hôtel-de-Ville? There were
a good many boys among them, fourteen or fifteen years old.
Some do not know how to load their muskets; others cannot
carry them. One of those who fired in the Rue de Paradis sat
down with a bump after the shot. Two drummers, killed at
the head of their columns, were placed in the Royal Printing
House, whose main doorway is shut. At this moment, barricades are being put up in the Rue des Quatre Fils and at the
corner of the little Rues de Bretagne, de Poitou, de Touraine,
and there are groups of people listening. A grenadier of the
National Guard passes by in uniform, his musket on his back,
looking about him uneasily. It is seven o'clock; from my
balcony in the Place Royale I can hear the sound of platoon-
firing.

Eight in the evening: I follow the boulevards as far as the
Madeleine. They are covered with troops. There are a few
National Guards at the head of each patrol. The Sunday
strollers mingle with all this infantry, all this cavalry. Here
and there, a cordon of soldiers quietly move the crowd from
one side of the boulevard to the other. There is a performance
at the Vaudeville.

One in the morning: The boulevards are deserted. Only the
regiments are left, camping at short distances apart. On my
way home I passed through the little streets of the Marais. All
is quiet and gloomy. The old Rue du Temple is as black as
pitch. The lanterns there have been smashed.

The Place Royale is a camp. There are four big fires before
the Town Hall, round which the soldiers are chatting and
laughing, sitting on their knapsacks. The flames silhouette
some of them and cast a glow over the faces of the others. The
green, fresh leaves of the spring trees rustle merrily above
the braziers.

I had a letter to post. I went about it cautiously, for everything looks suspicious in the eyes of these worthy National
Guards. I remember that at the time of the riots of April
1834 I passed a guardhouse of the National Guard with a
volume of the works of the Duc de Saint-Simon. I was denounced as a Saint-Simonian, and narrowly escaped being
murdered.

Just as I was going indoors again, a squadron of hussars,
held in reserve all day in the courtyard of the Town Hall,
suddenly came out and rode past me at a gallop, going in the
direction of the Rue Saint-Antoine. As I went upstairs, I
heard the horses' hooves fading into the distance.

Monday, 13 May 1839, eight in the morning.

Several companies of the National Guard have come and
joined the line regiments encamped in the Place Royale.

A number of men in smocks are walking about among the
National Guard, uneasily observed and observing. An omnibus comes out of the Rue du Pas-de-la-Mule. It is made to
go back. Just now, my floor-polisher, leaning on his broom,
said: 'Whose side shall I join?' He added a moment afterwards: 'What a filthy government this is! I have thirty
francs owing to me, and I cannot get anything out of the
people!'

The drums beat to arms.

I breakfast as I read the papers. Monsieur Duflot arrives.
He was at the Tuileries yesterday. It was the Sunday recep-
tion; the King looked tired; the Queen was in poor spirits.
Then he went for a walk round Paris. In the Rue du Grand-
Hurleur he saw a man who had been killed—a workman,

stretched out on the ground, in his Sunday clothes, his forehead pierced by a bullet. It was evening. By his side was a
lighted candle. The dead man had rings on his fingers, and
his watch in his fob-pocket, from which there hung a big
bunch of trinkets.

Yesterday at half-past three, at the first musket-shots, the
King sent for Marshal Soult, and said to him: 'Marshal, the
waters are becoming troubled. Some ministers must be fished
up.'

An hour later the Marshal came to the King and, rubbing
his hands, said, in his southern accent: 'This time, Sire, I
think we shall manage.'

Sure enough, there is a Ministry this morning in the *Moniteur*.

Midday: I go out. Firing can be heard in the Rue Saint-
Louis. The men in smocks have been turned out of the Place
Royale, and now only those people who live there are allowed
to enter the street. The riot is in the Rue Saint-Louis. It is
feared that the insurgents may penetrate one by one to the
Place Royale and fire on the troops from behind the pillars
of the arcade.

Two hundred and twelve years, two months, and two days
ago today, Beuvron, Bussy d'Amboise, and Buquet on the one
hand, and Boutteville, Deschapelles, and Laberthe on the
other, fought to the death with swords and daggers in broad
daylight, at this same time and in this same Place Royale.
Pierre Corneille was then twenty-one years of age. I hear a
National Guard express regret at the disappearance of the
railing which has just been stupidly pulled down, and whose
fragments are still at this moment lying on the pavement.

Another National Guard says: 'I myself am a Republican,
as is natural, for I am a Swiss.'

The approaches to the Place Royale are deserted. The firing
continues, very sustained, and very close at hand.

In the Rue Saint-Gilles, in front of the house occupied in

c

1784 by the famous Comtesse Lamothe-Valois, of the Diamond Necklace affair, a Municipal Guard bars my way.

I reach the Rue Saint-Louis by the Rue des Douze-Portes. The Rue Saint-Louis looks very odd. At one end can be seen a company of soldiers, who are blocking the whole street and advancing slowly, pointing their muskets. I am hemmed in by people running away in every direction. A young man has just been killed at the corner of the Rue des Douzes-Portes.

It is impossible to go any farther. I return in the direction of the boulevard. At the corner of the Rue du Harlay, there is a cordon of National Guards. One of them, who is wearing the blue Ribbon of July, suddenly stops me. 'You cannot pass!' And then his voice becomes milder: 'I really do not advise you to go that way, sir.' I look up: it is my floor-polisher.

I go on.

I come to the Rue Saint-Claude. I have only gone forward a few steps when I see everybody hurrying. A company of infantry has just appeared at the end of the street near the church. Two old women, one of whom is carrying a mattress, utter cries of terror. I continue to make my way towards the soldiers, who are barring the end of the street. Some young rogues in smocks are bolting in every direction near me. Suddenly the soldiers bring down their muskets and take aim. I have only just time to jump behind a street post, which at least protects my legs. I am fired at. No one falls in the street. I walk towards the soldiers, waving my hat to ask them not to fire again. As I come close to them, they open their ranks for me, I pass, and not a word is exchanged between us.

The Rue Saint-Louis is deserted. It looks as it does at four o'clock in the morning in summer: shops shut, windows shut, no one about, broad daylight. In the Rue du Roi-Doré, the neighbours are chatting in their doorways. Two horses, un-harnessed from some cart which has been turned into a barri-cade, pass up the Rue Saint-Jean-Saint-François, followed by a bewildered carter. A large body of National Guards and troops

of the line appear to be lying in ambush at the end of the Rue
Saint-Anastase. I make inquiries.

About half an hour ago seven or eight young workmen
came there, dragging muskets which they hardly knew how
to load. They were youths of fourteen or fifteen. They silently
loaded their arms in the midst of the people of the neighbourhood and the passers-by, who looked on as they did so, then
they broke into a house where there were only an old woman
and a little child. There they sustained a brief siege. The firing
in my direction was aimed at some of them who were running
away up the Rue Saint-Claude.

All the shops are closed, except the wine-shops where the
insurgents drank, and where the National Guards are drinking.

Three o'clock: I have just explored the boulevards. They
are crowded with people and soldiers. Platoon-firing can be
heard in the Rue Saint-Martin. In front of Fieschi's window I
saw a lieutenant-general in full uniform pass by, surrounded
by officers and followed by a squadron of very fine dragoons,
sabre in hand. There is a sort of camp at the Câteau d'Eau;
the actresses of the Ambigu are on the balcony of their green-
room, looking on. None of the boulevard theatres will be
giving a performance this evening.

All signs of disorder have disappeared in the Rue Saint-
Louis. The rioting is concentrated in the Central Market. A
National Guard said to me just now: 'There are over four
thousand of them behind the barricades over there.' I said
nothing in reply to the good fellow. At moments like this, all
eyes are magnifying glasses.

In a house being built in the Rue des Coutures-Saint-
Gervais, the builder's men have resumed work. A man has
just been killed in the Rue de la Perle. In the Rue des Trois-
Pavillons, I see some little girls playing at battledore and
shuttlecock. In the Rue de l'Écharpe there is a laundryman in
a fright, who says he has seen cannon go by. He counted eight.

Eight in the evening: The Marais remains fairly quiet. I gather that there are cannon in the Place de la Bastille. I go there, but cannot make anything out; the twilight is too deep. Several regiments stand in silent readiness, infantry and cavalry. The people are getting used to the sight of the wagons from which supplies are distributed to the men. The soldiers get ready to bivouac. The noise is heard of the wood for the night fires being unloaded into the street.

Midnight: Whole battalions are patrolling the boulevards. The bivouacs are lighted up everywhere and throw a glow as of a conflagration on the fronts of the houses. A man dressed as a woman has just passed rapidly by me, with a white hat and a very thick black veil, which completely hides his face. As the church clocks were striking twelve, I distinctly heard, amidst the silence of the city, two very long and sustained bursts of platoon-firing.

I listen as a long file of carts, making a heavy iron clatter, pass in the direction of the Rue du Temple. Are these cannon?

Two in the morning: I return home. I notice from a distance that the great bivouac fire lighted at the corner of the Rue Saint-Louis and the Rue de l'Écharpe has disappeared. As I approach, I see a man squatting in front of the fountain and holding something under the water. I look. The man looks uneasy. I see that he is extinguishing some half-burnt logs of wood; then he hoists them on to his shoulders and makes off. They are the last brands which the soldiers have left on the pavement on leaving their bivouacs. In fact, there is nothing left now but a few heaps of red ashes. The soldiers have returned to their barracks. The riot is over. It will at least have helped to keep a poor wretch warm next winter.

THE EXECUTION OF LOUIS XVI, 21 JANUARY 1793

1840

THERE are certain minute, characteristic details connected with the execution of Louis XVI which have never been recorded. They were recounted to me by an eye-witness[1] and are published here for the first time.

The scaffold was not erected, as is generally believed, in the very centre of the square, on the spot where the obelisk now stands, but at the spot which the decree of the Provisional Executive Council designates in these precise terms: 'between the *pied d'estal* and the Champs-Élysées.'

What was this pedestal? The present generations who have seen so many things pass away, so many statues crumble and so many pedestals fall, do not quite know how to interpret this very vague designation, and would be hard put to it to tell for what monument the mysterious stone which the Executive Council of the Revolution laconically calls the *pied d'estal* served as a base. This stone had carried the statue of Louis XV.

Let us note in passing that this strange square which has been called successively the Place Louis XV, the Place de la Révolution, the Place de la Concorde, the Place Louis XVI, the Place du Garde-Meuble and the Place des Champs-Élysées, and which failed to retain a single name, failed to retain a single monument either. It had the statue of Louis XV, which disappeared; an expiatory fountain which was to have cleansed the bloody centre of the square was projected, but not even the first stone was laid; a rough model of a

---

[1] This eye-witness was a certain Leboucher, who arrived in Paris from Bourges in December 1792, and was present at the execution of Louis XVI on 21 January 1793. He described the execution to Hugo in 1840. [Tr.]

monument to the Charter was made: we have never seen anything but the pedestal of this monument. Just when a bronze figure representing the Charter of 1814 was about to be erected, the July Revolution arrived with the Charter of 1830. The pedestal of Louis XVIII vanished like the pedestal of Louis XV. Now on this same spot we have placed the obelisk of Sesostris. It had taken the great desert thirty centuries to engulf half of it; how many years will the Place de la Révolution require to swallow it up altogether?

In the Year I of the Republic, what the Executive Council called the *pied d'estal* was nothing but a shapeless, hideous block. It was a sort of sinister symbol of royalty itself. Its ornaments of marble and bronze had been wrenched off; the bare stone was everywhere split and cracked; on the four sides there were broad gashes showing the places where the bas reliefs had been smashed with hammers. The history of the three royal lines had been similarly broken and mutilated on the sides of the old monarchy. At the most a remnant of the entablature could still be distinguished at the summit of the pedestal, and beneath the cornice a string of ovoli, rough and worn, surmounted by what architects call 'a chaplet of paternosters'. On the table of the pedestal one could see a heap of debris of all kinds, in which tufts of grass were growing here and there. This pile of nameless things had replaced the royal statue.

The scaffold was erected a few paces away from this ruin, a little to the rear of it. It was covered with long planks, laid transversely, which masked the framework. A ladder without banisters or balustrade was fitted to the back, and what one hesitates to call the head of this horrible construction was turned towards the Garde-Meuble. A basket of cylindrical shape, covered with leather, was placed at the spot where the head of the King was to fall, to catch it; and at one of the corners of the entablature, to the right of the ladder, there could be seen a long wicker basket prepared for the body, and on which one of the executioners, while waiting for the King, had laid his hat.

Imagine, now, in the middle of the square, these two lugubrious things, a few paces from each other: the pedestal of Louis XV and the scaffold of Louis XVI; that is to say, the ruins of royalty dead and the martyrdom of royalty living; around these two things four awe-inspiring lines of armed men, preserving a great empty square in the midst of a huge crowd; to the left of the scaffold, the Champs-Élysées, to the right the Tuileries, which, neglected and left at the mercy of the passer-by, had become a waste of dirt-heaps and mounds, and over these melancholy edifices, over these black, leafless trees, over this gloomy multitude, the icy, sombre sky of a winter morning, and you will have an idea of the appearance which the Place de la Révolution presented at the moment when Louis XVI, in the carriage of the Mayor of Paris, dressed in white and holding the Book of Psalms, arrived there to die at a few minutes after ten o'clock on 21 January 1793.

Strange excess of abasement and misery: the son of so many kings, robed and crowned like the kings of Egypt, was to be consumed between two layers of quicklime, and to this French royalty, which at Versailles had had a throne of gold and at Saint-Denis sixty sarcophagi of granite, there remained nothing but a platform of pine and a wicker coffin.

I shall not recount here the well-known details. Here are some which are unknown. The executioners numbered four; only two performed the execution; the third stayed at the foot of the ladder, and the fourth was on the wagon which was to convey the King's body to the Madeleine Cemetery and which was waiting a few feet from the scaffold. The executioners wore breeches, coats in the French style as modified by the Revolution, and three-cornered hats with enormous tricolour cockades.

They executed the King with their hats on, and it was without taking his hat off that Sanson, seizing by the hair the severed head of Louis XVI, showed it to the people, and for a few moments let the blood from it stream on to the scaffold.

At the same time his valet or assistant undid what were

called the *sangles* or straps; and, while the crowd gazed alter-
nately at the King's body, dressed entirely in white, as I have
said, and still attached, with the hands bound behind the back,
to the swing board, and at that head whose kind and gentle
profile stood out against the dark, misty trees of the Tuileries,
two priests, commissioners of the Commune, whom it had
instructed to be present as Municipal officials at the execution
of the King, sat in the Mayor's carriage laughing and chatting
loudly. One of them, Jacques Roux, derisively drew the other's
attention to Capet's fat calves and abdomen.

The armed men who surrounded the scaffold had only
swords and pikes; there were very few muskets. Most of them
wore large round hats or red caps. A few platoons of mounted
dragoons in uniform were mingled with these troops at intervals. A whole squadron of dragoons was ranged in battle
array beneath the terraces of the Tuileries. What was called
the Marseilles Battalion formed one of the sides of the square.

The guillotine—it is alway with repugnance that one writes
that hideous word—would strike today's professionals as very
badly constructed. The knife was simply hung from a pulley
fixed in the centre of the upper beam. This pulley and a rope
the thickness of a man's thumb constituted the whole apparatus.
The knife, which was not very heavily weighted, was of
small dimensions and had a curved edge, which gave it the
form of a reversed ducal horn or Phrygian cap. No hood was
provided to cover the King's head and at the same time to
hide and circumscribe its fall. All that crowd could see the
head of Louis XVI drop, and it was thanks to chance, thanks
perhaps to the smallness of the knife which reduced the
violence of the shock, that it did not bounce out of the basket
on to the pavement—a horrible incident which often occurred
at executions during the Terror. Nowadays murderers and
poisoners are decapitated more decently. Many 'improvements'
in the guillotine have been made.

At the spot where the King's head fell, a long rivulet of
blood streamed down the planks of the scaffold to the pavement. When the execution was over, Sanson threw the people

the King's coat, which was of white molleton, and in an instant it disappeared, torn by a thousand hands.

At the moment when the head of Louis XVI fell, the Abbé Edgeworth was still near the King. The blood spurted on him. He hastily donned a brown overcoat, descended from the scaffold, and plunged into the crowd. The first row of spectators opened before him with a sort of surprise mingled with respect; but after he had gone a few steps everybody's attention was still so concentrated on the centre of the square where the event had just taken place, that nobody took any further notice of the Abbé Edgeworth.

The poor priest, wrapped in his thick coat which concealed the blood with which he was covered, fled in horror, walking as if he were in a dream and scarcely knowing where he was going. However, with that sort of instinct which preserves sleepwalkers, he crossed the river, took the Rue du Bac, then the Rue du Regard, and thus managed to reach the house of Madame de Lézardière, near the Barrière du Maine.

There he took off his soiled clothing and remained for several hours in a state of collapse, without being able to collect a thought or utter a word.

Some Royalists who joined him, and who had witnessed the execution, surrounded the Abbé Edgeworth and reminded him of the farewell he had just addressed to the King: 'Son of St. Louis, ascend to Heaven!' These words, however, memorable though they were, had left no trace on the mind of him who had uttered them. 'We heard them,' said the witnesses of the catastrophe, still moved and trembling. 'It is possible,' he replied, 'but I do not remember.'

The Abbé Edgeworth lived a long life without being able to remember whether he really did utter these words.

Madame de Lézardière, who had been seriously ill for more than a month, was unable to bear the shock of the death of Louis XVI. She died during the very night of 21 January.

NAPOLEON'S ARRIVAL IN PARIS, 20 MARCH 1815

1840

HISTORY and contemporary memoirs have truncated, or badly related, or even omitted altogether, certain details of the arrival of the Emperor in Paris on 20 March 1815. But living witnesses are to be met with who saw them and who can rectify or complete them.

During the night of the 19th the Emperor left Sens. He arrived at Fontainebleau at three o'clock in the morning. About five o'clock, as day was breaking, he reviewed the few troops he had brought with him and those who had rallied to him at Fontainebleau itself. There were some from every corps, from every regiment, from every arm, a little of the Grand Army, a little of the Guard. At six o'clock, when the review was over, one hundred and twenty lancers mounted their horses and went on ahead to wait for him at Essonnes. These lancers were under the command of Galbois who is now a lieutenant-general, and who recently distinguished himself at Constantine.

They had been scarcely three-quarters of an hour at Essonnes, resting their horses, when the Emperor's carriage arrived. The escort of lancers were in their saddles in the twinkling of an eye and surrounded the carriage, which immediately started off again after changing horses. The Emperor stopped on the way at the large villages to receive petitions from the inhabitants and the submission of the authorities, and sometimes to listen to harangues. He was on the rear seat of the carriage with General Bertrand in full uniform sitting on his left. Colonel Galbois galloped beside the door on the Emperor's side; the door on Bertrand's side was guarded by a quartermaster of lancers called Ferrès, today a wine-shop keeper at Puteaux, a former hussar of great courage whom the Emperor knew personally and addressed by name. No one else on the road approached the Emperor. Everything that was intended for him passed through General Bertrand's hands.

Three or four leagues beyond Essonnes the imperial cortège found the road suddenly barred by General Colbert, at the head of two squadrons and three regiments echelonned towards Paris.

General Colbert had been the colonel of the very regiment of lancers from which the detachment escorting the Emperor had been drawn. He recognized his lancers and the lancers recognized him. They shouted: 'General, come over to us!' The General answered: 'Lads, do your duty, I am doing mine.' Then he wheeled round and went off to the right across country with a few riders who followed him. He could not have resisted; the regiments behind him were shouting: 'Long live the Emperor!'

This meeting delayed Napoleon for only a few minutes. He continued on his way. The Emperor, surrounded only by his one hundred and twenty lancers, thus reached Paris. He entered by the Barrière de Fontainebleau, took the broad avenue of trees which is on the left, the Boulevard du Mont-Parnasse, the other boulevards as far as the Invalides, then the Pont de la Concorde, the quay along the river and the gate of the Louvre.

At a quarter past eight in the evening he was at the Tuileries.

NAPOLEON'S FUNERAL
NOTES TAKEN ON THE SPOT

15 December 1840

I HAVE heard the drums beating to arms in the streets since half-past six in the morning. I go out at eleven. The streets are deserted, the shops shut; there is nobody to be seen except an old woman here and there. It is evident that all Paris has poured over to one side of the city like a liquid in a leaning vase. It is very cold, with a bright sun, and a light mist overhead. The gutters are frozen. As I reach the Pont Louis-Philippe a cloud descends and a few snowflakes, driven by the north wind, lash me in the face. Passing near Notre-Dame, I notice that the great bell is not ringing.

In the Rue Saint-André-des-Arts the feverish atmosphere of the holiday begins to manifest itself. For this is a holiday, the holiday of an exiled coffin returning in triumph. Three men of the lower classes, three of those poor workmen in rags who are cold and hungry all winter, are walking gaily in front of me. One of them jumps about, dances and performs a thousand absurd antics, shouting: *'Vive l'Empereur!'* Pretty grisettes, smartly dressed, pass by, led by their student companions. Cabs speed past in the direction of the Invalides. In the Rue du Four the snow thickens. The sky turns black. The snowflakes sprinkle it with white tear-drops. Heaven itself seems to wish to hang out mourning.

The storm, however, lasts only a short while. A pale streak of light whitens the corner of the Rue de Grenelle and the Rue du Bac, and there the Municipal Guards are stopping all vehicles. I pass by. Two great empty wagons driven by artillerymen come noisily from behind me, and return to their quarters at the end of the Rue de Grenellé just as I come out

on the Place des Invalides. Here I fear for a moment that all
is over, and that the Emperor has passed by, there are so
many people coming towards me who appear to be going
home. It is only the crowd being turned back by a cordon of
Municipal Guards on foot. I show my ticket for the first stand
on the left, and pass the barrier.

These stands are huge wooden structures, covering all the
grass-plots on the Esplanade from the quay to the railings.
There are three stands on each side.

On my arrival, the side of the stands on the right hides the
square from my view. I can hear a terrible, dismal noise. It
sounds like innumerable hammers beating time on the planks.
It is the hundred thousand spectators crowded on the stands,
who, frozen by the north wind, are stamping to keep themselves warm until the procession arrives.

I climb up on the stand. The sight which meets my eyes is
just as strange. The women, nearly all of them veiled and
wearing heavy boots, are hidden beneath great heaps of furs
and cloaks; the men are sporting extraordinary mufflers.

The decoration of the square is both good and bad. Shab-
biness dressing magnificence. Along the two sides of the
avenue there are two rows of figures, heroic, colossal, pale in
this cold sunlight, producing rather a good effect. They appear
to be of white marble; but this marble is plaster. At the far
end, opposite the building, stands the statue of the Emperor
in bronze; this bronze is also plaster. In each gap between the
statues there is a canvas pillar, painted and gilded in rather bad
taste, and surmounted by a brazier, at present filled with
snow. Behind the statues are the stands and the crowd; between the statues, a straggling file of National Guards; above
the stands, masts, on top of which there flutter grandly sixty
long tricolour pennants.

It seems that there has not been time to finish the decoration
of the principal entrance to the building. Above the railings a
sort of funereal triumphal arch of painted cloth and crape has
been run up, with which the wind plays as with old clothes
hung out to dry from the garret of a hovel. A row of poles,

plain and bare, rise above the cannon, and, from a distance, look like those small sticks which little children plant in the sand. Rags and tatters, which are supposed to be black drapery with silver spangles, flap and flutter feebly between these poles. In the background, the dome, with its flag and mourning drapery, sparkling with a metallic lustre, blurred by the mist in a brilliant sky, has a sombre, splendid look.

It is midday.

The cannon at the Invalides is fired at quarter-hour intervals. The crowd stamp their feet. Gendarmes, disguised in plain clothes, but betrayed by their spurs and the stocks of their uniforms, walk about here and there. In front of me a ray of sunshine lights up a rather poor statue of Joan of Arc, holding in her hand a palm-branch which she seems to be using as a shade, as if the sun were hurting her eyes.

A few yards from the statue a fire, at which a number of National Guards are warming their feet, is burning in a heap of sand.

From time to time military bandsmen invade a platform built between the two stands on the opposite side, perform a funeral flourish, then come down again hastily and disappear into the crowd, only to reappear the next moment. They leave the music for the wine-shop.

A hawker roams along the stand, selling dirges at a ha'penny each, and accounts of the ceremony. I buy two of these papers.

All eyes are fixed on the corner of the Quai d'Orsay, where the procession is due to appear. The cold adds to the feeling of impatience. Black and white puffs of smoke rise here and there through the misty shrubbery of the Champs-Élysées, and detonations can be heard in the distance.

Suddenly the National Guards hasten to arms. An orderly officer crosses the avenue at a gallop. A line is formed. Workmen place ladders against the pillars and start lighting the braziers. A salvo of heavy artillery booms out at the east corner of the Invalides; a cloud of dense yellow smoke, mingled with golden flashes, fills the whole of that corner. From where I am, I can see the guns being fired. They are

two fine old engraved cannon of the seventeenth century, and
one can hear the bronze in the noise they make. The procession
approaches.

It is half-past twelve.

At the far end of the esplanade, near the river, a double
row of mounted grenadiers, with yellow shoulder-belts,
solemnly appear. This is the Gendarmerie of the Seine. It is
the head of the procession. At this moment the sun does its
duty, and appears in all its glory. It is the month of Austerlitz.

After the bearskins of the Gendarmerie of the Seine and
the brass helmets of the Paris Municipal Guard come the tricolour pennants of the lancers, fluttering charmingly in the
air. Trumpets blow and drums roll.

A man in a blue smock climbs up the outside of the scaffolding of the stand opposite me, at the risk of breaking his neck.
No one helps him. A spectator in white gloves looks at him
but does not hold out a hand to him. The man, however,
reaches his destination.

The procession, including generals and marshals, looks magnificent. The sun, striking the cuirasses of the carabineers,
lights up a dazzling star on each breast. The three military
schools pass by with proud and solemn bearing, then the
artillery and infantry, as if they were going into action: the
ammunition wagons with their spare wheel at the rear, the
soldiers with their knapsacks on their backs. A short way off,
a great statue of Louis XIV, of ample dimensions and fairly
good style, gilded by the sun, seems to be viewing all this
splendour with amazement.

The mounted National Guard appear. Uproar in the crowd.
It is in fairly good order, though; but it is a regiment with no
record of fame, and this marks it out in a procession of this
kind. People laugh. I hear this dialogue: 'Just look at that fat
colonel! Look how he holds his sword!' 'Who is that fellow?'
'That is Montalivet.'

Interminable legions of the infantry of the National Guard
now march past, with arms reversed like the line regiments,
beneath the shadow of this grey sky. A mounted National

Guard, who drops his shako, and so gallops bareheaded for some time, to his intense annoyance, causes much amusement to the gallery, that is to say to a hundred thousand people.

From time to time the procession halts, then continues on its way. The lighting of the braziers is completed, and they smoke between the statues like great bowls of punch.

The crowd grows more attentive. Here is the black silver-fringed carriage of the chaplain of the *Belle-Poule*, inside which we can see a priest in mourning; then the great black velvet coach with mirror panels of the St. Helena Commission. Each of these two carriages is drawn by four horses.

Suddenly the cannon are fired simultaneously from three different points on the horizon. This triple sound encloses the ear in a sort of triangle, awe-inspiring and superb. Drums beat a salute in the distance. The Emperor's funeral carriage appears. The sun, obscured until this moment, reappears at the same time. The effect is remarkable.

In the distance, in the mist and sunlight, against the grey and russet background of the trees in the Champs-Élysées, between the great white ghostlike statues, a kind of golden mountain can be seen moving slowly along. All that we can distinguish of it as yet is a sort of luminous glitter, which makes now stars, now lightning, sparkle over the whole surface of the car. A mighty roar accompanies this apparition. It is as if the car were trailing the acclamations of the whole city behind it as a torch trails its smoke.

As it turns into the avenue of the Esplanade, it is halted for a few moments by some accident before a statue which stands at the corner of the avenue and of the quay. I have since ascertained that this statue was that of Marshal Ney.

At the moment when the funeral car appeared, it was half-past one.

The procession resumes its progress. The car moves forward slowly. We can begin to make out its shape.

Here are the saddle-horses of the marshals and generals who hold the cords of the Imperial pall. Here are the eighty-six legionaries bearing the banners of the eighty-six departments. Nothing could be more beautiful than this square, above which flutter a forest of flags. One might imagine that a field of gigantic dahlias was on the march.

Here comes a white horse covered from head to foot with a violet pall, accompanied by a chamberlain in pale blue, embroidered with silver, and led by two footmen, dressed in green, with gold lace. It is the Emperor's livery. A shudder goes through the crowd. *'It is Napoleon's charger!'* The majority really believe this. If the horse had been ridden for only two years by the Emperor, he would be thirty years old, which is a good age for a horse.

The fact is that this palfrey is a good old supernumerary horse, which for some ten years has played the charger in all the military ceremonies arranged by the Funeral Administration. This pseudo-charger carries on his back the genuine saddle of Bonaparte at Marengo: a crimson velvet saddle with a double row of gold lace, fairly well worn.

After the horse come the five hundred sailors of the *Belle-Poule*, in close, regular formation, young men for the most part, dressed for action, with round jackets, round varnished hats, each with his pistols in his belt, his boarding-axe in his hand, and at his side his sword, a cutlass with a broad handle of polished iron.

The salvoes continue. At this moment the story goes round the crowd that the first discharge of cannon at the Invalides blew off the legs of a Municipal Guard. By an oversight, the gun had not been unloaded. It is added that a man fell under the wheels of the funeral car on the Place Louis XV, and was crushed to death.

The car is now very near. It is almost immediately preceded by the officers of the *Belle-Poule*, under the command of the Prince de Joinville, on horseback. The Prince de Joinville's face is covered with a fair beard, something which strikes me as contrary to naval regulations. He is wearing for the first time the grand ribbon of the Legion of Honour. Until now he figured on the roll of the Legion only as a plain knight.

As it arrives immediately in front of me, the car meets some

D

momentary obstacle, and comes to a halt. It remains stationary for a few minutes between the statue of Joan of Arc and that of Charles V.

I can survey it at leisure. The overall effect has a certain grandeur. It is an enormous mass, gilded all over, its tiers rising pyramid-like above the four great gilt wheels which bear it. Under the violet pall, studded with bees, which covers it from top to bottom, some rather fine details may be observed; the salient eagles on the base, the fourteen Victories on the top-piece bearing on a golden tablet a dummy coffin. The real coffin is invisible. It has been deposited inside the basement, something which detracts from the emotional effect.

That is the grave defect of this car. It conceals what we would like to see, what France has demanded, what the people expect, what every eye seeks—Napoleon's coffin.

On the sham sarcophagus have been deposited the insignia of the Emperor, the crown, the sword, the sceptre, and the robe. In the gilded orifice which separates the Victories on the summit from the eagles on the base, we can clearly see, in spite of the gilding which is already flaking off, the joins in the deal planks. Another defect. This gold is merely imitation. Deal and paste-board, that is the reality. I would have preferred a genuine splendour for the Emperor's funeral car.

Nevertheless, the greater part of this sculptural composition has some boldness and artistic merit, although the concept of the design and the ornamentation hesitates between the Renaissance and the Rococo.

Two huge bundles of flags, conquered from all the nations of Europe, wave in splendid arrogance from the front and rear of the car.

The car, with its load, weighs twenty-six thousand pounds. The coffin alone weighs five thousand pounds.

Nothing more surprising and more magnificent could be imagined than the team of sixteen horses drawing the car. They are terrifying creatures, adorned with white plumes flowing down to their haunches, and covered from head to foot with splended caparisons of gold-cloth, leaving only their eyes visible, something which gives them an indescribable air of ghost horses.

Footmen in the Imperial livery lead this imposing cavalcade.

On the other hand, the worthy and venerable generals who hold the cords of the pall have an appearance as far removed from the fantastic as could possibly be imagined. In front, two marshals, the Duc de Reggio,[1] diminutive and blind in one eye, on the right; on the left, the Comte Molitor; in the rear on the right an admiral, the Baron Duperre, a stout jovial sailor; on the left a lieutenant-general, the Comte Bertrand—old, exhausted, broken-down, a noble and illustrious figure. All four wear the red ribbon.

The car, it should be added, was not intended to be drawn by more than eight horses. Eight horses is a symbolical number which has a significance in the ceremonial. Seven horses, nine horses, are a wagoner's team; sixteen horses are for a stone-mason's dray; eight horses are for an Emperor.[2]

[1] The Duc de Reggio is not really blind in one eye. A few years ago, as the result of a chill, the marshal had an attack of local paralysis which affected the right cheek and pupil. Since then he has been unable to open that eye. However, throughout this ceremony he displayed admirable courage. Riddled with wounds and seventy-five years of age, he remained in the open air, in a temperature of fourteen degrees, from eight o'clock in the morning until two o'clock in the afternoon, in full uniform and without a cloak, out of respect for his general. He made the journey from Courbevoie to the Invalides on foot, *on his three broken legs*, as the Duchesse de Reggio wittily said to me. The Marshal, in fact, having suffered two fractures of his right leg and one of the left, really has had three legs broken.

After all, it is remarkable that, out of so many veterans exposed for so long to this severe cold, no mishap should have happened to any one of them. Strange to say, this funeral did not bury anybody.

[2] 29 December 1840. It has since been ascertained that the magnificent saddle cloths of gold brocade which caparisoned the sixteen horses were of spun glass. An unworthy economy. An unseemly deception. This astonishing announcement may now be read in the newspapers:

'A large number of persons who came to the spun-glass warehouse at No. 97, Rue de Charonne, to see the imperial mantle which adorned the sides of Napoleon's funeral car, wished to keep a souvenir of the great ceremony by buying a few eagles from this mantle. The manager of the establishment, who in obedience to the Government's orders was obliged to refuse, is now in a position to accede to their request.'

So we have a bronze statue in plaster, solid gold Victories in pasteboard, an Imperial mantle in spun glass, and—a fortnight after the ceremony—eagles for sale. V.H.

The spectators on the stands went on stamping their feet until the catafalque passed before them. Only then did their feet fall silent. One can tell that a great thought is going through the crowd.

The car has resumed its progress, the drums beat a salute, the firing of the cannon quickens. Napoleon is at the gates of the Invalides. It is ten minutes to two.

Behind the bier there come in civilian dress all the survivors of the Emperor's household, then all the survivors of the soldiers of the Guard, clad in their glorious uniforms already unfamiliar to us.

The remainder of the procession, made up of regiments of the regular army and the National Guard, occupies, it is said, the Quai d'Orsay, the former Pont Louis XVI, the Place de la Concorde and the Avenue des Champs-Élysées as far as the Arc de l'Étoile.

The car does not enter the courtyard of the Invalides; the railings set up by Louis XIV are too low. It turns off to the right; sailors are seen reaching into the basement and emerging with the coffin, then disappearing under the porch erected at the entrance to the enclosure. They are in the courtyard.

Everything is over for the spectators outside. They get down noisily and hurriedly from the stands. Knots of people stop here and there in front of posters stuck to the boards and reading thus: *Leroy, victualler, Rue de la Serpe, near the Invalides. Choice wines and hot pastry.*

I can now examine the decoration of the avenue. Nearly all these plaster statues are bad. Some are ridiculous. The Louis XIV, which, at a distance looked imposing, is grotesque at close quarters. Macdonald is a good likeness. Mortier too. Ney would be if he had not been given such a high forehead. Moreover, the sculptor has made it exaggerated and ridiculous in the attempt to achieve a melancholy effect. The head is too large. In this connexion, it is said that in the hurry to improvise the statues, the measurements were given incorrectly.

On the day when they had to be delivered, the statuary sent in a Marshal Ney a foot too tall. What did the people of the Beaux-Arts department do? They sawed out of the statue a slice of the stomach twelve inches thick, and stuck the two pieces together again as well as they could.

The bronze-coloured plaster of the statue of the Emperor is stained and covered with spots which make the imperial robe look like a patchwork of old green serge.

This reminds me—for the generation of ideas is a strange mystery—that this summer, at Monsieur Thiers's residence, I heard Marchand, the Emperor's valet, say how Napoleon loved old coats and old hats. I understand and share this taste. For a brain which works, the pressure of a new hat is unbearable.

The Emperor, said Marchand, when he left France, took with him three coats, two frock-coats, and two hats; he got through his six years at St. Helena with this wardrobe; he did not wear any uniform.

Marchand added other curious details. The Emperor, at the Tuileries, seemed to change his clothes quickly and frequently. In reality this was not so. The Emperor usually wore civilian dress, that is to say breeches of white kerseymere, white silk stockings, shoes with buckles. But in the next room there was always a pair of riding-boots, lined with white silk up to and over the knees. When anything happened which made it necessary for the Emperor to mount on horseback, he took off his shoes, put on his boots, got into his uniform, and was transformed into a soldier. When he returned, he took off his boots, put on his shoes again, and became a civilian once more. The white breeches, the stockings and the shoes were never worn more than one day. The next day these Imperial cast-offs belonged to the valet.

It is three o'clock. A salvo of artillery announces that the ceremony at the Invalides is at an end. I meet B——. He has just come out. The sight of the coffin produced an indescribable impression.

The words which were spoken were simple and grand. The Prince de Joinville said to the King: 'Sire, I present to you the body of the Emperor Napoleon.' The King replied: 'I receive it in the name of France.' Then he said to Bertrand: 'General, place on the coffin the Emperor's glorious sword.' And to Gourgaud: 'General, place on the coffin the Emperor's hat.'

Mozart's *Requeim* had little effect. Beautiful music, already wrinkled with age. Music too, alas, becomes wrinkled with age!

The catafalque was finished only one hour before the arrival of the coffin. B—— was in the church at eight o'clock in the morning. It was as yet only half draped, and encumbered with ladders, tools, and workmen. The crowds were collecting during this time. Large gilded palms five or six feet in height were tried on the four corners of the catafalque. But when they had been put in position they were seen to produce a poor effect. They were removed.[3]

The Prince de Joinville, who had not seen his family for six months, went and kissed the hand of the Queen, and shook hands heartily with his brothers and sisters. The Queen received him solemnly and without effusiveness. As a Queen rather than as a mother.

During this time the archbishops, curés, and priests sang the *Requiescat in pace* around Napoleon's coffin.

The procession was splendid, but too exclusively military, good enough for Bonaparte, but not for Napoleon. All the institutions in the State should have figured in it, or at least

[3] 23 December. Since the transfer of the coffin, the church of the Invalides has been open to the public. There pass through it daily a hundred thousand persons, from ten o'clock in the morning until four o'clock in the afternoon. The lighting of the chapel costs the State 350 francs a day. M. Duchatel, Minister of the Interior (who it may be stated by the way is said to be a son of the Emperor), is loud in his complaints at this expense. V.H.

been represented. The fact is, the Government had been casual in the extreme. It was in a hurry to be done with the affair. Philippe de Ségur, who followed the car as a former aide-de-camp of the Emperor, told me how this morning at Courbevoie, on the banks of the river, with the thermometer standing at fourteen degrees, there was not even a waiting-room with a fire in it. Those two hundred veterans of the Emperor's household had to wait for an hour and a half in a kind of Greek temple exposed to the four winds.

The same neglect was shown with respect to the steamboats which brought the body from Le Havre to Paris, a journey remarkable nevertheless for the solemn, reverent attitude of the riverside populations. None of these boats was suitably fitted up. There was not enough food. There were no beds. Orders were given that no one should land. The Prince de Joinville was obliged to sleep, one of a party of twenty, on a table in a common room. Others slept underneath. People slept on the floor, and the more fortunate on benches or chairs. It seemed as if the authorities had been guilty of spite. The Prince complained openly of it, and said: 'In this affair all that emanates from the people is great, all that emanates from the government is petty.'

Wishing to reach the Champs-Élysées, I crossed the suspension bridge where I paid my sou. A real act of generosity, for the mob crowding on to the bridge neglects to pay.

The legions and regiments are in battle array in the Avenue de Neuilly. The avenue is decorated, or rather dishonoured, along its entire length by fearful statues in plaster representing figures of Fame and by triumphal columns crowned with golden eagles and placed on grey marble pedestals. The street boys amuse themselves by making holes in this marble which is made of cloth.

On each column, between two bundles of tricolour flags, can be seen the name and date of one of Bonaparte's victories.

An inferior theatrical-looking group occupies the top of the

Arc de Triomphe: the Emperor erect upon a car surrounded by figures of Fame, having on his right, Glory, and on his left, Grandeur. What is the meaning of a statue of grandeur? How can grandeur be expressed in a statue? By making it larger than the others? This is monumental nonsense.

This scenic effect, poorly gilded, faces towards Paris. By going to the other side of the Arc, one can see the back of it. It is a regular theatrical set piece. Seen from the Neuilly side, the Emperor, the Glories, and the Fames are simply pieces of framework clumsily shaped.

In this connexion, the figures in the Avenue des Invalides have been strangely chosen. The published list gives some bold and singular conjunctions of names. Here is one: *Lobau. Charlemagne. Hugues Capet.*

A few months ago, I was taking a walk along these same Champs-Élysées with Thiers, then Prime Minister. He would undoubtedly have managed the ceremony with greater success. He would have put his heart into it. He had ideas. He loves and appreciates Napoleon. He told me some anecdotes of the Emperor. Monsieur de Rémusat allowed him to see the unpublished memoirs of his mother. There are scores of amusing details in them.

The Emperor was good-natured and loved to tease people. Teasing is the malice of good men. Caroline, his sister, wanted to be a queen. He made her a queen—Queen of Naples. But the poor woman had endless troubles from the moment she had a throne, and became somewhat care-worn and faded. One day Talma was breakfasting with Napoleon—etiquette permitted Talma to come only to breakfast. Queen Caroline, who had just arrived from Naples, pale and fatigued, called to see the Emperor. He looked at her, then turned towards Talma, who was feeling very ill at ease between these two majesties. 'My dear Talma,' he said, 'women all want to be queens, but they lose their beauty in consequence. Look at Caroline. She is a queen; she is ugly.'

As I pass, the demolition is just being finished of the count-less stands, draped with black, and fitted with benches, which had been erected by speculators at the entrance to the Avenue de Neuilly. Upon one of them, facing the Beaujon garden, I read this notice: *Seats to let. Austerlitz grandstand. Apply to M. Berthellemot, Confectioner.*

On the other side of the Avenue, on a fairground booth adorned with two frightful pictorial signs representing, one the death of the Emperor, the other the encounter at Mazagran, I read another notice: *Napoleon in his coffin. Three sous.*

Some men of the people go by singing: 'Long live great Napoleon! Long live old Napoleon!' Hawkers make their way through the crowd, shouting: 'Tobacco and cigars!' Others offer the passers-by some kind of hot and steaming liquid out of a copper tea-urn covered with a black cloth. An old woman at a stall coolly pulls on her drawers in the midst of the hurly-burly.

About five o'clock, the funeral car, now empty, returns by way of the Avenue des Champs-Élysées to be set down under the Arc de Triomphe. This is a capital idea. But the splendid ghost-horses are tired. They walk slowly and wearily, in spite of all the drivers' efforts. Nothing stranger can be imagined than the shouts of *Hu-ho!* and *Dia-hu!* lavished on this im-perial but fantastic team.

I return home by the boulevards. The crowd there is im-mense; suddenly it falls back and looks round with a certain air of respect. A man passes proudly by in its midst. He is an old hussar of the Imperial Guard, a veteran of great height and robust appearance. He is in full uniform, with tight-fitting red trousers, a white waistcoat with gold braid, a sky-blue pelisse, a busby with a grenade and a bullion fringe, his sword at his side, his sabretache beating against his thighs, an eagle on his satchel. All round him the little children cry: *'Vive l'Empereur!'*

It is certain that the whole ceremony has been curiously scamped and bungled. The government seemed to be afraid of the ghost it had raised. It was as if the object was both to show and to hide Napoleon. Anything which would have been too grand or too touching was left out of sight. The real and grandiose were concealed beneath more or less splendid coverings, the imperial procession was hidden in the military procession, the army was hidden in the National Guard, the Chambers were hidden in the Invalides, and the coffin was hidden in the cenotaph.

On the contrary, Napoleon should have been treated frankly as a source of pride, and honoured royally and popularly as Emperor. Then strength would have been found just where a failure almost occurred.

Today, 11 March 1841, three months afterwards, I saw once more the Esplanade of the Invalides.

I had been to see an old officer who was ill. The weather was as fine as could be; the sun was warm and young; it was a day for the end rather than the beginning of spring.

The whole Esplanade is in confusion. It is littered with the ruins of the funeral. The scaffolding of the stands has been removed. The squares of grass which they covered have re-appeared, hideously cut up in every direction by the deep ruts of the builders' wagons. Of the statues which lined the triumphal avenue, only two remain standing—Marceau and Duguesclin. Here and there are heaps of stones, the remains of the pedestals. Soldiers, pensioners, apple-women, wander about amid all this fallen poetry.

A merry crowd was hurrying past the Invalides, on its way to see the artesian well. In a silent corner of the Esplanade stood two omnibuses, painted a chocolate colour—*Béarnaises*—bearing this inscription in large letters:

WELL AT GRENELLE SLAUGHTER-HOUSE

Three months ago they bore this one:

NAPOLEON'S FUNERAL AT THE INVALIDES

In the courtyard of the Invalides, the sun cheered and warmed the crowd of youngsters and old men, the most charming sight imaginable. It was public visiting day. There were crowds of sightseeers. Gardeners were clipping the hedges. The lilacs were bursting into bud in the pensioners' little gardens. A little boy of fourteen was singing at the top of his voice, sitting on the carriage of the last cannon on the right, the same one which killed a gendarme in firing the first funeral salvo on 15 December.

I should like to mention in passing that for the last three months these admirable sixteenth- and seventeenth-century pieces have been perched on hideous little cast-iron carriages, producing a most mean and wretched effect. The old wooden carriages, enormous, squat, and massive, were worthy supports for these gigantic and magnificent bronzes.

A bevy of children languidly supervised by their nursemaids, each of whom was leaning against her soldier, were playing among the twenty-four great culverins brought back from Constantine and Algiers.

These gigantic engines, at least, have been spared the indignity of *uniform* carriages. They lie flat on the ground on both sides of the gateway. Time has painted the bronze a light and pretty green colour, and they are covered with large patches of arabesques. Some of them, admittedly the least handsome, are of French manufacture. On the breach is the inscription: *François Durand. Metal-founder to the King of France at Algiers.*

While I was copying the inscription, a tiny little girl, pretty and fresh-complexioned, dressed all in white, amused herself by filling with sand, with her little pink fingers, the touch-hole of one of these bulky Turkish cannons. A pensioner, with bare sword, standing on two wooden legs, and no doubt guarding this artillery, looked at her doing this, and smiled.

Just as I was leaving the Esplanade, about three o'clock, a little group walked slowly across it. It was composed of a man dressed in black, with a mourning band on his arm and his hat, followed by three others, one of whom, dressed in a blue smock, was holding a little boy by the hand. The man with the mourning bands had under his arm a kind of whitish box, half hidden under a black cloth, which he carried as a musician carries the case containing his instrument. I went over to them. The man in black was an undertaker's mute; the box was a child's coffin.

The course taken by the little procession, parallel with the front of the Invalides, cut across that which three months ago was followed by Napoleon's hearse.

Today, 8 May, I returned to the Invalides to see the chapel of Saint-Jérôme, where the Emperor is temporarily placed. All traces of the ceremony of 15 December have disappeared from the Esplanade. The quincunxes have been cut out anew, but the grass has not yet grown again. There was some sunshine, accompanied now and then by clouds and rain. The trees were green and gay. The poor old pensioners were talking quietly to groups of youngsters, and walking round in their little gardens full of flowers. It is that delightful period of the year when the late lilacs have shed their petals and the early laburnums are in bloom.

The broad shadows of the clouds moved rapidly across the forecourt, where, under an archivolt on the first floor, there stands a plaster pedestrian statue of Napoleon, a rather pitiful counterpart to the equestrian Louis XIV boldly chiselled in stone over the great portal.

All round the court, below the eaves, are still stuck up, as the last traces of the funeral, the long narrow strips of black cloth in which had been painted in golden letters, three by three, the names of the generals of the Revolution and the Empire. But the wind is beginning to tear them down here and there. On one of these strips, whose loose end was floating in the air, I read these three names:

SAURET—CHAMBURE—HUG ...

The end of the third name had been torn and carried off by the wind. Was it *Hugo* or *Huguet*?

A few young soldiers were entering the church. I followed these *tourlourous*, as the phrase goes nowadays. For in wartime the soldier calls the citizen a *pékin*, and in peace-time the citizen calls the soldier a *tourlourou*.

The church was bare and cold, almost deserted. At the far end a large grey cloth, stretched from top to bottom, hid the enormous archivolt of the dome. Behind this covering could be heard the muffled and almost funereal sound of hammering.

I walked about for a little while reading on the pillars the names of all the warriors buried there.

All along the lofty nave above our heads, the flags conquered from the enemy, that splendid collection of rags and tatters, fluttered gently near the roof.

In the intervals between the blows of the hammers, I heard some whispering in a corner of the church. It was an old woman at confession.

The soldiers went out and myself behind them. They turned to the right along the Metz corridor, and we mingled with a fairly large and very well-dressed crowd going in that direction. The corridor leads to the inner courtyard in which the minor entrance to the dome is situated.

There, in the shadows, I found three more statues, of lead, taken from heaven knows where, which I remember having seen on this same spot as a child in 1815, at the time of the mutilation of buildings, dynasties, and nations which took place at that period. These three statues, in the worst Empire style, cold as allegory, gloomy as mediocrity, stand alongside the wall there, on the grass, among heaps of architectural capitals, with something about them of tragedies which have been hissed. One of them is leading a lion by a chain and represents Might. Nothing looks so lost and helpless as a statue standing on the ground without a pedestal; it looks like a horse without a rider, or a king without a throne. There are only two alternatives for the soldier—battle or death; there are only two for the king—the throne or the tomb; there are only two for the statue—to stand against the sky or to lie flat on the ground.

A statue on foot baffles the mind and puzzles the eye. One forgets that it is plaster or bronze, and that bronze does not walk any more than plaster, and one is tempted to say to this poor creature with a human face, so awkward and un-happy-looking in its ostentatious attitude: 'Now then, go on! Be off with you! Quick march! Keep going! Move! The ground is under your feet. What is stopping you? What is hindering you?' A pedestal does at least explain a lack of mobility. For statues as for men, a pedestal is a small space, narrow and respectable, with four precipices around it.

After passing the statues, I turned to the right and entered the church by the great door at the back which opens on to the boulevard. Several young women went through the doorway at the same time as myself, laughing and calling to each other. The sentry allowed us to pass. He was a bent and melancholy-looking old soldier, sword in hand, perhaps an old grenadier of the Imperial Guard, silent and motionless in the shadow, and resting the end of his worn wooden leg on a marble fleur-de-lis, half chipped out of the stone.

To get to the chapel where Napoleon is, one has to walk over a pavement tessellated with fleurs-de-lis. The crowd, the women, and the soldiers walked quickly. I entered the church with slow steps.

A pale, wan light from above, the light of a workshop rather than of a church, illuminated the interior of the dome. Immediately under the cupola, at the spot where the altar used to be and the tomb will be, and covered on the side of the aisle by a vast grey cloth, there stood the huge scaffolding used in the demolition of the baldachin erected under Louis XIV. No trace of this baldachin remained except the shafts of the six great wooden columns which used to support the head. These columns, destitute of capital or abacus, were still supported vertically by six logs which had been put in in place of the pedestals. The gold foliage, the spirals of which created the appearance of twisted columns, had already disappeared, leaving a black mark upon the six gilded shafts. The work-men perched here and there inside the scaffolding looked like great birds in an enormous cage.

Others, below, were tearing up the stone floor. Others again were coming and going in the church, carrying their ladders, whistling and chatting.

On my right, the chapel of Saint-Augustin was full of debris. Piles of huge, broken blocks of that splendid mosaic work in which Louis XIV had set his fleurs-de-lis and suns, concealed the feet of St. Monica and St. Alipa, looking astounded and shocked in their niches. The statue of Religion by Girardon, standing between the two windows, looked solemnly down at this confusion.

Beyond the chapel of Saint-Augustin, some large marble slabs, which had formed the flooring of the dome, placed vertically against each other, half hid the white, recumbent figure of a warrior beneath a rather high pyramid of black marble set in the wall. Underneath the warrior, in a gap between the flagstones, could be read these three letters—

UBA

It was Vauban's tomb.

On the other side of the church, opposite Vauban's tomb, was the tomb of Turenne. The latter had been treated with greater respect than the former. No accumulation of ruins rested against that great piece of sculpture, more pompous than funereal, better suited to the stage than to the church, in harmony with the cold, noble etiquette which ruled the art of Louis XIV. No palisade, no mound of rubbish prevented the passer-by from seeing Turenne dressed as a Roman Emperor dying from an Austrian bullet above the bronze bas-relief of the battle of Turckheim, or from reading this memorable date, 1675; the year in which Turenne died, the Duc de Saint-Simon was born, and Louis XIV laid the foundation-stone of the Hôtel des Invalides.

On the right, against the scaffolding of the dome and Turenne's tomb, between the silence of this sepulchre and the noise of the workmen, in a little barricaded and deserted chapel, I glimpsed, behind a railing, through the opening of a white arch, a group of gilded statues, placed there pell-mell, and doubtless torn from the baldachin, which seemed to be conversing in whispers about all this devastation. There were six of them, six winged and luminous angels, six golden phantoms, eerily illuminated by a pale stream of sunlight. One of these statues was pointing out to the others the chapel of Saint-Jérôme, gloomy and hung in mourning drapery, and seemed to be uttering in consternation the word: Napoleon. Above these six spectres, on the cornice of the little dome of the chapel, a great angel in gilded wood was playing a violoncello with eyes upturned to heaven, almost in the attitude which Veronese gives Tintoretto in *The Marriage at Cana*.

By this time, I had reached the threshold of the chapel of Saint-Jérôme.

A great archivolt, with a lofty door-curtain of rather shabby purple cloth, printed with a fretwork pattern, and with golden palm-leaves; at the top of the door-curtain, the imperial escutcheon in painted wood; on the left two bundles of tricolour flags, surmounted with eagles which looked like cocks touched up for the occasion; pensioners wearing the Legion of Honour and carrying pikes; the crowd silent and reverent, entering under the archway; at the far end, eight or ten paces down, an iron gateway painted bronze: on the gateway, which is lavishly and feebly decorated, lions' heads, gilt 'N's with a tinsel-like appearance, the arms of the Empire, the *main-de-justice* and the sceptre, the latter surmounted by a seated miniature of Charlemagne, crowned and with orb in hand; beyond the gateway, the interior of the chapel, an indescribably august, moving, and impressive sight: a hanging lamp, a golden eagle with widespread wings, its stomach glistening in the gloomy lamplight and its wings in a ray of sunshine: under the eagle, beneath a vast and dazzling bundle of enemy flags, the coffin, the ebony supports and brass handles of which were visible; on the coffin, the great Imperial crown like that of Charlemagne, the gold laurel diadem like that of Caesar, the purple velvet pall studded with bees; in front of the coffin, on a credence-table, the hat of St. Helena and the sword of Eylau; on the wall to the right of the coffin, in the centre of a silver shield the word *Wagram*; on the left in the centre of another shield another word, *Austerlitz* : all round on the wall, a hanging of purple velvet embroidered with bees and eagles; right at the top, on the spandrel of the nave, above the lamp, the eagle, the crown, the sword, and the coffin, a fresco, and in this fresco the angel of judgement sounding the trumpet over a sleeping St. Jerome—that is what I saw at a glance, and that is what a minute sufficed to engrave upon my memory for life.

The hat, low-crowned, wide-brimmed, little worn, trimmed with a black ribbon, out of which there peeped a small tricolour cockade, was lying on the sword, of which the chased gold hilt was turned towards the entrance to the chapel and the point towards the coffin.

There was a certain admixture of meanness in all this grandeur. The meanness was in the purple cloth, which was printed and not embroidered; in the pasteboard painted to look like stone; in the hollow iron made to look like bronze; in that wooden escutcheon; in those 'N's in tinsel; in that canvas Roman column, painted to look like granite; in those eagles which were almost cocks. The grandeur was in the spot, in the man, in the reality, in the sword, in the hat, in that eagle, in these soldiers, in that ray of sunlight.

The people were there as before an altar on which God was visible. But on leaving the chapel, after going a hundred yards, they went into the kitchen to see the great saucepan. Such is the nature of the people.

It was with profound emotion that I contemplated that coffin. I remembered that, less than a year before, in the month of July, a Monsieur —— presented himself at my house, and after telling me that he was in business as a cabinet-maker in the Rue des Tourelles and a neighbour of mine, begged me to give him my advice regarding an important and precious article which he was commissioned to make just then. As I am greatly interested in the progress which can be

E

made in that minor internal architecture which is called furnishing, I responded favourably to this request, and accompanied Monsieur —— to the Rue des Tourelles. There, after taking me through several large, well-filled rooms, and showing me an immense quantity of oak and mahogany furniture, Gothic chairs, writing-tables with carved rails, and tables with twisted legs, among which I admired a genuine old Renaissance cupboard inlaid with mother-of-pearl and marble, very dilapidated and very charming—the cabinet-maker showed me into a big workshop full of activity, bustle, and noise, where a score of workmen were busy with pieces of black wood which they had in their hands. In a corner of the workshop I saw a kind of large black ebony box, about eight feet long and three feet wide, fitted at each end with big brass rings. I went towards it. 'That,' said the employer, 'is precisely what I wanted to show you.' This black box was the Emperor's coffin. I saw it then, I saw it again today. I saw it empty, hollow, wide open. I saw it again full, inhabited by a great memory, closed for ever.

I remember that I contemplated the inside for a long time. I looked especially at a long pale vein in the ebony plank which formed the left-hand side, and I said to myself: 'In a few months the lid will be closed on this coffin, and my eyes will perhaps have been closed for three or four thousand years before it will be given to other human eyes to see what I see at this moment—the inside of Napoleon's coffin.'

Then I picked up all the pieces of the coffin which had not yet been fastened, and weighed them in my hands. The ebony was very fine and very heavy. The head of the establishment, in order to give me an idea of the general effect, had the lid put on the coffin by six men. I did not like the commonplace shape which had been given to the coffin, a shape given nowadays to all coffins, all altars, and all wedding caskets. I should have preferred Napoleon to sleep in an Egyptian tomb like Sesostris, or in a Roman sarcophagus like Merovaeus.

On the lid there shone in fairly large characters the name: Napoleon. 'What metal are these letters made of?' I asked the man. He replied: 'In copper, but they are going to be gilded.'

'These letters,' I said, 'must be in gold. In less than a hundred years, copper letters will have become oxydized and will have eaten into the woodwork of the coffin. How much would gold letters cost the State?' 'About twenty thousand francs, sir.' That very evening I called on Monsieur Thiers, who was then President of the Council, and I explained the matter to him. 'You are right,' said Monsieur Thiers, 'the letters shall be in gold; I will go and give the necessary orders.' Three days afterwards, the treaty of 15 July burst upon us; I do not know whether Monsieur Thiers gave the orders, whether they were executed, or whether the letters which are now on the coffin are gold letters.

I left the chapel of Saint-Jérôme as four o'clock was striking, and I said to myself as I went off. 'To all appearances, here is a tinsel N which shatters, eclipses, and supersedes the marble L's with their crowns and fleurs-de-lis of Louis XIV; but, in reality, it is not so. If this dome is narrow, history is wide. A day will come when Louis XIV will have his dome restored to him, and a sepulchre will be given to Napoleon.'

FIESCHI

14 April 1842

In the Boulevard du Temple just now, Fieschi's[1] house is being pulled down. The rafters of the roof have been stripped

[1] Giuseppe Fieschi (1790–1836), with two accomplices called Morey and Pepin, attempted to assassinate Louis-Philippe on 28 May 1835, firing an 'infernal machine' from the window of No. 50, Boulevard du Temple as the King and his suite were riding on their way to the Bastille to celebrate the anniversary of the 1830 Revolution. Several people were killed, including Marshal Mortier, and many wounded. Fieschi and his fellow-conspirators were sentenced to death and executed. [Tr.]

of their tiles. The windows, without glass or frames, reveal the interior of the rooms. At the back, through the windows at the corner of the yard, can be seen the staircase which Fieschi, Pepin, and Morey went up and down so many times with their hideous plan in their heads. The yard is crowded with ladders and scaffolding, and the ground floor is surrounded by a timber hoarding.

What can be seen of Fieschi's room appears to have been embellished and decorated by the different lodgers who have lived in it since. The walls and ceilings are covered with a paper sprinkled with a small greenish pattern, and on the ceiling there is an ornamental paper beading in the shape of a Y. This ceiling, however, has already been broken and cracked in several places by the builder's pick-axe.

On the subject of the Fieschi trial, the Chancellor himself, Monsieur Pasquier, has given me several details which are not generally known.

As long as Fieschi, after his arrest, thought that his accomplices were in sympathy with him, he remained silent. One day, he learnt from his mistress, Nini Lassave, the one-eyed woman, that Morey had said: 'What a pity the explosion did not kill him!' From that moment Fieschi was filled with hatred: he denounced Pepin and Morey, and was as assiduous in bringing about their ruin as he had previously been anxious to save them.

Morey and Pepin were arrested. Fieschi became a fervent ally of the prosecution. He entered into the most minute details, revealed everything, threw light on, traced, explained, unveiled, unmasked everything, concealed nothing, and never told a lie, not caring whether he was putting his head under the knife, provided the other two heads fell.

One day, he said to Monsieur Pasquier: 'Pepin is such a fool that he entered in his account-book the money he gave me for the machine, indicating what it was to be used for. Search his house. Take his account-book for the first six

months of 1835. You will find at the head of one page an entry
of this kind made with his own hand.' His instructions were
followed, the search was ordered, the book was found.
Monsieur Pasquier examined the book, the Public Prosecutor
examined the book; nothing was found. This seemed strange.
For the first time, Fieschi was at fault. He was told about this,
and said: 'Look again.' It was all in vain. The commissioners
of the Court were reinforced by an old examining magistrate,
whom this case made a Councillor at the Royal Court in Paris
(Monsieur Gaschon, whom Chancellor Pasquier, in telling me
all this, called Gâcon or Cachon). This judge, an expert, took
the book, opened it, and, within two minutes, found at the
top of a page, as stated, the memorandum Fieschi had mentioned. Pepin had simply struck it out carelessly, but it remained perfectly legible. The President of the Court of Peers
and the Public Prosecutor, out of a certain habit which it is
easy to understand, had not read the passages which were
struck out, and this memorandum had escaped them.

When it had been found, Fieschi was brought along and
Pepin was brought along, and they were confronted with each
other before the book. Consternation on Pepin's part, joy on
Fieschi's. Pepin faltered, grew confused, wept, talked of his
wife and three children. Fieschi triumphed. The interrogation
was decisive, and Pepin was lost. The sitting had taken a long
time; Monsieur Pasquier dismissed Pepin, took out his watch,
and said to Fieschi: 'Five o'clock! Come, that will do for
today. It is time for you to go and have your dinner.' Fieschi
leapt to his feet: 'Dinner? Oh I have dined today. I have cut
off Pepin's head!'

Fieschi was correct in the smallest particulars. He said one
day that at the time of his arrest he had a dagger on him. No
mention was to be found of this dagger in any of the deposi-
tions. 'Fieschi,' said Monsieur Pasquier, 'what is the use of
telling lies? You had no dagger.' 'Ah!' said Fieschi, 'when I
arrived at the guard-house, I took advantage of the moment
when the policemen had their backs turned to throw the
dagger under the camp-bed which I had been given. It must

still be there. Have a search made. Those gendarmes are a filthy lot. They never sweep underneath their beds.' A visit was made to the guard-house; the camp-bed was moved, and the dagger was found.

I was at the Peers' Court the day before his condemnation. Morey was pale and motionless. Pepin pretended to be reading a newspaper. Fieschi gesticulated, made speeches, laughed. At one moment, he rose and said: 'My lords, in a few days my head will be severed from my body; I shall be dead, and I shall rot in the earth. I have committed a crime, and I am rendering a service. I am going to expiate my crime, and you will gather the fruits of my service. After me, there will be no more riots, no more assassinations, no more disturbances. I tried to kill the King; I shall have succeeded in saving him.'

These words, the gesture, the tone of voice, the time, the occasion impressed me. The man struck me as courageous and resolute. I said so to Monsieur Pasquier, who answered me: 'He did not think that he was going to die.'

He was a bravo, a mercenary, nothing else. He had served in the ranks, and he mixed up his crime with heaven knows what military ideas. 'What you did was appalling,' Monsieur Pasquier told him, 'blowing up perfect strangers, people who had never done you any harm—innocent passers-by.' Fieschi coldly replied: 'That is what soldiers do in an ambush.'

THE DEATH OF THE
DUC D'ORLÉANS

14 July 1842

YESTERDAY, 13 July, the Duc d'Orléans died of an accident.

In this connexion, when one reflects upon the history of the last hundred and fifty years, an idea occurs to the mind. Louis XIV reigned, his son did not reign; Louis XV reigned, his son did not reign; Napoleon reigned, his son did not reign; Charles X reigned, his son did not reign; Louis-Philippe reigns, his son will not reign. This is an extraordinary fact! Six times in succession human foresight designates from amidst a whole people one person who is to reign, and it is precisely that person who does not reign. The fact is repeated with a dreadful and mysterious persistency. A revolution takes place, a universal upheaval of ideas which engulfs in a few years a past of ten centuries, and the whole social life of a great nation; this formidable commotion overturns everything except the fact to which we have referred; on the contrary, it causes that fact to spring up in the midst of all that it demolishes; a great Empire is established, a Charlemagne appears, a new world arises, but the fact goes on recurring; it appears to belong to the new world as well as to the old. The Empire falls, the old line returns; Charlemagne has vanished, exile takes the conqueror, and returns those who had been banished; revolutions form again and break out; dynasties change three times, event follows event, the tide ebbs and flows—and still the fact remains, intact, uninterrupted, unchanged, unbroken. Since monarchies have existed, the law has said: *the eldest son of the King always reigns*; and now for a hundred and forty years, the fact has answered: *the eldest son of the King never reigns*. Does it not seem as if this is a law which is revealing itself, and revealing itself, in the inexplicable order of human occurrences, with a degree of persistence and exactitude which up to now had belonged only to material facts? Would it not be frightening if certain laws of history were to be made manifest to men with the same precision, the same inflexibility and, so to speak, the same harshness, as the great laws of nature?

For the dying Duc d'Orléans a few mattresses were hurriedly thrown on the floor, and a bedside table was made of an old arm-chair turned upside down.

There was a battered stove behind the Prince's head. Pots

and pans and coarse earthenware vessels were arranged on a few boards hung along the wall. A large pair of shears, a fowling-piece, one or two cheap coloured pictures fastened with four nails, represented Mazagran, the Wandering Jew, and the Attempt of Fieschi. A portrait of Napoleon and a portrait of the Duc d'Orléans (Louis-Philippe) as a Colonel-in-Chief of the Hussars, completed the decoration of the wall. The flooring was a square of plain red bricks. Two old wardrobes propped up the Prince's death-bed on the left.

The Queen's chaplain, who assisted the vicar of Neuilly in giving the sacrament of Extreme Unction, is a natural son of Napoleon, the Abbé ——, who greatly resembles the Emperor, minus the air of genius.

Marshal Gérard was present at the death, in uniform; Marshal Soult, in a black coat, with his face like that of an old bishop; Monsieur Guizot, in a black coat; the King, in black trousers and a brown coat. The Queen was dressed in a violet silk gown trimmed with black lace.

20 July 1842

God has bestowed two gifts on man: hope and ignorance. Ignorance is the better of the two.

Every time the Duc d'Orléans, the Prince Royal, went to Villiers to his summer palace, he passed by a squalid-looking house, with only two upper storeys and a single window to each of these two storeys, and with a wretched shop, painted green, on the ground floor. This shop, which had no window looking on to the roadway, had only one door through which could be seen in the shadows a counter, a pair of scales, a few common wares displayed on the floor, and over which was painted in dirty yellow letters this inscription: *Grocery Stores.* It is not at all certain that the Duc d'Orléans, young, lighthearted, gay, and happy, ever noticed this door; but if he occasionally glanced at it while passing quickly along the road on his errands of pleasure, he probably regarded it as the door of some wretched shop, some sty, some hovel. It was the door of his tomb.

Today, Wednesday, I visited the spot where the Prince fell, exactly a week ago now. It is at that part of the road between the twenty-sixth and the twenty-seventh tree on the left, counting the trees from the intersection of the road with the circus at the Porte Maillot. The roadway is twenty-one paving stones wide from one side to the other. The Prince smashed his forehead on the third and fourth paving-stones on the left, near the edge. Had he been thrown eighteen inches farther, he would have fallen on the bare earth.

The King has had the two bloodstained paving-stones removed, and today, in spite of the mud of a rainy day, one could still distinguish the two new stones which have just been put in.

On the wall opposite, between the two trees, a cross has been cut in the plaster by some passer-by, with the date: 13 July 1842. Next to the date is written this word: *Martir* [*sic*].

From the spot where the Prince fell, the Arc de l'Étoile can be seen on the right, through a vista formed by the house and trees. On the same side, and within pistol-shot, there is a great white wall surrounded by sheds and rubbish, bordered by a moat and surmounted by a tangle of cranes, windlasses, and scaffoldings. These are the fortifications of Paris.

While I was examining the two paving-stones and the cross on the wall, a gang of schoolboys, all in straw hats, suddenly surrounded me, and these young, fresh-looking and merry faces gathered with carefree curiosity around the fatal spot. A few steps farther on a young nurse kissed and caressed a little baby, at the same time roaring with laughter.

The house in which the Prince died is No. 4, and is situated between a soap factory and a low eating-house and wine-shop. The shop on the ground floor was shut. Against the wall, on the right-hand side of the door, there was a rough wooden seat, on which two or three old women were basking in the sun. Over their heads, on the green-painted wall, a large bill was stuck, bearing these words: *Esprit Putot Mineral Water*. A pair of white calico curtains at the first-floor window seemed to indicate that the house was still occupied. A number of men, sitting drinking at tables in the neighbouring wine-shop, were laughing and talking noisily. Two doors farther on, on the house No. 6 nearly opposite the spot where the Prince was killed, this sign is painted in black letters: *Chanudet, stone-mason*.

Strangely enough, the Prince fell to the left, and the post-mortem examination showed that the body was bruised and the skull smashed on the right-hand side.

Monsieur Villemain (it was he himself who told me this the day before yesterday) arrived at the Prince's side barely half-an-hour after the accident. All the royal family were already there. On seeing Monsieur Villemain enter, the King hurried over to him and said: 'It was a terrible fall; he is still unconscious, but there is no fracture, the limbs are all supple and uninjured.' The King was right; the whole of the Prince's body was healthy and intact except the head, which, without any visible tear or cut, was broken under the skin like a plate, Villemain told me.

In spite of what has been said on the subject, the Prince neither wept nor spoke. The skull being shattered and the brain torn, this would have been impossible. There was only a little organic life left. The dying man did not see, feel, or suffer. Monsieur Villemain only saw him move his legs twice.

The left-hand side of the road is occupied by gardens and summer-houses; on the right-hand side there are only hovels.

On 13 July, when the Prince left the Tuileries for the last time, he passed, first of all, that human monument which evokes most powerfully the idea of endurance, the obelisk of Rameses; but he might have recalled that on this same spot the scaffold of Louis XVI had been erected. Next he passed that monument which evokes in most splendid fashion the idea of glory, the Arc de Triomphe de l'Étoile; but he might have recalled that the coffin of Napoleon had passed under this same arch. Five hundred yards farther on he passed a road which owes its ominous name to the insurrection of 6 October, fomented by Philippe Égalité against Louis XVI. This road is called the Route de la Révolte. Just as they entered it, the horses conveying the grandson of Égalité ran away, revolted, so to speak, and two-thirds of the way down this fatal road the Prince fell.

The Duc d'Orléans was called Ferdinand after his grandfather of Naples, Philippe after his father and grandfather of France, Louis after Louis XVI, Charles after Charles X, and Henri after Henri V. On his death certificate, his Sicilian name of Rosolino was omitted (was this by design?). I confess I regretted the omission of this pleasing name, which recalled Palermo and St. Rosalie. It was feared that it might be considered ridiculous. Rosolino sounds charming to poets and whimsical to commonplace people.

As I was coming home about six o'clock in the evening, I noticed a bill printed in large letters, stuck here and there on the walls, with the words: *Fête at Neuilly, 3 July*.

KING LOUIS-PHILIPPE

28 June 1844

THE King told me that Talleyrand said to him one day:
'You will never be able to do anything with Thiers, although he would make an excellent tool. He is one of those men one cannot use unless one is able to satisfy them. Now, he will never be satisfied. It is a pity for him, as for you, that in our times he cannot be made a cardinal.'

Talking about the fortifications of Paris, the King told me how the Emperor Napoleon learned the news of the taking of Paris by the Allies.

The Emperor was marching on Paris at the head of his guard. Near Juvisy, at a place in the Forest of Fontainebleau where there is an obelisk ('which I never see without feeling heavy at heart,' the King told me), a courier coming to meet Napoleon brought him the news of the capitulation of Paris. Paris had been taken. The enemy had entered the city. The Emperor turned pale. He hid his face in his hands and remained like that, motionless, for a quarter of an hour. Then, without saying a word, he turned about and took the road back to Fontainebleau.

General Athalin witnessed this scene and described it to the King.

July 1844

A few days ago the King said to Marshal Soult (in the presence of others):

'Marshal, do you remember the siege of Cadiz?'

'Indeed I do, Sire. I swore enough before that accursed Cadiz. I besieged the place and I was forced to go away as I had come.'

'Marshal, while you were before it, I was inside it.'

'I know, Sire.'

'The Cortes and the English Cabinet offered me the command of the Spanish army.'

'I remember.'

'The offer was a serious one. I hesitated for a long time. To bear arms against France! For my family, it is possible; but against my country! I was greatly perplexed. At that point, you asked me, through a trusty person, for a secret interview in a little house situated on the Cortadura, between the city and your camp. Do you remember that, Marshal?'

'Perfectly, Sire. In fact the day was fixed and the interview arranged.'

'And I did not turn up.'

'That is so.'

'Do you know why?'

'I have never known.'

'I will tell you. As I was getting ready to go to meet you, the commander of the English squadron, having heard about it somehow or other, suddenly came to see me and warned me that I was about to fall into a trap; that Cadiz being impregnable, they despaired of seizing me, but that at the Cortadura I would be arrested by you; that the Emperor wanted to make of the Duc d'Orléans a parallel case to that of the Duc d'Enghien, and that you would have me shot immediately. Now, really,' added the King with a smile, 'your hand on your conscience, were you going to shoot me?'

The Marshal remained silent for a moment, then replied, with a smile no less inscrutable than the King's:

'No, Sire; I wanted to compromise you.'

The conversation turned to some other subject. A few minutes later the Marshal took leave of the King, and the King, as he watched him walking away, said with a smile to the person who heard this conversation:

'Compromise! Compromise! Today they call that compromise! The truth is, he would have had me shot!'

August 1844

A month or two ago the King went to Dreux. It was the anniversary of the death of the Duc d'Orléans. The King had chosen this day to put the coffins of his relatives in the family vault in order.

Among them was a coffin which contained all the bones of the princes of the House of Orleans which the Duchesse d'Orléans, the King's mother, had been able to collect after the Revolution, when they had been violated and dispersed. The coffin, placed in a separate vault, had recently been smashed in by the fall of an arch. The debris of the arch, stones and plaster, had become mingled with the bones.

The King had the coffin brought to him and opened. He was alone in the vault with the chaplain and two aides-de-camp. Another coffin which was bigger and stronger had been prepared. The King himself, with his own hands, took the bones of his ancestors out of the broken coffin one after another, and arranged them carefully in the new coffin.

He would not allow anyone else to touch them. Now and then he counted the skulls and said: 'This is Monsieur le Duc de Penthièvre. This is Monsieur le Comte de Beaujolais.' Then, to the best of his ability, and as far as he was able, he completed each group of bones.

This ceremony lasted from nine o'clock in the morning until seven o'clock in the evening without the King taking either rest or nourishment.

16 August 1844

Yesterday, the 15th, after dining at Monsieur Villemain's country house near Neuilly, I called on the King.

The King was not in the drawing-room where there were only the Queen, Madame Adélaïde, and a few ladies, among them Madame Firmin-Rogier, who is charming. There were a good many visitors, including the Duc de Broglie and Monsieur Rossi, with whom I had just been dining, Monsieur de Lesseps, who recently distinguished himself as consul at Barcelona, Monsieur Firmin-Rogier, and the Comte d'Agout.

I bowed to the Queen, who spoke to me at length about the Princesse de Joinville, who was delivered the day before yesterday, and whose baby arrived on the same day as the news of the bombardment of Tangier by its father. It is a little girl. The Princesse de Joinville spends the whole day kissing her and saying: 'How sweet she is!' with that soft southern accent which the teasing of her brothers-in-law has not yet caused her to lose.

While I was talking to the Queen, the Duchesse d'Orléans came in, dressed in black, and sat beside Madame Adélaïde, who said to her: 'Good evening, dear Hélène.'

A moment afterwards, Monsieur Guizot, in black, wearing a chain of decorations and a red ribbon in his buttonhole and the badge of the Legion of Honour on his coat, and looking pale and grave, crossed the room. I shook hands with him and he said:

'I have been looking for you in vain these past few days. Come and spend a day with me in the country. We have a lot to talk about. I am at Auteuil, No. 4, Place d'Agueneau.'

'Will the King come tonight?' I asked him.

'I do not think so,' he replied. 'He is with Admiral de Mackau. The news is serious. He will be occupied all the evening.'

Then Monsieur Guizot went away.

It was nearly ten o'clock. I was about to follow his example and was already in the antechamber when one of Madame Adélaïde's ladies of honour, sent by the Princesse, came and told me that the King wished to speak with me and asked me to stay. I returned to the drawing-room which had become almost empty.

A moment later, as ten o'clock was striking, the King came in. He wore no decorations and had a preoccupied look.

As he passed by he said to me:

'Wait until I have gone my rounds; we shall have a little more time when everybody has left. There are only four people here now and I have only four words to say to them.'

Sure enough, he spent only a moment with the Prussian Ambassador and Monsieur de Lesseps, who had brought him a letter from Alexandria concerning the strange abdication of the Pasha of Egypt.

Everybody took his leave, and then the King came over to me, grasped me by the arm and led me into the large waiting-room where he sat down, offering me a red sofa which is between two doors opposite the fireplace. Then he started talking, rapidly and energetically, as if a weight were being lifted from his mind.

'Monsieur Hugo, I am pleased to see you. What do you think of the situation? It is all very serious, or rather it looks very serious. But in politics, I know, one sometimes has to take into account what looks serious as much as what is serious. We made a mistake in taking on that confounded protectorate of Tahiti. We thought we were doing something popular for France, and we have done something embarrassing for the world. The popular effect was poor; the embarrassing effect is enormous. Why did we have to saddle ourselves with Tahiti (the King pronounced it Taëte)? What did that pinch of tobacco seeds in the middle of the ocean matter to us? What is the use of lodging our honour four thousand leagues away in the box of a sentry insulted by a savage and a madman? On the whole there is something laughable about it. When all is said and done it is a small matter and nothing big will come of it. Sir Robert Peel has spoken thoughtlessly. He has acted like a silly schoolboy. He has diminished his reputation in Europe. He is a serious man, but capable of foolish actions. And then he does not know any languages. Unless he is a genius there are bound to be gaps in the ideas of a man who is not a linguist. Now, Sir Robert is no genius. And—would you believe it?—he does not know French. Consequently he does not understand anything about France. French ideas pass in front of him like shadows. He is not malevolent, no; he is not open, that is all. He has spoken unthinkingly. I judged him to be what he was forty years ago. It was forty years ago that I saw him for the first time. He was a young man then and secretary to the Earl of ——. I did not quite catch the name. The King was talking quickly.) I often visited that house. I was living in England then. When I saw young Peel I felt that he would go a long way, but that he would stop. Was I mistaken? There are some Englishmen, and of the highest rank, who understand nothing about the French. Like that poor Duke of Clarence, who later became William IV. He was just a sailor. One must beware of the sailor mentality, as I often say to my son Joinville. A man who is just a sailor is nothing on land. Well, this Duke of Clarence used to say to me: "Duc d'Orléans, a war between France and England is necessary every twenty years. History shows it." I would reply: "My dear duke, of what use are people of intelligence if they allow mankind to do the same foolish things over and over again?" The Duke of Clarence, like Peel, did not know a word of French.

'What a difference between those men and Huskisson! You know, Huskisson who was killed on a railway line. He was a masterly man, if you like. He knew French and liked France. He had been my comrade at the Jacobins' Club. I don't mean that in bad part. He understood everything. If there were a man like him in England now, he and I would ensure the peace of the world. Monsieur Hugo, we will do it without him. I will do it alone. Sir Robert Peel will reconsider what he has said. He said that! Does he even know why or how?

'Have you seen the English Parliament? You speak from your place, standing among your colleagues; you are carried away; more often than not you say what the others think rather than what you think yourself. There is a magnetic communication. You are subjected to it. You rise.' Here the King rose and imitated the gestures of an orator speaking in Parliament. 'The assembly ferments all round and close to you; you let yourself go. On this side somebody says: "England has suffered a gross insult," and on that side: "With gross indignity." It is simply applause that you look for on both sides. Nothing more. But that is bad. It is dangerous. It is harmful. In France our tribune, which isolates the orator, has many advantages.

'Of all the English statesmen I have known, only one was able to resist that influence of assemblies. That was Mr. Pitt. Mr. Pitt was a celever man, although he was very tall. He had an awkward air and spoke hesitatingly. His lower jaw weighed a hundredweight. Hence a certain slowness which inevitably brought prudence into his speeches. Besides, what a statesman Pitt was! They will do justice to him one of these days, even in France. They still harp on Pitt and Coburg. But that is something which will pass. Mr. Pitt knew French. To carry on politics properly we must have Englishmen who know French and Frenchmen who know English.

F

'Look here, I am going to England next month. I shall be very well received: I speak English. And then Englishmen appreciate the fact that I have studied them thoroughly enough not to hate them. For one always begins by hating the English. This is a superficial effect. I esteem them, and pride myself on the fact. Between ourselves, there is one thing I am afraid of in going to England, and that is an excessively warm welcome. I shall have to avoid an ovation. Popularity there would make me unpopular here. But there is another difficulty. I must not get a bad reception either. Badly received there, I should be ridiculed here. Oh, it is not easy to move when one is Louis-Philippe, is it, Monsieur Hugo?

'However, I shall try to manage it better than that great fool the Emperor of Russia, who went riding full gallop in search of a fall. There's an idiot for you. What a simpleton! He is nothing but a Russian corporal, busy with a boot-heel and a gaiter button. What an idea to arrive in London on the eve of the Polish ball! Do you thing I would go to England on the eve of the anniversary of Waterloo? What is the use of looking for trouble? Nations don't alter their ideas just for princes.

'Monsieur Hugo, Monsieur Hugo, intelligent princes are very rare. Look at the Pasha of Egypt, who had a good mind and who abdicates, like Charles V who, although he was a genius, committed the same foolish action. Look at the idiotic King of Morocco! What a job to govern in the midst of this mob of bewildered Kings! But they won't force me into committing the great mistake of going to war. They are pushing me towards it, but they won't push me into it. Listen to this and remember it: the secret of maintaining peace is to look at everything from the good side and nothing from the bad. Oh, Sir Robert Peel is a strange man to speak so wildly. He doesn't know how strong we are. He doesn't think!

'The Prince of Prussia made a very true remark to my daughter in Brussels last winter: "What we envy France is Algeria. Not on account of the territory, but on account of the war. It is a great and rare good fortune for France to have at her door a war which does not trouble Europe and which is making an army for her. We as yet have only review and parade soldiers. When a collision occurs we shall have only soldiers who have been made by peace. Only France, thanks to Algiers, will have soldiers made by war."

'That is what the Prince of Prussia said, and it was true.

'Meanwhile, we are making children too. Last month it was my daughter of Nemours, this month it is my daughter of Joinville. She has given me a princess. I would have preferred a prince. In view of the fact that they are trying to isolate my house among the royal houses of Europe I must think of future alliances. Well, my grandchildren will marry among themselves. This little girl who was born yesterday won't lack cousins, nor consequently a husband.'

Here the King laughed, and I rose. He had spoken almost without interruption for an hour and a quarter. I had only said a few words here and there. During this sort of long monologue Madame Adélaïde passed by as she retired to her apartments. The King said to her: 'I will join you presently,' and continued his conversation with me. It was nearly half-past eleven when I left the King.

It was during this conversation that the King asked me:

'Have you ever been to England?'

'No, Sire.'

'Well, when you do go—for you will go—you will see how strange it is. There is nothing there which resembles France. Over there you will find order, arrangement, symmetry, cleanliness, boredom, clipped trees, pretty cottages, well-mown lawns, and profound silence in the streets. The passers-by are as serious and silent as ghosts. When, being French, and alive, you speak in the street, those ghosts look round at you and murmur with an indescribable mixture of gravity and disdain: "French people!" When I was in London I was walking arm-in-arm with my wife and sister. We were chatting, but not talking very loudly, for we are well-bred persons, you know; yet all the passers-by, bourgeois and men of the people, turned round to look at us, and we could hear them muttering behind us: "French people! French people!"'

September 1844

King Louis-Philippe said to me the other day:

'I have been in love only once in the whole of my life.'

'And with whom, Sire?'

'With Madame de Genlis.'

'Ah! But she was your tutor.'

The King laughed and replied:

'As you say. And a strict tutor, I can tell you. She brought up my sister and myself quite ferociously. Roused at six in the morning, winter and summer alike; fed on milk, roast meat, and bread; never any dainties, never any sweets; plenty of work and no play. It was she who accustomed me to sleep on boards. She made me learn a great variety of manual skills; thanks to her I can work a little at every trade, including that of a barber-surgeon. I can bleed my man like Figaro. I am a cabinet-maker, a groom, a mason, a blacksmith. She was systematic and severe. As a child I was afraid of her; I was a weak, lazy, cowardly boy; I was afraid of mice! She made me quite a bold man, with a fair amount of spirit. As I grew up, I perceived that she was very pretty. I did not know what was the matter with me when she was present. I was in love, but I never suspected it. She, who was an adept in the matter, understood, and guessed what it was at once. She treated me very badly. It was at the time when she was sleeping with Mirabeau. She constantly said to me: "Come, now, Monsieur de Chartres, you great booby, why are you always at my skirts?" She was thirty-six years old and I was seventeen.'

The King, who saw that I was interested, continued.

'Madame de Genlis has been much talked about and little known. She has had children ascribed to her of whom she was not the mother, Pamela and Casimir. This is how it was:

she loved everything that was beautiful or pretty, she liked to have smiling faces around her. Pamela was an orphan whom she took in on account of her beauty. Casimir was the son of her porter. She thought the child charming; his father used to beat him. "Give him to me," she said one day. The man consented, and that is how she got Casimir. In a little while Casimir became the master of the house. She was old then. Pamela she had in her youth, in our own time. Madame de Genlis worshipped Pamela. When we had to flee the country, Madame de Genlis set out for London with my sister and a hundred louis in money. She took Pamela to London. The ladies were very poor and lived meanly in furnished rooms. It was winter-time. I can assure you, Monsieur Hugo, they did not dine every day. The tastiest morsels were for Pamela. My poor sister sighed and was the victim, the Cinderella. That is how it was. My sister and Pamela, in order to economize the wretched hundred louis, slept in the same room. There were two beds, but only one blanket. My sister had it at first; but one evening Madame de Genlis said to her: "You are strong and healthy; Pamela is very cold; I have put the blanket on her bed." My sister was indignant, but did not dare to rebel; she contented herself with shivering every night. Besides, my sister and myself loved Madame de Genlis.'

Madame de Genlis died three months after the July Revolution. She lived just long enough to see her pupil King. Louis-Philippe was to some extent her handiwork; she had educated him as though she had been a man, and not a woman. She had positively refused to crown her work with the supreme education of love. A strange thing this in a woman with so few scruples, that she should have shaped the heart, and then disdained to complete her work.

When she saw the Duc d'Orléans King, she simply said: 'I am very pleased.'

Her last years were spent in poverty, almost in destitution. It is true that she had no skill in management, and threw her money about. The King often went to see her; he visited her right up to the last days of her life. He and his sister, Madame

Adélaïde, never ceased to pay Madame de Genlis every kind of respect and deference.

Madame de Genlis merely complained of what she called the King's stinginess. She said: 'He was a Prince, I made a man of him; he was clumsy, I made a handy man of him; he was a bore, I made an entertaining man of him; he was a coward, I made a brave man of him; he was stingy, I could not make a generous man of him. Liberal if you like; generous, no.'

September 1844

Monsieur Guizot goes out every day after breakfast, at midday, and spends an hour at the residence of the Princesse de Liéven, in the Rue Saint-Florentin. In the evening he returns and, except on official days, he spends the whole evening there.

Monsieur Guizot is fifty-seven years old; the Princess is fifty-eight. With regard to this, the King said one evening to Monsieur Duchâtel, the Minister of the Interior: 'Hasn't Guizot a friend to advise him? Let him beware of those north-country women. He does not know what they are like. When a north-country woman is old, and gets hold of a man younger than herself, she sucks him dry.' Then the King burst out laughing. Monsieur Duchâtel, who is fat and stout, who wears whiskers, and who is forty-five, turned crimson.

October 1844

The King, when at home in the evening, does not usually wear any decoration. He is dressed in a brown coat, black trousers, and a waistcoat of black satin or white piqué. He has a white cravat, silk open-work stockings, polished shoes. He wears a grey toupee only slightly concealed, and arranged in the style of the Restoration. No gloves. He is gay, good-natured, affable, and chatty.

His visit to England delighted him. He spoke to me about it for an hour and a half, with much gesticulation, accompanied by many imitations of English pronunciation and mannerisms.

'I was very well received,' he said. 'Crowds of people, acclamations, salvoes of artillery, banquets, ceremonies, fêtes, visits from the Corporation, an address from the City of London, nothing was wanting. In all this, two things especially touched me. Near Windsor, at a posting stage, a man who had run after my carriage came and stood close to me at the window, shouting: "Long Live the King!" in French. Then he added, also in French: "Sire, welcome to the home of this ancient people; you are in a country which knows how to appreciate you." That man had never seen me before and will never see me again. He expects nothing of me. It seemed to me as though he was the voice of the people. This affected me more than any other compliment. In France, at the stage beyond Eu, a drunkard, seeing me pass, shouted: "There is the King who has come back; it is all right now; the English are satisfied, and the French will be at peace." The contentment and peace of the two peoples, that indeed was my aim. Yes, I was well received in England. And, if the Emperor of Russia compared his reception with mine, it must have been quite painful to him, he who is so vain. He went to England before me to prevent me from paying my visit. It was a foolish thing to do. He would have done better to go after me. They would then have been obliged to treat him in the same way. In London, for instance, he is not liked. I do not know whether they would have got the members of the Corporation to take the trouble to go and see him. Those aldermen are very stolid.'

Louis-Philippe used to make fun of the elder Monsieur Dupin, who, thinking to heighten the refinements of Court language, calls Madame Adélaïde, the King's sister, *Ma belle demoiselle*.

Saint-Cloud, November 1844

The King yesterday looked tired and care-worn. When he saw me, he led me into the apartment behind the Queen's room and said to me, as he showed me a large tapestry couch, with parrots worked on it in medallions: 'Let us sit down on these birds.' Then he took my hand and said, in a rather bitter, plaintive voice:

'Monsieur Hugo, I am misunderstood. I am said to be proud, I am said to be clever. That means that I am a traitor. It grieves me. I am simply an honest man. I go straight ahead. Those who are acquainted with me know that I am not wanting in frankness. Thiers, when he was working with me, told me one day when we were in disagreement: 'Sire, you are cunning and proud, but I am more cunning than you.'' "The proof that that is not so," I replied, "is that you tell me so." Monsieur de Talleyrand said to me one day: "You will never make anything of Thiers, who otherwise would be an excellent instrument. But he is one of those men who can only be used if you satisfy their requirements. And he will never be satisfied. The misfortune for him as well as for you is that there is no longer any possibility of his being a Cardinal." Thiers is clever, but he has too much of the conceit of a self-made man. Guizot is better. He is a man of weight, a fulcrum; the species is a rare one, and I appreciate it. He is superior even to Casimir Périer, who had a narrow mind. His was the soul of a banker, sealed to the ground like a strong-box. Ah! how rare is a true minister! They are all like schoolboys. The attendances at the Council are irksome to them; the most important affairs are dealt with at a gallop. They are in a hurry to be off to their departments, their commissions, their offices, their gossiping. In the period after 1830 they had a look of uneasiness and humiliation when I presided. Moreover, no real appreciation of power, little basic grandeur, no consistency in aim, no persistency of will. They leave the Council like children leaving a classroom. On the day he left the Ministry, the Duc de Broglie jumped for joy in the Council chamber.

Marshal Maison arrived. "What is the matter with you, my dear duke?" "Marshal, we are leaving the Ministry." "You entered it like a wise man," said the Marshal, who had a sense of humour, "and you leave it like a madman." The Comte Molé, now, had a way of yielding to me and resisting at one and the same time. "I share the King's opinion as to the general question, but not as to the expediency." Monsieur Hugo, if you only knew how things happen sometimes at the Council! The Right of Search treaty, the famous Right of Search, would you believe it, was not even read at the Council. Marshal Sébastiani, at that time Minister, said: "Pray read the treaty, gentlemen." I said: "My dear Ministers, pray read the treaty." "Oh, we have not time, we know what it is; let the King sign," they said. And I signed.'

THE ATTEMPT OF LECOMTE

31 May 1846

THE Court of Peers has been summoned to try the case of another attempt on the person of the King.

On 16 April last the King went for a drive in the forest of Fontainebleau, in a charabanc. Beside him was Monsieur de Montalivet, and behind him were the Queen and several of their children. They were returning home about six o'clock, and were passing the walls of the Avon enclosure, when two shots were fired from the left. No one was hit. Rangers, gendarmes, some officers of hussars who were escorting the King, all sprang forward. A groom climbed over the wall and seized a man whose face was half masked with a neckerchief. He was an ex-Ranger of the Crown forests, who had been dismissed from his post eighteen months before for a grave dereliction of duty.

1 June 1846, midday

The orators' tribune and the President's chair have been removed.

The accused is seated on the spot where the tribune usually stands, with his back to a green baize curtain, hung there for the trial, between four gendarmes with grenadiers' hats, yellow shoulder-straps, and red plumes. In front of him are seated five barristers, with white bands at their necks and black robes. The one in the centre has the ribbon of the Legion of Honour, and grey hair. It is Maître Duvergier, the President of the Corporation of Barristers. Behind the prisoner, red benches, occupied by spectators, fill the semicircle where the Chancellor usually presides.

The accused is forty-eight years of age; he does not look more than about thirty-six. He has nothing in his face which would suggest the deed which he has done. It is one of those calm, almost insignificant faces which impress favourably rather than otherwise. General Voirol, who is sitting beside me, says to me: 'He looks a decent fellow.' However, a sombre expression gradually spreads over his face, which is quite handsome, although of a vulgar type, and he takes on the appearance of an ill-natured fellow. From where I am, his hair and moustache appear black. He has a long face with ruddy cheeks. He keeps his eyes downcast nearly all the time; when he raises them, every now and then, he looks right up at the ceiling; if he were a fanatic, I should say up to Heaven. He has a black cravat, a white shirt, and an old black frock-coat, with a single row of buttons and no ribbon, although he belongs to the Legion of Honour.

General Berthuzène leans over and tells me that yesterday Lecomte remained quiet all day, but that he flew into a temper when he was refused a new black frock-coat which he had asked for 'to appear in before the High Court'. This is a trait of character.

While the names of the peers were being called over his eyes wandered here and there. To the preliminary questions of the Chancellor he replied in a low voice. Some of the peers called out: 'Speak up!' The Chancellor told him to turn towards the Court.

The witnesses were brought in, among them one or two women, very stylishly dressed, and some peasant women. They are on my right, in the lobby on the left of the tribune. Monsieur Decazes walks about among the witnesses. Monsieur de Montalivet, the first witness, is called. He is wearing the red ribbon, together with two stars, one of a foreign order. He comes in limping on account of his gout. A footman, in a russet livery with a red collar, assists him.

I have examined the articles brought forward in support of the indictment, which are in the right-hand lobby. The gun is double-barrelled, with twisted barrels, the breech decorated with arabesques in the Renaissance style; it is almost a fancy weapon. The smock worn by the assassin is blue and fairly old. The neckerchief with which he hid his face is of cotton, coffee-coloured, with white stripes. To each of these articles there is attached a small card bearing the signatures of the prosecuting officials and the signature of Pierre Lecomte.

5 June 1846

During an interval in the trial I observed the man from close quarters. He looks his age. He has the tanned skin of a huntsman and the faded skin of a prisoner. When he speaks, when he becomes excited, when he stands upright, he looks strange. His gestures are abrupt, his attitude fierce. His right eyebrow rises towards the corner of his forehead and gives him an indescribably wild and diabolical appearance. He speaks in a quiet but firm voice.

At one point, explaining his crime, he said:

'I stopped on the 15th of April at the Place du Carrousel. It was raining. I stood under a projecting roof, looking at some engravings. There was a conversation going on in the adjoining shop, where there were three men and a woman. I listened without meaning to. I felt sad. Suddenly I heard the name of the King; they were talking about the King. I looked at the men. I recognized them as servants at the Palace. They said the King would be going the following day to Fontaine-bleau. At that instant my idea occurred to me. It came to me clear and terrible. The rain stopped. I put my hand out from under the projecting roof. I found that it had stopped raining, and I walked away. I went home to my little room, to my bare, wretched room. I remained there alone for three hours. I mused, I pondered, I was very unhappy. I kept on thinking about my plan. And then the rain started coming down again. The weather was gloomy; a strong wind was blowing; the sky was nearly black. I felt like a madman. Suddenly I got up. It was settled. I had made up my mind. That is how the idea came into my head.'

At another point, when the Chancellor said that there was no motive for the crime, he said:

'What do you mean? I wrote to the King, once, twice, three times. The King did not reply. And then . . .'

He did not finish what he was saying; but his fist clutched the rail fiercely. At that moment he was terrifying. He was a real savage. He sat down. He was calm again. Calm and fierce.

While the Public Prosecutor was speaking, he moved about like a wolf and looked furious. When his counsel (Duvergier) spoke, tears came into his eyes. They ran down his cheeks, heavy and clearly visible.

This is how it all happens. On his name being called in a loud voice by the clerk of the Court, each peer rises and pronounces sentence, also in a loud voice.

The thirty-two peers who voted before me all declared for the parricide's penalty.[1] One or two mitigated this to capital punishment.

[1]A man condemned to 'the parricide's penalty' was taken to the guillotine barefoot, with his head covered with a black veil, and exposed on the scaffold while the death-sentence was read out. The cutting off of his right hand, which had hitherto formed part of the penalty, had been abolished by 1846. [Tr.]

When my turn came, I rose and said:

'Considering the enormity of the crime and the futility of the motive, it is impossible for me to believe that the delinquent acted in the full possession of his moral liberty, of his will. I do not think he is a human creature with an exact perception of his ideas and a clear consciousness of his actions. I cannot sentence this man to any other punishment but life imprisonment.'

I said these words in a very loud voice. At the first words all the peers turned round and listened to me in a silence which seemed to invite me to continue. I stopped short there, however, and sat down again.

The calling of the names continued.

The Marquis de Boissy said:

'We have just heard some solemn words. The Vicomte Victor Hugo has given utterance to an opinion which deeply impresses me, and to which I give my support. I think, with him, that the delinquent is not in full possession of his reason. I declare for life imprisonment.'

The calling of the names continued with the lugubriously monotonous rejoinders: 'Capital punishment. . . . The parricide's penalty.'

Proceeding according to the dates at which the members of the House took their seats, the list came down to the oldest peers. The Vicomte Dubouchage being called in his turn, said:

'Already uneasy in my mind during the trial, on account of the manner of the accused, but fully convinced by Monsieur Victor Hugo's observations, I declare that, in my opinion, the delinquent is not of sound mind. The Vicomte Hugo gave the reasons for this opinion in a few words, but in a way which appeared to me conclusive. I support him in his vote, and I declare, like himself, for life imprisonment.'

The other peers, of whom only a very few remained, all voted for the parricide's penalty.

The Chancellor, the last to be called, rose and said:

'I declare for the parricide's penalty. Now a second vote

will be taken. The first vote is only provisional, the second alone is final. All are, therefore, at liberty to retract or confirm their votes. An opinion worthy of careful consideration in itself, and not less worthy of consideration owing to the quarter from which it emanates, has been expressed with authority, although supported by a very small minority, during the course of the voting. I think it right to declare here that during the long investigation preceding the trial, an investigation lasting seven weeks, I saw the accused every day. I examined him, pressed him, questioned him, and, as old parliamentarians say, "turned him round" in every direction. Never for a single moment did his perception falter. I always found that he reasoned correctly within the frightful logic of his deed, without any sign of either mental derangement or repentance. He is not a madman. He is a man who knows what he wanted to do, and who admits what he has done. Let him suffer the consequences.'

The second roll-call began. The number of peers voting for the parricide's penalty increased. When my name was called, I rose. I said:

'The Court will appreciate the scruples of one in whose anguished conscience such terrible questions are suddenly agitated for the first time. This moment, my lords, is a solemn one for all, for no one here more than for myself. For the past eighteen years I have had fixed and definite ideas on the subject of irreparable penalties. You are familiar with those ideas. As a mere author, I have published them; as a politician, with God's help, I will apply them. As a general rule, irreparable penalties are repugnant to me; in no particular instance do I approve of them. I have listened closely to the Chancellor's observations. They are weighty, coming from so eminent a mind. I am struck by the imposing unanimity of this imposing assembly. But, while the Chancellor's opinion and the Court's unanimity are a great deal from the point of view of reasoning, they are nothing in the face of one's conscience. Before the speeches began, I read, re-read, and studied all the evidence; during the trial, I studied the attitude, the looks, and the gestures of the accused, and scrutinized his soul. Well, I tell this Court of just men, and I tell the Chancellor, whose opinion carries so much weight, that I stand by my vote. The accused has led a solitary life. Solitude is good for great, and bad for little minds. Solitude deranges those minds which it does not enlighten. Pierre Lecomte, a solitary man with a small mind, was necessarily destined to become a savage man with a deranged mind. The attempt on the King, the attempt on a father, at such a time, when he was surrounded by his family; the attempt on a group of women and children, death dealt out haphazardly, twenty possible crimes inextricably added to a deliberate crime—there is the deed. It is monstrous. Now let us examine the motive. Here it is: a deduction of twenty francs out of an annual allowance, a resignation accepted, three letters left unanswered. How can one fail to be struck by such a juxtaposition and such an abyss? I repeat, in conclusion, in the presence of these two extremes, the most heinous of crimes, the most insignificant of motives, it is evident to me that the thing is absurd, that the mind which has made such a juxtaposition and bridged such an abyss, is an illogical mind, and that this criminal, this assassin, this wild and solitary man, this fierce savage being, is a madman. To a doctor, perhaps, he is not a madman; to a moralist he certainly is. I would add that here expediency is in harmony with justice, and that it is always well to dissociate human reason from a crime which revolts against Nature and shakes the foundations of society. I stand by my vote.'

The peers listened to me with profound and sympathetic attention. Monsieur de Boissy and Monsieur Dubouchage stood firm, as I did.

There were 232 voters. This is how the votes were distributed:

196 for the parricide's penalty;
33 for capital punishment;
3 for life imprisonment.

The whole Chamber of Peers may be said to have been displeased at the execution of Lecomte. He had been condemned in order that he might be reprieved. It was an opportunity for clemency which the peers had held out to the King. The King seized such opportunities eagerly, and the Chamber knew this. When it learned that the execution had actually taken place, it was surprised, almost hurt.

Immediately after the condemnation, the Chancellor and Chief President Franck-Carré were summoned by the King. Monsieur Franck-Carré was the peer who had been delegated to draw up the case. They went to the Palace in the Chancellor's carriage. Monsieur Franck-Carré, although he had voted for the parricide's penalty, was openly in favour of a reprieve. The Chancellor also leant in this direction, although he would not declare himself on the subject. On the way he said to President Franck-Carré: 'I directed the investigation, I directed the prosecution, I directed the trial. I had some influence on the vote. I will not give any opinion on the subject of a reprieve. I have enough responsibility as it is. They will do what they like.'

In the King's study he respectfully adopted the same attitude. He declined to express any definite opinion on the subject of a reprieve. President Franck-Carré was explicit. The King guessed what the Chancellor's opinion was.

Maître Duvergier had taken a liking to his client, as a barrister always does to the client he has to defend. This is only to be expected. The Public Prosecutor ends up by hating the accused, and the counsel for the defence by loving him. Lecomte was sentenced on a Friday. On the Saturday, Monsieur Duvergier went to see the King. The King received him in a friendly manner, but said: 'I will think about it; I will consider it. It is a serious matter. A danger to me is a danger to all. My life is of great consequence to France, so that I must defend it. However, I will think the matter over. You know that I hate the death penalty. Every time I have to sign the dismissal of an appeal for a reprieve I am the first to suffer. All my inclinations, all my instincts, all my convictions

are on your side. However, I am a constitutional King; I have
Ministers who decide. And then of course I must think a little
of myself too.'

Monsieur Duvergier left the King's presence deeply distressed. He saw the King would not grant a reprieve.

The Council of Ministers was unanimously in favour of the
execution of the sentence of the Court of Peers.

On the following day, Sunday, Monsieur Duvergier received an express letter from the Keeper of the Seals, Martin
du Nord, informing him that *the King had thought fit to
decide that the law should take its course.* He was still under
the influence of the first shock of hope shattered, when a
second express letter arrived.

In this letter the Keeper of the Seals informed the President
of the Corporation of Barristers that the King, wishing to
grant the condemned man, Pierre Lecomte, a *further* token of
his good will, had decided that the annual pension of the said
Lecomte should revert to his sister for her lifetime, and that
His Majesty had placed a sum of three thousand francs at the
sister's immediate disposal for her assistance. 'I thought,' said
the Keeper of the Seals, in conclusion, 'that it would be agree-
able to you to communicate yourself this evidence of the royal
favour to the unfortunate woman.'

Monsieur Duvergier thought he had made some mistake in
reading the first letter. 'A *further* token,' he said to one of his
friends who was present. 'I was mistaken, then. The King
must have granted a reprieve.' But he re-read the letter, and
saw that he had read it only too correctly. *A further token* remained inexplicable to him. He refused to accept the commission which the Keeper of the Seals had asked him to
undertake.

As for Lecomte's sister, she refused the three thousand francs
and the pension; she refused them with a certain bitterness
and also a certain dignity. 'Tell the King,' she said, 'that I
thank him. I would have thanked him better for something
else. Tell him that I do not forget my brother so quickly as to
take his spoils. This is not the boon that I expected of the

G

King. I need nothing. I am very unhappy and poor, I am nearly starving of hunger, but it pleases me to die like this, since my brother died like that. He who causes the death of the brother has no right to support the sister.'

Monsieur Mérilhou played a sadly active part during the whole of this case. He was a member of the Commission of the Peers during the preliminary investigation. He wanted to omit from the brief for the prosecution the letter in which Doctor Gallois spoke of Lecomte as a madman. It was at one moment proposed to suppress the letter.

Lecomte displayed a certain courage. At the last moment, however, on the night preceding the execution, he asked, about two o'clock, to see the Public Prosecutor, Monsieur Hébert, and Monsieur Hébert, on leaving him after a conversation lasting a quarter of an hour, said: 'He has completely collapsed; his mind is gone.'

12 June 1846

I dined yesterday at the house of Monsieur Decazes with Lord Palmerston and Lord Lansdowne.

Lord Palmerston is a stout, short, fair man, who is said to be a wit. His face is full, round, broad, red, merry, and shrewd, and slightly vulgar. He was wearing a red ribbon and a star which I think is that of the Bath.

The Marquis of Lansdowne offers a striking contrast to Lord Palmerston. He is tall, dark, spare, grave, and courteous, with an air of breeding: a gentleman. He had a star on his coat, and round his neck a dark-blue ribbon on which there hung a gold-enamelled decoration, in the shape of a wheel surmounted by the Irish harp.

Monsieur Decazes introduced these two gentlemen to me. We spoke for a few minutes about Ireland, cereals, and the potato disease.

'Ireland's disease is graver still,' I said to Lord Palmerston.

'Yes,' he replied; 'the Irish peasants are very wretched. Now *your* peasants are happy. But you are favoured by the skies. What a climate France has!'

'Yes, my Lord,' I answered; 'but you are favoured by the sea. What a citadel England is!'

Lady Palmerston is graceful and talks well. She must have been charming at one time. She is no longer young. Lord Palmerston married her four years ago, after a mutual passion which had lasted thirty years. I conclude from this that Lord Palmerston belongs a little to history and a great deal to romance.

At table, I was between Monsieur de Montalivet and Alexandre Dumas. Monsieur de Montalivet was wearing the cross of the Legion of Honour, and Alexandre Dumas the cross of an order which he told me was that of St. John, and which I believe to be Piedmontese.

In conversation with Monsieur Montalivet I broached the subject of the event of 16 April. He was, as everyone knows, sitting beside the King in the charabanc.

'What were you talking about with the King when the explosion occurred?' I asked.

'I cannot remember,' he replied. 'I took the liberty of questioning the King on this subject. He could not remember either. Lecomte's bullet destroyed something in our memory. All I know is that while our conversation was not important we were very intent on it. If it had not absorbed our attention we would certainly have noticed Lecomte when he stood up above us to fire: the King at all events would have done so, for I myself had my back turned slightly in order to speak to the King. All that I remember is that I was gesticulating at the time. When the first shot was fired, someone in the suite cried: "It is a sportsman unloading his gun." I said to the King: "A strange kind of sportsman to fire the remains of his powder at kings." As I finished speaking, the second shot went off. I cried: "It is an assassin!" "Oh!" said the King, "not so fast, we must not judge too hastily. Let us wait. We shall find out what it was." You recognize the King in that, do you not? Calm and serene in the presence of the man who had just fired at him; almost kindly. At that moment the Queen touched me gently on the shoulder; I turned round.

Without saying a word, she showed me the wadding of the gun which had fallen into her lap, and which she had just picked up. There was a certain calmness about that silence of hers which was solemn and touching. The Queen, when the carriage leans over a little, trembles for fear it will be overturned; she makes the sign of the cross when it thunders; she is afraid of a display of fireworks; she alights when a bridge has to be crossed. When the King is fired on and she is present, she is calm.'

A VISIT TO THE CONCIERGERIE

I REMEMBER that on Thursday, 10 September 1846, St. Patient's day, I decided to go to the Académie. There was to be a public meeting for the award of the Montyon prize, with a speech by Monsieur Viennet. Arriving at the Institut, I climbed the staircase in some perplexity. In front of me, running up the stairs boldly and cheerfully, with the nimbleness of a schoolboy, there was a member of the Institut in full dress, with his coat buttoned up, tight-fitting and nipped in at the waist, a lean, spare man, with a lively step and a youthful figure. He turned round. It was Horace Vernet. He had a huge moustache, and three crosses of different orders hanging from his neck. In 1846 Horace Vernet was certainly over sixty years of age.

Arriving at the top of the staircase, he entered. I felt neither as young nor as bold as he, and I did not enter.

In the street outside the Institut, I met the Marquis of B——. 'You have just come away from the Académie?' he asked. 'No,' I replied; 'one cannot come away if one has not gone in. And you, how is it you are in Paris?' 'I have just come from Bourges.' The Marquis, an ardent Legitimist, had been to see Don Carlos, the son of him who took the title of Charles

V. Don Carlos, whom the faithful called Prince of the Asturias, and afterwards King of Spain, and who was known to European diplomacy as the Comte de Montemolin, looked with some annoyance on the marriage of his cousin, Dona Isabella, with the Infante Don Francisco d'Assiz, Duke of Cadiz, which had just been concluded at that very time. He had shown the Marquis how surprised he felt, and even let him see a letter addressed by the Infante to him, the Comte de Montemolin, in which this sentence occurred: 'I will not think of my cousin as long as you remain between her and me.'

We shook hands, and Monsieur de B—— left me.

As I was returning along the Quai des Morfondus, I passed St. Louis's old round towers and I felt an urge to visit the prison of the Conciergerie.

I could not say how the idea came into my head unless it was that I wanted to see how man had contrived to render hideous inside what is so magnificent outside, or unless it was that I had a desire to substitute a visit to the Conciergerie for a meeting of the Académie, in imitation of Frédérick Lemaître who, acting in *Rober Macaire*, announced one fine day on the poster that that evening the fifth act would be replaced by a balloon.

I accordingly turned to the right, into the little courtyard, and rang at the grating of the doorway. The door opened and I gave my name. I had my Peer's medal with me. A door-keeper was put at my disposal, to serve as a guide wherever I wished to go.

The first impression which strikes one on entering a prison is a feeling of darkness and oppression, a diminution of light and air, something ineffably nauseous and insipid, intermingled with the funereal and the lugubrious. A prison has its odour just as it has its *chiaroscuro*. Its air is not air, its daylight is not daylight. Iron bars have some power, it would seem, over those two free and heavenly things, air and light.

The first room we came to was none other than St. Louis's old guardroom, a huge hall divided into a large number of compartments for the requirements of the prison. Everywhere there are pointed arches and pillars with capitals, all scraped, pared, levelled, and marred by the hideous taste of the architects of the Empire and the Restoration. I make this remark once and for all, the whole building having been treated in the same fashion. In this guardroom one could still see on the right-hand side the nook where the pikes were stacked, marked out by a pointed moulding in the corner between the two walls.

The outer office in which I stood was the spot where the 'toilet' of condemned criminals used to take place. The office itself was on the left. In this office there was a very polite old fellow, buried under a heap of cardboard boxes and surrounded by cupboards, who rose as I entered and took off his cap, lighted a candle and said:

'You would probably like to see Héloïse and Abélard?'

'Good Heavens,' I said, 'there is nothing I should like better.'

The old man took the candle, pushed to one side a green case bearing this inscription: '*Discharges for the month*,' and showed me in a dark corner behind a big cupboard a pillar with a capital depicting a monk and a nun back to back, the nun holding in her hand an enormous phallus. The whole thing was painted yellow, and was called Héloïse and Abélard.

The good man continued:

'Now that you have seen Héloïse and Abélard, you would probably like to see the condemned cell?'

'Certainly,' I said.

'Show the gentleman the way,' said the good man to the turnkey.

Then he returned to his cases. This peaceful creature keeps the register of the sentences and terms of imprisonment.

I went back to the outer office, where I admired as I passed a very large and handsome shell-work table in the brightest and prettiest Louis XV taste, with a marble border; but dirty, hideous, daubed with paint which had once been white, and relegated to a dark corner. Then I passed through a gloomy room encumbered with wooden bedsteads, ladders, broken panes of glass, and old window-frames. In this room the turn-key opened a door with a dreadful noise of heavy keys and drawn bolts, and said: 'Here it is, sir.'

I went into the condemned cell.

It was a fairly large place, with a low arched ceiling, and paved with St. Louis's old stone flooring, square blocks of lias-stone alternating with slabs of slate. There were paving-stones missing here and there. A fairly large semi-circular vent-hole, protected by its iron bars and projecting shaft, admitted a pale and wan sort of light. There was no furniture, except an old cast-iron stove from the time of Louis XV, decorated with panels in relief, which it was impossible to distinguish owing to rust, and in front of the skylight, a large arm-chair in oak which was in fact a toilet. The chair was of the period of Louis XIV, and covered with leather, which was partly torn away and exposing the horsehair. The stove was on the right of the door. My guide told me that when the cell was occupied a folding bed was placed at the back. A gendarme and a warder, relieved every three hours, watched the condemned man day and night, standing the whole time, without a chair or bed, so that they might not fall asleep.

We returned to the outer office, which led to two more rooms, the parlour of the privileged prisoners who were able to receive their visitors without standing behind a double row of iron bars, and the *salon* of the barristers, who were entitled to communicate freely and in private with their clients. This '*salon*', for so it was described in the inscription over the door, was a long room, lighted by an opening in the wall, furnished with long wooden benches, and similar to the other parlour.

It seems that some young barristers had in certain cases been guilty of abusing the privilege of a legal tête-à-tête. Female thieves and poisoners are occasionally very good-looking. The abuse had been discovered, and the '*salon*' had been provided with a glazed doorway. In this way it was possible to see, although not to hear.

At this point the Governor of the Conciergerie, a Monsieur Lebel, came up to us. He was a venerable old man, with a shrewd look in his eye. He wore a long frock-coat, with the ribbon of the Legion of Honour in his buttonhole. He apologized for not having ascertained before that I was in the place, and asked me to allow him to accompany me on the tour of inspection which I wished to make.

The outer office led through a gateway into a long, wide, and spacious vaulted passage.

'What is that?' I asked Monsieur Lebel.

'That,' he said, 'used to be connected with St. Louis's kitchens. It was very useful to us during the riots. I did not know what to do with my prisoners. The Prefect of Police asked me: "Have you plenty of room just now? How many prisoners can you accommodate?" I replied: "I can accommodate 200." They sent me 350, and then said to me: "How many more can you accommodate?" I thought they were joking. However, I made room by using the Women's Infirmary. "You can," I said, "send me 100 prisoners." They sent me 300. This rather annoyed me, yet they said: "How many more can you find room for?" This time I replied: "You can send as many as you like." Sir, they sent me 600! I installed them here; they slept on the floor on trusses of straw. They were very excitable. One of them, Lagrange, the Republican from Lyons, said to me: "Monsieur Lebel, if you will let me see my sister, I promise you I will make everybody here keep quiet." I allowed him to see his sister; he kept his word, and my roomful of 600 devils became a little heaven. My Lyons men remained well behaved and charming until the day when, the House of Peers having taken up the matter, they were brought in contact, during the official inquiry, with the Paris rioters, who were in Sainte-Pélagie. The latter said to them: "You must be mad to remain quiet like that. Why, you should complain, you should shout, you should be frenzied." My Lyons men now became frenzied, thanks to the Parisians. They became absolute devils. Oh, what trouble I had! They said to me: "Monsieur Lebel, it is not because of you, but because of the Government. We want to show our teeth to the Government." And Reverchon stripped naked.'

'He called that showing his teeth, did he?' I asked Monsieur Lebel.

In the meantime, the turnkey had opened the great gate at the far end of the corridor, then other gates and heavy doors, and I found myself in the heart of the prison.

Through the railed arches I could see the men's exercise yard. It was a fairly large oblong courtyard, above which towered on every side St. Louis's high walls, now plastered and disfigured.

A number of men were walking up and down in groups of two or three; others were sitting in the corners, on the stone benches which surround the yard. Nearly all wore prison dress—large jackets with linen trousers; two or three, however, wore frock-coats. One of the latter was still clean and sedate-looking, and had a certain town-bred air about him. He was the wreck of a gentleman.

This yard had nothing sinister about it. It is true that the sun was shining brightly, and that everything looks pleasant in the sun—even a prison. There were two flower beds with some trees, which were small but very green, and between the two beds, in the middle of the yard, there was an ornamental fountain with a stone basin.

This yard was formerly the cloister of the Palace. The Gothic architect had surrounded it on all four sides with a gallery with pointed arches. The modern architects have filled these arches with masonry; they have built floors and partitions in them and made two storeys. Each arcade made one cell on the ground floor and one on the first floor. These cells, clean and fitted with timber floorings, had nothing very repulsive about them. Nine feet long by six feet wide, a door opening into the corridor, a window overlooking the ground, iron bolts, a large lock and a railed opening in the door, iron bars to the window, a chair, a bed in the corner on the left of the door, covered with coarse linen and coarse blanketing, but very carefully and neatly made, that is what these cells were like.

It was recreation time. Nearly all the cells were open, the men being in the yard. Two or three, however, remained closed, and some of the prisoners, young workmen—shoemakers and hatters, for the most part—were working inside, making a great noise with their hammers. They were, I was told, hard-working and well-conducted prisoners, who preferred to do some work rather than go out for exercise.

The quarters of the privileged prisoners were above. The cells were a little bigger, and as a result of the greater liberty enjoyed here at a cost of sixteen centimes a day, a little dirtier. As a general rule, in a prison, the greater the cleanliness the less liberty there is. These wretched creatures are so constituted that their cleanliness is the token of their servitude. They were not alone in their cells; there were sometimes two or three together; there was one large room in which there were six. An old man with a kindly, honest-looking face was reading in this room. He raised his eyes from his book when I entered, and looked at me like a country priest reading his breviary and sitting on the grass with the sky above him. I made inquiries, but I could not discover of what this good man was accused.

Monsieur Lebel called my attention, in the yard, to the spot where a prisoner had made his escape a few years before. The right-angle formed by the two walls of the yard at the northernmost end had been sufficient for the man's purpose. He had planted his back in this corner and hoisted himself up solely by the muscular force of his shoulders, elbows, and heels, as far as the roof, where he had caught hold of a stove-pipe. If this stove-pipe had given way under his weight, he would have been a dead man. Reaching the roof, he had climbed down again into the outer enclosure and fled. All this in broad daylight. He was captured again in the Palais de Justice. His name was Bottemolle. 'An escape like that deserved better luck,' said Monsieur Lebel. 'I was almost sorry to see him brought back.'

At the entrance to the men's yard there was, on the left, a little office reserved for the chief warder, with a table placed at a right-angle before the window, a leather-covered chair,

and all kinds of cardboard boxes and papers upon the table.
Behind this table and chair was an oblong space about eight
feet by four. It was the site of the cell formerly occupied by
Louvel.[1] The wall which divided it from the office had been
demolished. At a height of about seven feet the wall ended,
and was replaced by an iron grating reaching to the ceiling.
The cell was lighted only through this and the window in the
door, the light coming from the corridor and the office and
not from the courtyard. Through this grating and through the
window of the door Louvel, whose bed was in the far corner,
was watched night and day. For all that, two turnkeys were
installed in the cell itself. When the wall was pulled down, the
architect had the door preserved—a low door, armed with a
big square lock and round bolt—and had it built into the
outer wall. It was there that I saw it.

I remember that in my early youth I saw Louvel cross the
Pont-au-Change on the day he was taken to the Place de
Grève. It was, I think, in the month of June. The sun was
shining brightly. Louvel was in a cart, with his arms tied
behind his back, a blue coat thrown over his shoulders, and
a round hat on his head. He was pale. I saw him in profile.
His whole face suggested a sort of earnest ferocity and violent
determination. There was something cold and grim in his
appearance.

Before we left the men's quarters, Monsieur Lebel said:
'Here is a curious spot.' And he took me into a round,
vaulted room, fairly high, about fifteen feet in diameter, without any window or opening in the wall, and lighted only
through the doorway. A circular stone bench ran all round
the room.

'Do you know where you are now?' asked Monsieur Lebel.

'Yes,' I replied.

I recognized the famous torture chamber. This room occupies the ground floor of the crenellated tower, the smallest of
the three round towers on the quay.

[1] Louis-Pierre Louvel (1783–1820) assasinated the Duc de Berry in 1820.
[Tr.]

In the centre was a sinister, strange-looking object. It was a sort of long, narrow table of lias-stone, joined with molten lead poured into the crevices, very heavy, and supported on three stone pillars. This table was about two and a half feet high, eight feet long, and twenty inches wide. Looking up, I saw a big rusty iron hook fastened in the round stone which forms the keystone of the arch.

This object is the rack. A leather covering used to be put over it, on which the victim was stretched. Ravaillac[2] remained for six weeks on this table, with his feet and hands tied, bound at the waist by a strap attached to a long chain hanging from the ceiling. The last ring of this chain was fastened to the hook which I could still see fixed above my head. Six gentlemen guards and six guards of the Provost's department watched him night and day.

Damiens[3] was guarded like Ravaillac in this chamber, and tied down on this table during the whole time occupied by the investigation and the trial of his case.

Desrues, Cartouche, and Voisin were tortured on this table.[4]

The Marquise de Brinvilliers[5] was stretched out on it stark naked, fastened and, so to speak, quartered by four chains attached to her four limbs, and there suffered the frightful 'extraordinary torture by water' which caused her to ask: 'How are you going to put that great barrel of water into this little body?'

A whole dark history is there, having filtered, so to speak, drop by drop into the pores of these stones, these walls, this vault, this bench, this table, this pavement, this door. It is all there; it has never left the place. It has been shut up there, it has been bolted up. Nothing has escaped, nothing has

---

[2] François Ravaillac (1578–1610) assassinated Henri IV. [Tr.]

[3] Robert-François Damiens (1715–57) tried to assassinate Louis XV and was quartered. [Tr.]

[4] Antoine-François Desrues (1744–77) was a poisoner. Cartouche (1693–1721) was a highwayman who was broken on the wheel on the Place de Grève. Voisin was Catherin Desayes, know as La Voisin, a poisoner who was beheaded and burnt in 1680. [Tr.]

[5] Marie Madeleine d'Aubray, the Marquise de Brinvilliers (1630–76), was a poisoner who was beheaded and burnt on the Place de Grève. [Tr.]

evaporated; no one has ever spoken, related, betrayed, revealed anything of it. This crypt, which is like an inverted funnel, this case made by the hands of man, this stone box, has kept the secret of all the blood it has drunk, of all the shrieks it has stifled. The frightful occurrences which have taken place in the judges' den still palpitate and live there and exhale all sorts of horrible miasmas.

What a strange abomination this chamber is, and this tower placed in the very middle of the quay, without any moat or wall to separate it from the passer-by! Inside, the saws, the boots, the racks, the wheels, the pincers, the hammers knocking in the wedges, the hiss of flesh touched with the red-hot iron, the spluttering of blood on the live embers, the cold questions of the magistrates, the desperate shrieks of the tortured man; outside, four paces away, citizens coming and going, women chattering, children playing, tradespeople selling their wares, vehicles rolling along, boats on the river, the roar of the city, air, sky, sun, liberty!

It is a sinister thought that this windowless tower has always seemed silent to the passer-by; it made no more noise than it does now. How thick these walls must be for the noise of the street not to have reached the tower, and for the noise of the tower not to have reached the street!

I contemplate this table in particular with a curiosity filled with awe. Some of the prisoners had carved their names on it. Near the centre, there were eight or ten letters beginning with an M and forming an illegible word which were cut fairly deep. At one end the name *Merel* had been written with a punch. (I quote from memory and may be mistaken, but I think that is the name.)

The wall was hideous in its nakedness. It seemed as if one could feel its fearful, pitiless solidity. The paving was the same kind of paving as in the condemned cell; that is to say, St. Louis's old black and white stones in alternate squares. A large square brick stove had taken the place of the old furnace for heating the instruments of torture. This room is used in winter-time as a place of warmth for the prisoners.

We then went on to the women's building. After being in the prison for an hour, I was already so accustomed to the bolts and bars that I no longer noticed them, any more than the air, peculiar to prisons, which suffocated me when I went in. It would therefore be impossible for me to say how many doors were opened to enable us to walk from the men's to the women's quarters. I cannot remember. I only recall that an old woman, with a nose like a bird of prey, appeared at a gate and opened it for us, asking if we wished to look round the yard. We accepted the offer.

The women's exercise-yard was much smaller and much gloomier than that of the men. There was only one bed of shrubs and flowers, a very narrow one, and I do not think there were any trees. Instead of the ornamental fountain there was a wash-house in the corner. A female prisoner, with bare arms, was inside washing her clothes. Eight or ten women were sitting in the yard in a group, talking, sewing, and working. I raised my hat. They stood up and looked at me inquisitively. Most of them seemed to belong to the lower middle class, and looked like small shopkeepers of about forty. That appeared to be about the average age. There were, how-ever, two or three young girls.

Next to the yard there was a little room into which we entered. There were two young girls there, one sitting, the other standing. The one who was sitting looked ill; the other was nursing her.

I asked: 'What is the matter with this girl?'

'Oh, it is nothing,' said the other, a tall, rather handsome brunette with blue eyes; 'she is ofen like this. She is feeling faint. This often happened to her at Saint-Lazare. We were there together. I look after her.'

'What is she charged with?' I continued.

'She is a maid. She stole six pairs of stockings from her employers.'

Just then the invalid turned pale and fainted. She was a poor girl of sixteen or seventeen.

'Give her some air,' I said.

The tall girl took her in her arms like a child, and carried her into the yard. Monsieur Lebel sent for some ether.

'She stole six pairs of stockings,' he said, 'but it is her third offence.'

We went back into the yard. The girl was lying on the stones. The women gathered round her and gave her the ether to smell. The old wardress took off her garters, while the tall dark girl unlaced her clothing. As she undid her stays, she said:

'This comes over her every time she puts on stays. I'll give you stays, you little fool!'

In those words, *little fool*, there was a gentle, sympathetic note.

Monsieur Lebel felt the sick girl's pulse. I took the opportunity to slip a five-franc piece into her hand.

All the women exclaimed: 'She is coming to! Poor dear!'

'It's because her garters were taken off,' said one.

'It's because her stays were undone,' said another.

'It's because she breathed some ether,' said a third.

'It's because the Governor felt her pulse,' said the wardress.

The tall brunette bent over to me and whispered to me: 'It's because you gave her five francs.'

We left the place.

One of the peculiarities of the Conciergerie is that all the cells occupied by regicides since 1830 are in the women's quarters.

I entered, first of all, the cell which had been occupied by Lecomte, and which had just been tenanted by Joseph Henri.[6] It was a very large room, well lighted, with nothing of the cell about it but the stone floor, the door, armed with the biggest lock in the Conciergerie, and the window, a large railed opening opposite the door. This room was furnished as follows: in the corner near the window a boat-shaped mahogany bedstead, four and a half feet wide, in the most imposing Restoration style; on the other side of the window, a

---

[6] Joseph Henri, like Lecomte, tried to assassinate Louis-Philippe in 1846. [Tr.]

mahogany writing-table; near the bed, a mahogany chest of drawers with lacquered rings and handles; on the chest of drawers a looking glass, and in front of the looking glass a mahogany clock in the form of a lyre, the face gilded and chased; a square mat at the foot of the bed; four mahogany chairs covered with Utrecht velvet; between the bed and the writing table, a china stove. This furniture, with the exception of the stove, which would shock the taste of ordinary people, is a rich shopkeeper's dream. Joseph Henri was dazzled by it. I asked what had become of that poor madman. After being transferred from the Conciergerie to the Prison of La Roquette, he had set out that very morning, in the company of eight thieves, for the convict-prison of Toulon.

The window of this cell looked out on the women's exercise yard. It was fitted with a rusty old shaft full of holes. Through these holes one could see what was going on in the yard, an amusement for the prisoner not altogether without drawbacks for the women, who thought they were alone and safe from observation there.

Next door was the cell formerly occupied by Fieschi and Alibaud.[7] Ouvrard, who was the first to occupy it, had had a marble chimney-piece installed in it (St. Anne marble, black with white veins) and a large wooden partition, making a bed-room and dressing-room. The furniture was mahogany and very similar to that in Joseph Henri's room. After Fieschi and Alibaud, this cell had been occupied by the Abbé de Lamen-nais and the Marchioness de Larochejacquelein, then Prince Louis Napoleon, and finally, that 'stupid Prince de Berghes', as Monsieur Lebel put it.

Opposite these two cells was the entrance to the Women's Infirmary, a long wide room, too low-ceilinged for its size. There were a score of beds there, with no one in them. I expressed surprise at this.

'I hardly ever have any invalids,' said Monsieur Lebel. 'In the first place, the prisoners only stay here a short time. They

[7] Louis Alibaud (1810–36) tried to assassinate Louis-Philippe on 25 June 1836 and was executed on 11 July. [Tr.]

come to await their trial, and go away immediately afterwards; if acquitted, to liberty; if convicted, to their destination. As long as they are here the anticipation of their trial keeps them in a state of excitement, which leaves room for nothing else. Yes, they have no time to get ill in; they have another sort of feverishness than fever. At the time of the cholera epidemic, which was also the great period of riots, I had 700 prisoners here. They were everywhere, in the doorways, in the offices, in the waiting-rooms, in the yards, on the beds, on straw, on the paving-stones. I thought: Good Heavens! I only hope I do not have the cholera on top of all this. Sir, I did not have a single prisoner fall ill.'

There is certainly a moral in these facts. They show that strong mental excitement is a preservative against all ailments. In times of pestilence, while sanitary and hygienic measures should not be neglected, the people should be entertained with grand fêtes, grand spectacles, moving experiences. If no one troubled about the epidemic, it would disappear.

When, in the cells on the opposite side, there was some prisoner guilty of an attempt on the person of the King, the Women's Infirmary was converted into a guard-room. Here fifteen or twenty warders were installed, kept *incommunicado* like the prisoner himself, seeing no one, not even their wives, and this all the time the preliminary investigation lasted, sometimes six weeks, sometimes two months.

'That is what I do,' added Monsieur Lebel, from whom I had these details, 'when I have regicides.'

This phrase came to his lips in the most natural manner possible; ;to; him it was a sort of habit to *have regicides*.

'You spoke,' I said, 'in a contemptuous manner of the Prince de Berghes. What do you think of him?'

He wiped his eye-glasses on his sleeve, and replied:

'Oh, I do not think anything of him; he was a poor simpleton, well bred, with excellent manners and a gentle expression, but a fool. When he arrived here I put him first of all in this Infirmary, which is a big room, so that he might have space and air. He sent for me. "Is my case a serious one, sir?" he

H

asked. I stammered a few embarrassed words. "Do you think," he went on, "that I shall be able to leave this evening?" "Oh, no," I said. "Well, tomorrow then? "Nor tomorrow," I replied. "What! Do you really think they will keep me here for a week?" "Perhaps longer." "Longer than a week! Longer than a week! Then my case really is a serious one? Do you think my case is serious?" He walked up and down, repeating this question, to which I made no reply. His family, however, did not abandon him. The Duchesse his mother, and the Princesse his wife, came to see him every day. The Princesse, a very pretty little woman, asked if she might share his prison cell. I gave her to understand that this was impossible. When all is said and done, what was his offence? Forgery, certainly; but without any motive. It was an act of stupidity, nothing more. The jury found him guilty because he was a prince. If he had been some rich merchant's son he would have been acquitted. After he was sentenced to three years' imprisonment he was left here for some time with me, and then transferred to a sanatorium, where a whole wing was reserved for his exclusive use. He has been there nearly a year now, and he will be left there for another six months; then he will be pardoned. So that while his being a prince damaged him at his trial, it helps him in prison.'

As we were going along a passage, my guide stopped me and drew my attention to a low door about four-and-a-half feet high, armed with a huge square lock and a big bolt, very similar to the door of Louvel's cell. It was the door of Marie-Antoinette's cell, the only part of her prison which had been preserved just as it was, Louis XVIII having converted her cell into a chapel. It was through this door that the Queen went to the Revolutionary Court; it was through this door too that she went to the scaffold. The door no longer turned on its hinges. Since 1814 it had been fixed in the wall.

I have said that it had been preserved just as it was, but I was mistaken. It was daubed with a fearful nankeen-coloured paint; but this is of no consequence. What sanguinary souvenir is there which has not been painted either a yellow or a rose colour?

A moment later I was in the chapel which had once been her cell. If one could have seen there the bare stone floor, the bare walls, the iron bars at the opening, the Queen's folding bed and the gendarme's camp bed, together with the historic screen which separated them, it would have created a profound feeling of emotion and an indescribable impression. Instead one saw a little wooden altar, which would have been a disgrace to a village church, a coloured wall (yellow, of course), small stained-glass windows, as in a Turkish café, a raised wooden platform, and on the wall two or three abominable paintings, in which the bad style of the Empire struggled with the bad taste of the Restoration. The entrance to the cell had been replaced by an archivolt cut in the wall. The vaulted passage along which the Queen walked to the Court had been walled up. There is a respectful vandalism that is even more revolting than vindictive vandalism, because of its stupidity.

Nothing was to be seen there of what the Queen's eyes had seen, unless it was a small portion of the paved flooring, which the boards fortunately did not entirely cover. This floor was an old-fashioned, chevroned pavement of bricks, set on edge, with the narrow side uppermost.

A straw-bottomed chair, placed on the platform, marked the spot where the Queen's bed had stood.

Coming away from this venerable spot, profaned by foolish piety, I went into a large room next door, which had been the priests' prison during the Terror, and which had been converted into the chapel of the Conciergerie. It was very mean-looking and very ugly, like the Queen's chapel-cell. The Revolutionary Court held its sittings above this room.

While walking about in the depths of the old building, I noticed here and there, through openings in the walls, huge cellars, mysterious deserted halls, with portcullises opening on to the river, fearful dungeons, dark passages. In these crypts spiders' webs abounded, as well as mossy stones, sickly gleams of light, vague, distorted forms. I would ask Monsieur Lebel:

'What is this place?' He would reply: 'This is no longer used.' What had it been used for?

We had to go back through the men's yard: as we were crossing it, Monsieur Lebel pointed out to me a staircase near the latrines. It was here that a murderer called Savoye, who had been condemned to the galleys, had hanged himself only a few days before, from the banister rails.

'The jury have made a mistake,' the man had said. 'I ought to have been condemned to death. I will settle the matter.'

He 'settled' it by hanging himself.

He was under the special supervision of a prisoner who had been made a warder to watch him, and whom Monsieur Lebel dismissed.

While the Governor of the Conciergerie was giving me these details a fairly well-dressed prisoner came up to us. He seemed to wish to be spoken to. I asked him a few questions. He was a young fellow who had been an embroiderer and lace-maker, then assistant to the Paris executioner, what was formerly called the 'headsman's valet', and finally, he said, a groom in the King's stables.

'Sir,' he said to me, 'please ask the Governor not to have me put into prison dress, and to leave me my *fainéant*.' This word which has to be pronounced *faignant*, means overcoat in the latest slang. He had, in fact, quite a good coat. I obtained permission for him to keep it, and I got him into conversation.

He spoke very highly of Monsieur Sanson, the executioner, his former master. Monsieur Sanson lived in the Rue du Marais-du-Temple, in an isolated house, whose Venetian shutters were always closed. He had a great many callers. Scores of English people went to see him. When visitors called at Monsieur Sanson's, they were introduced into an elegant reception-room on the ground floor, entirely furnished in mahogany, in the middle of which there was an excellent piano, usually open, and provided with pieces of music. Shortly afterwards Monsieur Sanson arrived and asked his visitors to be seated. The conversation turned on one topic and another. Generally, the English visitors asked to see the guillotine. Monsieur Sanson granted this request, no doubt for a consideration, and took the ladies and gentlemen to the next street (the Rue Albouy, I think), to the house of the scaffold-manufacturer. There was a shed at this place, where the guillotine stood all the time. The strangers gathered round it, and it was made to *work*. Trusses of hay were guillotined.

One day an English family consisting of the father, the mother, and three pretty daughters, fair and rosy-cheeked, presented themselves at Sanson's house. It was in order to see the guillotine. Sanson took them to the carpenter's and worked the instrument. The knife fell and rose again several times at the request of the young ladies. One of them, however, the youngest, was not satisfied with this. She made the executioner explain to her, in the minutest detail, what is called the *toilet of the condemned*. Still she was not satisfied. At last she turned hesitatingly towards the executioner.

'Monsieur Sanson,' she said.

'Mademoiselle?' said the executioner.

'What is done when the man is on the scaffold? How is he tied down?'

The executioner explained the horrible business to her, and said: 'We call that *putting him in the oven*.'

'Well, Monsieur Sanson,' said the young lady, 'I want you to put me in the oven.'

The executioner started. He gave an exclamation of surprise. The young lady insisted.

'It is a fancy which has taken me,' she said, 'to be able to say that I have been tied down on it.'

Sanson spoke to the father and mother. They replied:

'As she has taken a fancy to have it done, do it.'

The executioner had to give in. He made the young lady sit down, tied her legs with a piece of string, and her arms behind her back with a rope, fastened her to the swinging plank, and strapped her on with the leather strap. Here he wanted to stop.

'No, no, there is something more,' she said.

Sanson then swung the plank down, placed the head of the

young lady in the dreadful neckpiece, and closed it over her neck. Then she declared she was satisfied.

When he told the story afterwards, Sanson used to say: 'I thought she was going to say: *"There's something more, Make the knife fall."* '

Nearly all the English visitors ask to see the knife which cut off Louis XVI's head. This knife was sold as scrap, in the same way as all the other guillotine-knives when they are worn out. The English refuse to believe it, and offer to buy it from Monsieur Sanson. If he had cared to take up this trade, there would have been as many of Louis XVI's knives as of Voltaire's walking sticks.

From his anecdotes of Sanson, my informant, who said he had formerly been a groom at the Tuileries, wanted to go on to anecdotes of the King. He had heard the King talking to the ambassadors, etc. . . . I told him not to put himself out. I remembered that he was a Gascon and an embroiderer and his political revelations struck me as high-class *passementerie*.

Up to 1826, the Conciergerie had no other entrance but a gate opening into the courtyard of the Palais de Justice. It was through this gate that criminals condemned to death came out. In 1826 the doorway was made which is to be seen on the quay between the two great round towers. These two towers, like the tower of the torture chamber, had a room on the ground floor without a window. The two grotesque Gothic arches, without a *voussoir* or an equilateral triangle for a base, which are still admired here to this day and which are masterpieces of ignorance, were opened in these splendid walls by a sort of stonemason called Peyre, who held the office of architect to the Palais de Justice, and who mutilated, dishonoured, and disfigured the building as may be seen.

These two rooms, now lighted, make two fine round apartments. Their walls are decorated with inlaid Gothic arches, of admirable purity, resting on exquisite brackets. These charming triumphs of architecture and sculpture were never intended to see the light of day, and were intended, strangely enough, for horror and darkness.

The first of the two rooms, the nearer to the men's yard,
had been converted into a dormitory for the warders. There
were a dozen beds in it arranged like the rays of a star round
a stove placed in the centre. Above each bed a plank fixed in
the wall across the delicate mullions of the architecture, held
the personal belongings of the warders, generally consisting of
a brush, a trunk, and an old pair of boots. Over one of the
beds, however, next to the pair of boots, which was not wanting in a single case, was a pile of books. I noticed this; it was
explained to me. It was the library of a warder called Peiset,
to whom Lacenaire[8] had imparted literary tastes. This man,
seeing Lacenaire constantly reading and writing, first admired
and then consulted him. He was not unintelligent; Lacenaire
advised him to study. Some of the books which were there
were Lacenaire's. Lacenaire had given them to him. Peiset
had bought a few other old books on the quays; he took the
advice of Lacenaire, who said 'Read this', or 'Do not read that'.
By degrees, the jailer became a thinker, and it was thus that
an intelligence had been awakened and opened by that hideous
breath.

The other room could only be entered by a door which bore
this inscription: 'Entrance reserved for the Governor.' Mon-
sier Lebel graciously opened it for me, and we found ourselves
in his *salon*.

This apartment had in fact been transformed into the
Governor's 'drawing-room'. It was almost identical with the
other, but differently furnished. This drawing-room was an
extraordinary hotch-potch. The architecture of St. Louis, a
chandelier which had belonged to Ouvrard, hideous wallpaper in the Gothic arches, a mahogany writing-desk, some
articles of furniture with unbleached calico coverings, an old
portrait of a magistrate without either case or frame and
nailed askew to the wall, some engravings, some heaps of
paper, a table looking like a counter: altogether a room
which partook of a palace, a prison-cell, and a back-shop. It

[8] Pierre-François Lacenaire (1800–36) was a notorious murderer who left
some highly readable memoirs of doubtful authenticity. [Tr.]

was criminal, magnificent, ugly, ridiculous, sinister, royal, and vulgar.

It was into this room that the visitors of the privileged prisoners were shown. At the time of his detention, which had left a great many traces at the Conciergerie, Monsieur Ouvrard used to see his friends here. The Prince de Berghes used to see his wife and mother here.

'What does it matter to me if they receive their visitors here?' said Monsieur Lebel. 'They think themselves in a drawing-room, and they are none the less in a prison.'

The worthy man seemed convinced that the Duchesse and the Princesse de Berghes must have thought they were in a drawing-room.

It was there too that the Chancellor, the Du Pasquier, used to prepare the preliminaries of the official inquiries confided to him in respect of trials before the House of Peers.

The Governor's lodgings communicated with this room. They were very mean and ugly-looking. The sort of den which served as his bedroom depended entirely on the doors for light and air, that is to say as far as I could see, for I went through quickly. It was clean, but of a rather musty cleanliness, and had all sorts of odds and ends in the corners, and old-fashioned knick-knacks, and all those trifles one sees in the rooms of elderly people. The dining-room was larger, and had windows. Two or three attractive young ladies were sitting there on straw-bottomed chairs, working under the supervision of a lady of about fifty. They rose with a modest, gentle air as I passed, and their father, Monsieur Lebel, kissed them on the forehead.

Nothing stranger could be imagined than this sort of Anglican vicarage, surrounded by the infamous interior of a prison, and walled in as it were and preserved in all its purity in the midst of every vice, every crime, every disgrace, and every shame.

'But,' I said to Monsieur Lebel, 'what has become of the hall of the chimney-pieces? Where is it?'

He appeared to turn this question over in his mind like a person who does not understand.

'The hall of the chimney-pieces? Did you say the hall of the chimney-pieces?'

'Yes,' I said, 'a great hall which was under the waiting-room, with four huge chimney-pieces, built in the thirteenth century, in the four corners. Why, I distinctly remember coming to see it some twenty years ago with Rossini, Meyerbeer, and David d'Angers.'

'Ah!' said Monsieur Lebel. 'I know what you mean. That is what we call St. Louis's kitchens.'

'Well, St. Louis's kitchens then, if that is what you call them. But what has become of that hall? Apart from the four chimney-pieces, it had some handsome pillars supporting the roof. I have not seen it so far. Has your architect, Monsieur Peyre, hidden it away?'

'Oh, no. Only he did some alterations in it for us.'

These words, quietly spoken, made me shudder. The hall of the chimney-pieces was one of the most remarkable monuments of the royal and domestic architecture of the Middle Ages. What might not a creature like the architect Peyre have done with it? Monsieur Lebel continued:

'We scarcely knew where to put our prisoners during the time when they have to undergo their preliminary examination. Monsieur Peyre took St. Louis's kitchens and turned them into a splendid waiting-room with three compartments— one for men, one for women, and one for children. He did this in the best manner possible, and he did not damage the old hall to any great extent, I can assure you.'

'Will you take me there?' I asked Monsieur Lebel.

'Gladly.'

We went along some long, wide, low, narrow corridors. Here and there we came across a staircase crowded with gendarmes, and in the midst of a bunch of policemen and warders we saw a poor wretch whom the ushers were handing on to each other, at the same time saying this word: 'Disposable.'

'What does that word mean?' I asked my guide.

'It means that there is a man whom the examining

magistrate has done with, and who is at the disposal of the gendarme.'

'To set him free?'

'No, to take him back to prison.'

Finally the last door opened.

'Here you are,' said the Governor, 'in the room you were looking for.'

I looked around.

I was in darkness.

I had a wall in front of my eyes.

My eyes, however, gradually became accustomed to the darkness, and after a few moments I distinguished on my right, in a recess, a lofty, splendid chimney-piece, in the shape of an inverted funnel, built of stone and resting, by means of an open buttress of the most exquisite style, against a pillar which stood in face of it.

'Ah,' I said, 'here is one of the chimney-pieces. But where are the others?'

'This is the only one,' replied Monsieur Lebel, 'which remains intact. Of the three others, two have been completely destroyed and the third mutilated; that was necessary to build our waiting-rooms. Similarly we had to fill up the spaces between the pillars with stone-work. We had to put up partitions. The architect preserved this chimney-piece as a specimen of the architectural style of that time.'

'And,' I added, 'of the folly of the architects of our time. The hall has gone, partitions have appeared, and out of four chimney-pieces three have been destroyed. And this was done under Charles X. This is what the sons of St. Louis have done with the souvenirs of St. Louis.'

'It is true,' continued Monsieur Lebel, 'that the waiting-rooms might very well have been placed elsewhere. But then you see they did not think of that, and this hall was available. However, they arranged it very well. It is divided by stone walls into longitudinal compartments, each lighted by one of the windows of the old hall. The first is that of the children. Would you like to go in?'

A turnkey opened a heavy door with a peep-hole in it, by means of which a watch could be kept on the waiting-room, and we went in.

The children's waiting-room was an oblong room, a parallelogram, provided with two stone benches on the two longest sides. There were three boys there. The eldest was a fairly big boy. He looked about seventeen, and was dressed in frightful yellowish rags.

I spoke to the youngest, who had a fairly intelligent, though enervated and sullen face.

'How old are you, my boy?'

'Twelve, sir.'

'What have you done to be in here?'

'I took some peaches.'

'Where?'

'In a garden at Montreuil.'

'By yourself?'

'No, with my friend.'

'Where is your friend?'

He pointed to one of the others, who was dressed like himself in the prison material, and was a little bigger than he was, and said: 'There he is.'

'You climbed a wall, then?'

'No, sir. The peaches were on the ground, in the road.'

'You just bent down?'

'Yes, sir.'

'And picked them up?'

'Yes, sir.'

At this point Monsieur Lebel leaned towards me and said: 'He has already been taught his lesson.'

It was obvious, in fact, that the child was lying. There was neither honesty nor decision in his gaze. He looked at me stealthily, as a sharper examines his victim, and what is more, with that delighted expression of a child who is fooling a man.

'You are not telling the truth, my lad,' I said.

'Yes, I am, sir.'

This 'Yes, I am, sir,' was said with that kind of impudence

in which one feels that everything is missing, even assurance.
He added boldly:

'And for that I have been sentenced to three years' imprisonment. But I am appealing.'

'Haven't your relatives come to claim you?'

'No, sir.'

'And was your friend sentenced too?'

'No, his relatives claimed him.'

'So he is a better boy than you?'

The boy hung his head.

Monsieur Lebel said to me: 'He has been sentenced to
three years' detention in a House of Correction, to be brought
up there—acquitted, that is to say, for not having acted "with
understanding". The misfortune of all these little scamps is
to be under sixteen years of age. They do everything they can
to persuade the authorities that they are sixteen, and guilty
with understanding; you see, when they are sixteen years and
one day old they are punished with a few months' imprisonment for their pranks. If they are a day under sixteen, they
have three years' detention at La Roquette.'

I gave a small sum of money to those poor little wretches
who, perhaps, were only wanting in education. All things considered, society is more guilty towards them than they are
towards society. We can ask them: 'What have you done with
our peaches?' Very well. But they can reply: 'What have you
done with our intelligence?'

'Thank you, sir,' said the youngster, putting the money in
his pocket.

'I would have given you twice as much,' I told him, 'if you
had not told a lie.'

'Sir,' replied the boy, 'I have been sentenced, but I am
appealing.'

'It was bad to take peaches, but it was worse to tell a lie.'

The child did not seem to understand.

'I am appealing,' he said.

We left the cell, and as the door was closing the boy
followed us with his eyes, still repeating: 'I am appealing.'

The two others had not said a word.

The second compartment was reserved for men and was exactly similar to the first. I did not go in, but contented myself with looking through the peep-hole. It was full of prisoners, among whom the turnkey pointed out to me a youth with a pleasant face, reasonably well dressed, and wearing a thoughtful expression. This was a certain Pichery, the ringleader of a gang of thieves who were going to be tried in a few days' time.

The third slice cut out of St. Louis's kitchens was the women's jail. It was thrown open to me. I saw only seven or eight inmates, all over forty years old, with the exception of a youngish woman who still retained some remains of good looks. This poor creature hid herself behind the others. I understood this bashfulness, and I neither asked nor permitted any questions.

All kinds of women's oddments—baskets, bags, work-bags, pieces of knitting—littered the stone benches. There were also some big pieces of brown bread. I picked up one piece. It was the colour of manure, smelt very nasty, and stuck to my fingers like birdlime.

'What is this?' I asked Monsieur Lebel.

'It is the prison bread.'

'But it is horrible!'

'Do you think so?'

'Look at it yourself.'

'It is supplied by a contractor.'

'Who makes his fortune out of it, I imagine.'

'Monsieur Chavet, the Secretary of the Prefecture, has to examine the bread. He considers it very good, so good that he has it on his own table.'

'Monsieur Chavet,' I said, 'is wrong to judge the bread eaten by the prisoners by the bread he receives himself. Just because the speculator sends him good bread every day, that does not prove that he is not sending filth to the prisoners.'

'You are right. I will speak to him about it.'

I learnt afterwards that the quality of the bread had been looked into and that an improvement had been made.

On the whole, there was nothing remarkable about this cell, unless it was that the walls were covered all over with inscriptions. Here are the three which stood out promiently in bigger letters than the others: *'Corset.—I have been sentenst to six months for vagabondige.'—'Love for life.'*

The three doors of the compartment opened on to the same passage, a long dark corridor, at the two ends of which, like two stone tiaras, were the rounded forms of the two chimney-pieces which had been preserved, and of which, as I have already said, there was only one which was complete. The second had lost its principal ornament—its buttress. Of the others, all that remained visible was the sites on which they had stood in the corners of the children's compartment and the women's compartment.

It was on the easternmost of these two latter chimney-pieces that the curious figure of the demon Mahidis was carved. The demon Mahidis was a Persian devil whom St. Louis brought back from the Crusades. He was to be seen upon the chimney-piece with his five heads, for he had five heads, and each of these five heads had composed one of those songs which are called *ragas* in India, and which are the oldest music known.

These ragas are still celebrated and dreaded throughout Hindustan, on account of their magic powers. There is no juggler who is bold enough to sing them. One of these ragas, sung at midday, makes the night fall instantly, and conjures up from the ground a huge circle of darkness, which spreads as far as the voice of the singer will carry.

Another is called the Ihupuck raga. Whoever sings it perishes by fire. Legend has it that the Emperor Akbar one day was smitten by a desire to hear this raga sung. He sent for a famous singer called Naïk-Gopaul, and said to him:

'Sing me the Ihupuck raga.'

Thereupon the poor singer, trembling from head to foot, fell on his knees before the Emperor. The Emperor had his whim and was inflexible. The only concession the singer could obtain was to be allowed to go and see his family for the last time. He set out, returned to his home-town, made his will, embraced his old father and mother, took leave of all that he loved in the world, and returned to the Emperor.

Six months had passed. Eastern kings have melancholy and tenacious whims.

'Ah, there you are, minstrel,' said Shah Akbar, in a sad but friendly voice. 'Welcome. You are going to sing me the Ihu-puck raga.'

Naïk-Gopaul trembled and implored once more.

But the Emperor was inexorable. It was winter-time. The Jumna was frozen over; people were skating on it. Naïk-Gopaul had the ice broken and got into the water up to his neck.

He started singing. At the first stanza the water became warm; at the second stanza the ice melted, at the third stanza the river began to boil. Naïk-Gopaul was cooking; he was covered with blisters. Instead of singing, he started shouting:

'Mercy, Sire.'

'Go on,' said Akbar, who was no mean lover of music.

The poor wretch went on singing. His face turned crimson, his eyes started out of his head, but he continued to sing while the Emperor listened in ecstasy. Finally a few sparks shot out of the singer's hair, which was standing on end.

'Mercy!' he cried, for the last time.

'Sing!' said the Emperor.

He began the last stanza with a howl of pain. Suddenly flames burst forth from his mouth, then from his entire body, and the fire consumed him in the midst of the water.

That is one of the habitual effects of the music of the demon Mahidis, who was represented on the demolished chimney-piece.

He had a wife called Parbutta, who is the author of what the Hindus call the sixth raga. Thirty *raginis*, a music of a feminine and inferior character, were dictated by Boimba. It was these three devils or gods who invented the gamut of twenty-one notes which forms the basis of the music of India.

As we were going out, three gentlemen in black coats, escorted by a turnkey, passed near us; they were visitors.

'Three new members of the Chamber of Deputies,' Monsieur Lebel informed me in a whisper.

They had whiskers and high cravats, and spoke like provincial academicians. They were full of admiration, and went into ecstasies over the work which had been done in the way of embellishing the prison and making it suitable for the requirements of justice.

One of them maintained that Paris was growing remarkably beautiful, *thanks to the architects of taste who were modernizing* [sic] *the ancient buildings*: and he asserted that the Académie Français ought to make these embellishments the subject of a prize competition in poetry. This set me thinking, that, sure enough, Monsieur Peyre had done for the Palais de Justice what Monsieur Godde has done for Saint-Germain-des-Prés, and Monsieur Debret for Saint-Denis; and while Monsieur Lebel was giving some instructions to the warders, I wrote with a pencil on a pillar of the hall of chimney-pieces some verses on the subject which I might submit if ever the Académie should open the competition desired by these gentlemen, and which, I hope, would secure the prize.

I finished just as Monsieur Lebel turned round. He showed me to the outer door, and I emerged.

As I was coming away, somebody in a group of men in smocks behind me, who appeared to be waiting on the quay, said:

'There is a fellow who has just been discharged. He is a lucky devil.'

It seems that I looked like a thief. However, I had spent two hours at the Conciergerie, the sitting of the Académie must still be in progress, and I reflected with considerable inward satisfaction that if I had gone to it I should not have been 'discharged' so early.

LORD NORMANBY

6 January 1847

THE Marquis of Normanby, the British Ambassador, said to me yesterday: 'When the secret history of the Cracow affair is known, it will be known that Russia said to Austria: "Take Cracow, will you? You won't? Well then, I will take it." Austria yielded.'

'In that case,' I said, 'her audacity is obedience, her violence cowardice, her usurpation an abdication.'

Lord Normanby is a man of about fifty, tall, fair, with an extremely English appearance—he could scarcely look more English—elegant, graceful, high bred, good-natured, and dandyish. He has been Viceroy of Ireland and Home Secretary in England. He is the author of two or three novels of 'high life'. He wears a blue ribbon over his white tie, and a diamond star on his dress-coat. He speaks French with difficulty but wit.

Lord Normanby spoke to me about O'Connell who, in 1847, is beginning to break up. His seventy-three years are weighing him down, in spite of his great height and broad shoulders. This man, of such violent and bitter eloquence is, in a drawing-room, obsequious, full of compliments, modest to the point of humility, mild to the point of affectation. Lord Normanby said to me: 'O'Connell is affected.'

O'Connell has an old family mansion in County Kerry where he goes to shoot for two months in the year, receiving guests and entertaining them like an old country squire, providing, Lord Normanby told me, a ' wild hospitality'.

His eloquence, made for the masses and for Ireland, had little influence on the Commons of England. However, he had two or three great successes in Parliament. But the platform suited him better than the tribune.

I

DINNER AT SALVANDY'S

14 January 1847

YESTERDAY, Thursday, I dined at the house of Monsieur de Salvandy, the Minister of Public Instruction. There were present Lord Normanby, the British Ambassador; the Duc de Caraman, a young nobleman, intelligent and artless, very much absorbed in philosophic studies; Dupin the elder, with his rough bourgeois air; Monsieur de Rémusat, the Academician of eight days standing, a man with a keen mind and an impartial intelligence; Monsieur Gay-Lussac, the chemist, whom fame has made a Peer of France, and to whom nature has given the face of a worthy peasant; the other chemist, Monsieur Dumas, a man of talent, his hair rather too elaborately curled, and displaying very prominently the ribbon of a Commander of the Legion of Honour; Sainte-Beuve, short and bald; Alfred de Musset, with his youthful air, his fair beard, his equivocal opinions, and his intelligent face; Monsieur Ponsard, a man of thirty-two, with regular features, large dull eyes, and a rather narrow forehead, all this framed in a black beard and black hair, a good-looking man for shop-girls, a great poet for the bourgeois; Monsieur Michel Chevalier, with his close-cropped head, his receding forehead, his bird-like profile, and his slim figure; Alfred de Vigny, another fair man, with a bird-like profile but with long hair; Viennet, with his grimace; Scribe, with his peaceful air, rather anxious about a play of his which was being presented the same evening at the Gymnase, and which failed; Dupaty, upset by his fall of the 7th at the sitting of the Académie; Montalembert, with his long hair and English appearance, mild and disdainful; Philippe de Ségur, a gay, easy talker, with an aquiline nose deep-sunk eyes, and grey hair combed in imitation of the

Emperor; General Fabvier and Rapatel in full uniform, Rapatel with his round homely face, Fabvier with his flat-nosed lion's face; Mignet, smiling and cold; Gustave de Beaumont, with his dark, firm, and energetic face; Halévy, always timid; the astronomer Leverrier, rather red-faced; Vitet, with his tall figure and his smile, which is kindly, although it bares his teeth; Monsieur Victor Leclerc, the candidate for the Académie, who had been rejected that morning; Ingres, the table coming up to his chin, so that his white tie and his Commander's ribbon seemed to emerge from the table-cloth; Pradier, with his long hair and the look of a man of forty at the age of sixty; Auber, with his head on one side, his polite manners, and his two crosses in his button-hole.

I was sitting beside Lord Normanby, who is a very amiable man, even though he is the Ambassador of ill-humour; I called his attention to the fact that the end of the table was composed of Ingres, Pradier, Auber—painting, sculpture, and music.

Madame de Salvandy had Lord Normanby on her right and Monsieur Gay-Lussac on her left. Monsieur de Salvandy had Monsieur Dupin on his right and Monsieur de Rémusat on his left.

RELATIONS WITH ENGLAND

5 February 1847

Yesterday I was at the Tuileries. There was a performance there. After the opera, everybody went into the side-rooms where the buffet had been set up, and started conversing.

During the day Monsieur Guizot had made a very noble, very fine, and very spirited speech in the Chamber of Deputies about our budding dispute with England. There was a great deal of talk about this speech. Some approved, others condemned. Baron de Billing passed close to me, with a lady whom I could not see on his arm.

'Good evening,' he said. 'What do you think of the speech?' I replied: 'I am pleased with it. I am glad to see that at last we are holding up our heads again in this country. Some people say that this boldness is imprudent, but I do not think so. The best way not to have a war is to show that one is not afraid of it. See how England gave in to the United States two years ago; she will give in in the same way to France. Let us be firm, and others will be gentle; if we are gentle, others will be insolent.'

At that moment the lady on his arm turned towards me, and I recognized the wife of the British Ambassador. She looked very displeased. She said:

'Oh, Monsieur!'

I replied:

'Ah, Madame!'

And the war ended there. God grant that that may be the only exchange of words between the Queen of England and the King of France!

THE DEATH OF
MADEMOISELLE MARS

20 February 1847

OPENING of the Théâtre-Historique. I left the theatre at half-past three in the morning.

21 March 1847

Mademoiselle Mars was the only living person represented in the statuary of the porch of the Théâtre-Historique.

Madame d'A——, hearing about this, said:

'This places her among the dead; she has not long to live.'

Mademoiselle Mars died on 20 March, a month to a day after the opening of the Théâtre-Historique. She was sixty-nine years of age; two years older than Mademoiselle George. Mademoiselle Mars was fifty-two years old when she created the part of Doña Sol, a character supposed to be seventeen.

She leaves a son, in the banking house of Gontard. No letters announcing her death have been sent out, owing to the difficulty of putting:

'*Mademoiselle* Mars is dead. Her son regrets to inform you of the fact.'

26 March 1847

I have been at Mademoiselle Mars's funeral.

I arrived at twelve o'clock. The hearse was already at the Madeleine. There was a huge crowd, and the brightest sun imaginable. It was the day of the flower-market in the square outside the church. I made my way with considerable difficulty as far as the steps, but there it was impossible to go any further; the only door was blocked: no one could get in.

In the dark interior of the church, through the dazzling light of midday, I could see the ruddy stars of the tapers arranged round a tall black catafalque. The paintings on the ceiling formed a mysterious background.

I could hear the dirges, the sound of which reached as far as where I stood, and all around me the remarks and shouts of the crowd. There is nothing so sad as a funeral; one sees only people who are laughing. Everybody greets his neighbour gaily and talks about his affairs.

The church and the doorway were hung with black drapery, with an escutcheon of silver lace containing the letter M. I went over to the hearse, which was covered with black velvet, with the same letter M in silver lace. A few tufts of black feathers had been scattered over the place intended for the coffin.

The people of Paris are like the people of Athens—frivolous but intelligent. There were men in smocks there, with their sleeves rolled up, who said some cogent and forceful things about the stage, art, and poetry. They looked for and named the famous personalities in the crowd. These people must have glory. When there is no Marengo or Austerlitz, they love and must have their Dumas and their Lamartines. These men are like a light towards which all eyes turn eagerly.

I remained under the peristyle, sheltered from the sun by a column. One or two poets came and joined me and stood around me—Joseph Autran, Adolphe Dumas, Auguste Maquet. Alexandre Dumas came over to us with his son. The crowd recognized him by his thick head of hair, and murmured his name.

About one o'clock the coffin emerged from the church, together with the congregation. Remarks broke forth from among those outside:

'Ah, there's Bouffé!'

'But where's Arnal?'

'There he is.'

"Look, those men in black are the *sociétaires* of the Théâtre-Français!'

'The Théâtre-Français has come to its own funeral.'

'Look at Frédérick Lemaître; he is giving his arm to Clarisse Miroy.'

'Yes, and Rachel over there is giving her arm to Madame Doche.'

'There are some women—Madame Volnys, Madame Guyon, Rose Chéri.'

'That's Déjazet; she's getting on in years; this ought to make her think.'

And so on, and so forth.

The hearse moved off, and we all followed on foot. In our rear came some ten mourning carriages and a few open carriages with some actresses inside them. There were a good ten thousand people on foot. They formed a dark wave which appeared to push the hearse forward, jolting its huge black plumes.

On both sides of the boulevard there were more crowds lining the route. Women in red bonnets were sitting on a kind of step formed by the pavements, smiling; the balconies were crowded with people. Near the Porte Saint-Martin I left the procession and went away musing.

FÊTE AT THE
DUC DE MONTPENSIER'S

6 July 1847

MONSIEUR DE MONTPENSIER gave a fête this evening in the Parc des Minimes, in the Bois de Vincennes.

It was splendid and delightful. The fête cost the Prince 200,000 francs. In the Bois a host of tents had been erected, borrowed from the government repository and the French Museum of Arms, some of which were of historical interest. This alone cost ten thousand francs. There was the tent of the Emperor of Morocco, taken at the Battle of Isly, and exhibited three years ago at the Tuileries on a wooden platform constructed in the big pool; the tent of Abd-el-Kader, taken with the Smala, a beautiful thing with red and yellow arabesques embroidered in satin; another tent of the Bey of Constantine, of a wonderfully elegant shape; and finally the tent given to Napoleon by Sultan Selim.

The latter eclipsed all the others. From the outside it looked like an ordinary tent, remarkable only for having in the canvas some little windows—three on each side—whose frames were made of rope. The inside was superb. One found oneself inside a great chest of gold brocade; on this brocade there were flowers and countless fancy devices. On looking closely at the cords of the windows, one discovered that they were made of the most magnificent gold and silver lace; each window had its awning of gold brocade; the inner lining of the tent was of silk, with broad red-and-blue stripes. If I had been Napoleon, I should have liked to place my iron bed in this tent of gold and flowers, and to sleep in it on the eve of Wagram, Jena, and Friedland.

These splendid tents were disfigured by some fearful mahogany furniture scattered around inside them.

Monsieur de Montpensier received his guests very graciously.

Dancing took place in a huge marquee, where the princesses remained. They were all there, with the exception of the Duchesse d'Orléans. The Duc d'Aumale had come back from Brussels on purpose to take part in the fête.

Queen Maria Christina was there with her daughter, Madame de Montpensier. The *Reyna gobernadora* has some remains of beauty, but she is too stout and her hair is quite grey.

The tables were laid out under some other tents; there were ample refreshments, and buffets everywhere. The guests, although numbering more than four thousand, were neither crowded nor few and far between. Nowhere was there a crush. There were not enough ladies.

The fête had a splendid military character. Two huge cannon of the time of Louis XIV formed the pillars of the entrance. The gunners of Vincennes had constructed here and there columns of pikes with pistols for chapters.

The main avenue of the park was lit by coloured glass lamps; one might imagine that the emerald and ruby necklaces of the wood-nymphs were to be seen among the trees.

Sap-matches burned in the thickets and cast their glow over the wood. There were three tall poplar trees illuminated against the dark sky in a fantastic manner which was most impressive. The branches and leaves stirred in the wind amidst a brilliant scenic display of lights.

Along each side of the great avenue was a row of Gothic panoplies from the Artillery Museum; some with their backs against the oaks and the lime-trees, others erect and with the visor shut seated on dummy steeds, with caparisons and coats-of-arms, trappings and dazzling chamfrons. These steel statues, masked and motionless in the midst of the festivities, and covered with flashes and streams of light, had something dazzling and sinister about them.

Quadrilles were danced to vocal music. There could be nothing more charming than these youthful voices singing melodies among the trees in soft, deep tones; one might have fancied the guests to be enchanted knights, halted for ever in this wood while listening to the song of the fairies.

Everywhere in the trees there hung coloured lanterns, which looked like luminous oranges. Nothing stranger could be imagined than this illuminated fruit which had suddenly appeared on the branches.

From time to time trumpet-blasts drowned in triumphant tones the buzz of the festivities.

At the end of the avenue the gunners had hung a great star of the Legion of Honour, constructed of ramrods. They had arranged in the thickets, in the form of benches and chairs, piles of cannonballs, Paixhan mortars, and howitzers. Two huge siege-pieces guarded the cross of honour. Beneath it there were busts of the King and Queen.

Amidst all this moved a crowd of people, among whom I saw Auber, Alfred de Vigny, Alexandre Dumas with his son, Taylor, Théophile Gautier, Thiers, Guizot, Rothschild, the Comte Daru, President Franck-Carré, Generals Gourgaud, Lagrange, Saint-Yon, the Duc de Fézensac, Hébert, Keeper of the Seals, the Prince and Princesse de Craon, Lord Normanby, Narvaez, Duc de Valence, and a host of peers and ambassadors. The dust was terrible.

Two Arabs in white burnouses were there, the Cadi of Constantine and Bou-Maza. Bou-Maza has fine eyes but an ugly gaze, a well-shaped mouth but a dreadful smile: he looks treacherous and ferocious; there is something of the fox and the tiger about this man. I thought, however, that his face took on quite a fine expression at a moment when, thinking there was no one near him in the wood, he went up to the tent of Abd-el-Kader and stood looking at it. He appeared to be saying to it:

'What are you doing here?'

Bou-Maza is a young man; he looks about twenty-five years of age.

About one o'clock in the morning some fireworks were let off, and the wood was illuminated with Bengal lights. Then supper was served at the Princesses' table; all the ladies sat down to supper, the gentlemen remaining standing. Afterwards, dancing was resumed.

I am sorry I was unable to stay to the end. Through the dark branches, amidst those flagging festivities, those waning lights, those expiring illuminations, those wearied dancers, those women covered with flowers, diamonds, and dust, those pale faces, those drooping eyelids, those rumpled dresses, I should have liked to see that first gleam of daylight appear, so pale and dismal.

However, I think that, I know not why, the memory of this fête will remain: it has left a certain uneasy feeling in my mind. For a fortnight previously it had been talked about and had provided the people of Paris with a major topic of conversation. Yesterday, from the Tuileries to the Barrière du Trône, a triple row of onlookers lined the quays, the streets, and the Faubourg Saint-Antoine as the carriages of the guests passed by. Every few moments this crowd hurled at the gilded and bedizened passengers in their carriages shouts of disgust and hate. It was like a cloud of hatred around that transient splendour.

Everyone on his return related what had happened to him. Louis Boulanger and Achard had been booed; Tony Johannot's carriage had been spat into; mud and dirt had been thrown into General Harvaez's open carriage. Théophile Gautier, so calm and impassive, so Turk-like in his resignation, had been plunged into pensive gloom by these incidents.

It would not seem, however, that this great fête had anything impolitic about it, or that it should have proved unpopular. On the contrary, the Duc de Montpensier, by spending 200,000 francs, must have caused the expenditure of a million. That makes, in this period of poverty, a sum of 1,200,000 francs put in circulation for the people's benefit; they ought to be gratified. Well, they are not. Luxury is necessary to great states and to great civilizations, but there are times when the people must not be allowed to see it.

But what is luxury which is not seen? This is a problem. Magnificence in the background, profusion in the dark, a display which does not show itself, a splendour which dazzles nobody's eyes; is this possible? It has to be considered, however. When the people have luxury paraded before them in days of dearth and distress, their minds, which are those of children, jump a number of steps at once; they do not say to themselves that this luxury enables them to earn a living, that this luxury is useful to them, that this luxury is necessary to them; they say to themselves that they are suffering and that these people are enjoying themselves; they ask why all these things are not theirs, they examine these things not in the light of their poverty which requires work and consequently requires rich people, but in the light of their envy. Do not suppose that they conclude that luxury will give them so many weeks' wages and so many good days' employment. No, they, too, want not the work, not the wages, but leisure, pleasure, carriages, horses, lackeys, duchesses. It is not bread they require, but luxury. They stretch out their trembling hands towards these shining realities which would turn into shadows if they were to touch them.

The day on which the poverty of the many seizes on the riches of the few, darkness falls and there is nothing left, nothing for anybody. This is a real danger. When the crowd looks with these eyes at the rich, it is not ideas which occupy every mind, but events.

What specially irritates the people is the luxury of Princes and young men; it is, in fact, all too obvious that the former have not had the need, and the latter have not had the time, to earn it. This strikes them as unjust, and exasperates them; they do not reflect that the inequalities of this life prove the equality of the next.

Equilibrium, equity: these are the two aspects of the law of God. He shows us the first aspect in the world of matter and of the body; He will show us the second in the world of souls.

THE TESTE AND CUBIÈRES TRIAL

July 1847

ON the evening of the day when the judicial committee of peers decided to prosecute Monsieur Teste, chance willed it that the Chancellor had to go to Neuilly with the Bureau of the Chamber to present to the King a bill which had been passed.

The Chancellor and the Peers of the Bureau (among whom was the Comte Daru) found the King in a furious temper. He had been informed of the prosecution of Monsieur Teste. As soon as he caught sight of them, he strode towards them.

'What's the meaning of this, Chancellor?' he said. 'Wasn't one of my former Ministers enough for you? Must you have a second? You have taken Teste now. So that after I have spent seventeen years in France setting up authority once more, in one day, in one hour, you allow it to be cast down again. You destroy the whole work of my reign! You debase authority, power, the government. And *you* do that, you, the Chancellor of the House of Peers!' And so on, and so forth.

The squall was a violent one. The Chancellor was very firm. He resolutely stood up to the King. He said that doubtless politics had to be considered, but that it was also necessary to take justice into account; that the Chamber of Peers too had its independence as a legislative power, and its sovereignty as a judicial power; that this independence and sovereignty must be respected, and if need be, would enforce respect; that moreover, in the present state of public opinion it would have been a very serious matter to refuse satisfaction to it; that it would be doing an injury to the country and to the King not to do what public opinion demanded and justice required; that there were times when it was more prudent to advance than to retreat, and that finally what had been done was done.

'And well done,' added Daru.

'We shall see,' said the King.

And from anger he relapsed into uneasiness.

8 July 1847

Half-past twelve. The Court enters. A crowd in the galleries. Nobody in the reserved galleries except Colonel Poizat, the governor of the Palace. In the diplomatic galleries two persons only, Lord Normanby, the British Ambassador, and Count de Lœvenhœlm, the Swedish Minister.

The accused are brought in. Three tables covered with green baize have been placed facing the Court; at each of these tables there is a chair, and behind there is a bench for the counsel. President Teste sits down at the middle table, General Cubières at the right-hand table, Parmentier at the left-hand table. All three are dressed in black.

Parmentier entered some time after the two peers. Teste, who is a Commander of the Legion of Honour, has the rosette of the decoration in his button-hole; Cubières, who is a Grand Officer, the plain ribbon. Before sitting down, the General chats for a moment to counsel then, with a preoccupied air, glances through the volume of documents relating to the case. He looks much as usual. Teste is pale and calm. He rubs his hands like a man who is pleased with himself. Parmentier is stout and partly bald, with white hair, a red face, a hooked nose, a mouth like a sabre-cut, thin lips: the appearance of a rascal. He wears a white tie, as does also President Teste. The General wears a black tie.

The three accused do not look at each other. Parmentier casts his eyes down, and affects to be playing with the gold chain of his watch, which he displays with the ostentation of a country bumpkin against his black waistcoat. A young man with a thin black moustache, who is said to be his son, sits down on his left.

Questioned as to his position in life, Teste rises and says: 'I thought it would not be proper to bring to this bar the honours which have been conferred on me.' (This makes an impression on the Court.) 'Yesterday I placed them in the King's hands.' (This makes a very favourable impression.)

The indictment is read out. It sets forth the following facts:

Parmentier, Director of the Mines of Gouhenans, alleges that he remitted to General Cubières 94,000 francs for the purpose of obtaining from Monsieur Teste, the Minister of Public Works, a salt-mine concession. Monsieur Teste emphatically denies having received this sum. Parmentier is only too willing to believe that it was intercepted, and that he was thus defrauded of it either by Monsieur Cubières or another shareholder in the mines, Monsieur Pellapra, who appears to have acted as go-between from the General to Monsieur Teste. Parmentier is accused of corruption; Cubières and Pellapra of corruption and fraud; Teste of 'having received gifts and presents to perform an act pertaining to his functions not subject to payment'.

Pellapra has fled. Cubières, Teste, and Parmentier are present before the Court.

While the indictment is being read, Cubières hides his face and forehead in his left hand, and follows the reading of the volume which has been circulated. Teste also follows it, annotating his copy with a steel pen. He has put on his spectacles. From time to time he takes snuff from a big boxwood snuff-box, and chats with his counsel, Monsieur Paillet. Parmentier looks very attentive.

10 July 1847

This is what I can make out of it after the two first days.

I have spoken to General Cubières four or five times in my life, and to President Teste once only, and yet in this case, I am as interested in their fate as if they were friends of mine of twenty years' standing. Why? I will say it at once. It is because I believe them to be innocent.

'I believe' is not strong enough; I see them to be innocent

This view may, perhaps, be modified, for this case changes like the waves and alters its appearance from one moment to the next; but at the present time, after much perplexity, after many transitions, after many painful intervals, in which my conscience has more than once trembled and shuddered, I am convinced that General Cubières is innocent of the act of fraud, that President Teste is innocent of the act of corruption.

What is this case then? To my mind, it can be summed up in two words; commission and blackmail; commission deducted by Pellapra, blackmail perpetrated by Parmentier. The commission, tainted with fraud and swindling, was the cause of the act alleged in the indictment; blackmail was the cause of the scandal. Hence the whole case.

I have no leaning towards guilt which is not invincibly proved to me. My inclination is to believe in innocence. As long as there remains in the probabilities of a case a possible refuge for the innocence of the accused, all my theories, I will not say incline, but rush, towards it.

Sunday, 11 July 1847

The Court is not sitting today. The second and third hearings were devoted to the examination of the accused.

At the opening of Friday's sitting letters were read out which had been unexpectedly communicated by Messieurs Léon de Malleville and Marrast, and which appear to throw a strong light on this trial. The defendants came in looking pale and dejected, Parmentier, however, showing more assurance than the others.

Monsieur Teste listened to the reading of the new documents with his elbow on the table and half hiding his face in his hand; General Cubières with his eyes cast down; Parmentier with perceptible embarrassment.

The examination began with the General.

Monsieur Cubières has a doll-like face, an undecided look, a hesitant manner of speaking, red cheeks; I believe him to be innocent of fraud; however, I am not profoundly convinced. During the examination he was standing, and gently tapping the table with the tip of a wooden paper knife, with a look of extreme calm. The Public Prosecutor, Monsieur Delangle, a rather commonplace lawyer, treated him once or twice with insolence; Cubières, a veteran of Waterloo, did not manage to find a single rejoinder with which to rebuke him. I felt for him. In the Court's opinion he is already convicted.

The first part of the examination was badly conducted. There was only one expression of opinion at the refreshment bar. The Chancellor is a remarkable, exceptional old man, but when all is said and done, he is eighty-two years of age; at eighty-two a man does not face either a woman or a crowd.

Parmentier, interrogated after the General, spoke easily, with a sort of vulgar glibness which was sometimes witty, at other times shrewd, always skilful, never eloquent. He is an obvious, artless scoundrel. He is not aware of this himself. This shameless creature has a twisted mind, and exposes his nakedness just as Venus would. A toad which fancies it is beautiful is a repulsive sight. He was hissed. At first he either did not hear or did not understand; however, he ended up by understanding; then beads of perspiration appeared on his face; every now and then, when the assembly showed its disgust, he nervously wiped the streaming surface of his bald head, looked around him with a certain air of entreaty and bewilderment, feeling that he was doomed and trying to redeem himself. Yet he continued speaking and exposing his moral defects, while murmurs of indignation drowned his words, and his anguish increased. At that moment I felt pity for the wretched man.

Monsieur Teste, who was examined yesterday, spoke like an innocent man; frequently he was extremely eloquent. He was was not an advocate, he was a real man who was suffering, who was tearing out his very vitals and exposing them to view before his judges, saying: 'See there!' He moved me deeply. While he was speaking, it suddenly occurred to me that this whole affair might be explained by a fraud committed by Pellapra.

Teste is sixty-seven years old; he has a southern accent, a

large, expressive mouth, a high forehead giving him an intellectual look, and deep-set eyes which sparkle now and then;
his whole constitution is bowed and crushed, but he is energetic for all that. He moved about, waved his arms, shrugged
his shoulders, smiled bitterly, took snuff, glanced through his
papers, annotated them rapidly; held in check the Public
Prosecutor or the Chancellor, shielded Cubières, who is his
ruin, showed his contempt for Parmentier, who is defending
him; threw out witicisms, interruptions, replies, complaints,
shouts. He was turbulent yet ingenuous, overcome with
emotion, yet dignified. He was clear, rapid, persuasive, be-
seeching, menacing; full of anguish without any trepidation,
moderate and violent, haughty and tearful.

At one point he stirred me to the depths. His very soul
found expression in the cries which he uttered. I was tempted
to rise and say to him: 'You have convinced me; I will leave
my seat and sit on the bench beside you; will you let me be
your counsel?'—And then I restrained myself, thinking that
if his innocence continued to be apparent to me, I should
perhaps be more useful to him as a judge among his judges.

Pellapra is the pivot on which the case turns. Teste seems
to be sincerely upset at his flight. If Pellapra returns all will
be clear. I ardently hope that Teste is innocent, and that if
innocent he will be saved.

When the Court rose I followed him with my eyes as he
went out. He slowly and sadly crossed the benches of the peers,
looking right and left at these chairs, which perhaps he will
never occupy again. Two ushers who are guarding him walked
with him, one in front of him and the other behind him.

12 July 1847

The aspect of the case has suddenly changed. Some fresh
documents[1] have appeared, which are terribly damaging to

---

[1] A letter from Madame Pellapra, signed Émilie Pellapra. Six notes written
by Teste and recognized by him (he took them in his trembling hand said:
'They are mine.'). An extract from Pellapra's accounts which appear to show
that he had remitted the 94,000 francs to Teste. V.H.

Teste. Cubières rises, and confirms the authenticity and importance of these documents. Teste replies haughtily and energetically, but for all that his confidence has diminished. His mouth contracts; I feel uneasy about him. I begin to be afraid that he has been deceiving us all. Parmentier listens, almost with a smile, and with his arms casually folded. Teste sits down again, and takes a vast number of pinches of snuff from his big boxwood snuff-box, then wipes the perspiration from his forehead with a red silk handkerchief. The Court is greatly excited.

'I can imagine what he is suffering by what I am suffering myself,' Monsieur de Pontécoulant said to me.

'What torture this is!' said General Neigre.

'It is like a guillotine blade falling slowly,' said Bertin de Vaux.

Excitement is at fever pitch among the members of the Court and the public. All are anxious not to miss a single word. The peers call out to every witness: 'Speak up! Speak up! We can't hear.' The Chancellor begs the Court to consider his great age.

The heat is unbearable.

The stockbroker Goupil gives his evidence. Teste looks agitated.

Monsieur Charles Dupin questions the stockbroker. Teste listens to him, and applauds him with a smile. It would be impossible to imagine anything more pitiful than this smile.

On this occasion, the private conference was held before the sitting, in the old Chamber. The peers buzzed like a swarm of bees. The Chancellor came to the bench where I was sitting, and spoke to me about matters connected with the Académie; then about the trial, and how tired and distressed he felt, saying how pleasant a meeting of the Académie was after a sitting of the Court of Peers.

In his evidence, Monsieur Legrand, the Under-Secretary of State for Public Works, described Teste as 'a person sitting behind me'. Teste shrugged his shoulders.

After the serious evidence given by the notary Roquebert, Teste's face took on an agonized expression.

When the document from the Treasury was produced, he flushed, wiped his forehead in anguish, and turned towards his son. They exchanged a few words, then Teste started fingering his papers again, and the son buried his head in his hands.

In one hour, Teste has aged ten years; his head wobbles, his lower lip twitches. Yesterday he was a lion; today he is a dotard.

Everything in this case moves by fits and starts. Yesterday I saw Teste was innocent; today I see that he is guilty. Yesterday I admired him; today I would be tempted to despise him if he were not so wretched. But I no longer feel anything but pity for him.

This trial is one of the most terrible spectacles which I have ever witnessed in my life. It is a moral dismemberment. What our forefathers saw eighty years ago on the Place de Grève, on the day Damiens was executed, we have seen today, on the day President Teste was executed in the Court of Peers. We have seen a man tortured with hot irons and dismembered in the spirit. Every hour, every minute, something was torn from him; at twelve o'clock his distinction as a magistrate; at one o'clock his reputation as an upright Minister; at two o'clock his conscience as an honest man; half an hour later, the respect of others; a quarter of an hour afterwards, his own self-respect. In the end, he was nothing but a corpse. All this lasted six hours.

For my own part, as I said to Chief President Legagneur, I doubt whether I shall have the heart, even if Teste is convicted and guilty, to add any punishment whatever to this unparalleled chastisement, to this frightful torment.

13 July 1847

As I entered the cloakroom, the Vicomte Lemercier, who was there, said to me: 'Have you heard the news?'

'No.'

'Teste has attempted to commit suicide and failed.'

It was true. Yesterday evening at nine o'clock Monsieur Teste fired two pistol-shots at himself; he fired the two shots simultaneously, one with each hand. One he aimed into his mouth, and the cap missed fire; the other at his heart, and the bullet rebounded, the shot being fired from too close a distance.

The Chancellor read in the private conference the official documents reporting the incident; they were read again afterwards at the public sitting. The pistols were deposited on the table of the Court. They are two very small pistols, brand new, with ivory butts.

Teste, having failed to kill himself, refuses to appear again before the Court. He has written the Chancellor a letter in which he abandons his defence, 'the documents produced yesterday leaving no room for contradiction'. This is the language of a lawyer, not of a man; a man would have said: 'I am guilty.'

When we entered the Court, Monsieur Dupin the elder, who was sitting behind me on the Deputies' bench, said to me:

'Guess what book Teste sent for to kill time with?'

'I don't know.'

'*Monte-Cristo!* "Not the first four volumes," he said, "I have read them." '

Monte-Cristo was not to be found in the library of the House of Peers. It had to be borrowed from a public reading-room, which only had it in periodical parts. Teste spends his time reading these parts.

My neighbour, the Duc de Brancas, who is a kind and worthy old man, says to me:

'Do not oppose the condemnation. It is God's justice which is being done.'

Last night, when General Cubières was informed that Teste had fired two pistol-shots at himself, he wept bitterly.

I note that today is a fateful day, 13 July.

The seat lately occupied by Teste is empty at the sitting. The clerk of the court, La Chauvinière, reads the indictment. Monsieur Cubières listens with an air of profound sadness, then hides his face in his hand. Parmentier holds his head down the whole time. Yesterday's events—Teste's attempted suicide, and his letter to the Chancellor—completely destroy Parmentier's abominable line of defence.

At ten minutes past one Public Prosecutor Delangle rises to address the Court. He twice repeats in the midst of general emotion: 'Messieurs les Pairs . . .' then stops short, and continues: 'The trial is over.'

The Public Prosecutor had spoken for only ten minutes.

It is a curious fact that Teste and Delangle have been closely associated throughout their lives, Delangle following Teste, and in the end prosecuting him. Teste was the Batonnier of the bar; Delangle held that office immediately after him. Teste was appointed President of the Court of Appeal; Delangle entered the same court as Advocate-General. Teste is accused, Delangle is Public Prosecutor.

I now understand the conversation between the father and son which I noticed yesterday when the document from the Treasury was produced. The father said to the son: 'Give me the pistols.' The son handed them to him, and then buried his head in his hands. It is in this way, I think, that this sombre tragedy must have happened.

At the opening of the sitting the Chancellor reads a letter in which Cubières resigns his position as a peer.

The question is put as to whether the accused are guilty.

'Is Cubières guilty of fraud?'—Unanimously: 'No.'

On the question of corruption:

'Is Teste guilty?'—Unanimously: 'Yes.'

'Is Cubières guilty?'—Unanimously, with the exception of three votes: 'Yes.'

'Is Parmentier guilty?'—Unanimously: 'Yes.'

The sentences:

Teste is sentenced to civic degradation, unanimously, with the exception of one vote.

On the question of the fines, I rose in my turn, and said:

'I wish to punish a guilty man; I do not wish to punish a family, that is to say, innocent persons. The restitution of the money received would be sufficient to my mind. No fine. My lords, the example is not in a fine; the example is in the terrible things which you have seen; the example is in the terrible act which you have just committed. A fine debases the example. It puts a question of money in the place of a question of honour.'

Teste was condemned to pay a fine of 94,000 francs.

At half-past six a fresh letter from General Cubières is read out, in which he states that he has asked to be placed on the retired list. Every few moments the unhappy man throws something overboard.

15 July 1847

At half-past twelve the calling of the names takes place. The court is profoundly and painfully agitated.

The law officials call for the full severity of the law against Cubières; the dukes are more humane.

The Court proceeds to pass sentence.

On the question whether Teste should be imprisoned, I said:

'My lords, the guilty man has already been sufficiently punished. At the present moment he is sixty-seven years of age; in five years he will be seventy-two. I will say no more. No imprisonment!'

Teste is sentenced to three years' imprisonment.

With regard to Cubières and the penalty of civic degradation, when my turn came, I said:

'I can feel that the Court is weary, and I myself am suffering from disturbing emotions. I rise none the less. I have studied, as you have, my lords, with whatever intelligence and power of attention I may have, all the documents in this deplorable case. I have examined the facts. I have contrasted the persons. I have endeavoured to penetrate not only into the heart of the case, but into the heart of these men you are trying at this moment. Well, this is the conclusion I have arrived at: to my mind, General Cubières was led astray. Led astray by Pellapra, defrauded by Parmentier. In these circumstances there has been, I acknowledge, weakness—a deplorable, inexcusable, even gravely culpable weakness—but after all, only weakness, and weakness is not baseness, and I do not wish to punish weakness with infamy. I must admit, and the Court will pardon this admission, that during the many hours that this unfortunate case has occupied our minds, I imagined that you were going to render a different decision in your omnipotent and sovereign justice. I would have liked to leave in his terrible isolation the pitiful and grandiose figure of the principal defendant. This man, who, by dint of talent, has contrived—a miracle which, for my part, I would always have thought impossible—to be great in his abasement and touching in his shame: this man I would have liked to punish simply with civic degradation. And I would have preferred to add nothing to this fearful penalty; in such a case an addition is a diminution. For the weak and unfortunate General Cubières, I would have liked a sentence of deprivation, for a given period of time, of the civic and civil rights mentioned in Article 401. And finally, for the men of money, I would have liked money penalties; for the miscreants, humiliating penalties; for Parmentier, a fine and imprisonment. For these men of such diversity of guilt, I would have wished for a diversity of penalties, which your omnipotence would allow you to decree, and the observance of this proportion between crime and the punishment seemed to me to be in accordance with conscience and, I will add, although this concerns me less, in accordance with public opinion. In your wisdom you have decided otherwise. I bow to your wisdom, but I beg you none the less to approve my remaining of the same opinion. In an assembly in which there are so many men of importance who have occupied, or who will yet occupy, the highest functions in the State and the government, I understand, I honour, I respect that noble feeling of outraged decency which leads you to inflict unusually heavy penalties in this serious case, and to afford not only the most just but also the most cruel satisfaction to public opinion. I, gentlemen, am not a lawyer, I am not a soldier, I am not a public official; I am an ordinary taxpayer, I am a member, like anyone else, of the great crowd from which emanates that public opinion to which you defer; and it is because of this, it is because I am simply this, that I am perhaps qualified to say to you: Enough! Stop! Go as far as the limits of justice; do not overstep them. The example has been set. Do not destroy that isolation of the condemned man Teste, which is the principal aspect, the great moral lesson of the trial. As long as it was a question only of that unhappy man, I spoke to you merely in the lanuage of pity! I speak to you now in the language of equity, solemn and austere equity. I beg you, give credit to General Cubières for his sixty years of honourable life, give credit to him for the agony he has suffered, for those four years of torture which he endured at Parmentier's villainous hands, for this public exposure on that bench for four days; give him credit for that unjust accusation of fraud, which was also a torture to him; give him credit for his generous unwillingness to save himself by ruining Teste; give him credit, finally, for his heroic conduct on the battle-field of Waterloo, where I regret that he did not remain. I formally propose to sentence Monsieur Cubières to the penalty provided by Article 401, together with Article 42, that is to say, to a suspension of civil and civic rights for ten years. I vote against civic degradation.'

At seven o'clock there are still eighty peers who have not voted. The Chancellor proposes an adjournment until to-morrow. Objections are raised. An adjournment while voting is taking place! Monsieur Cauchy cites a precedent from the Quénisset trial. Uproar. The adjournment is carried.

16 July 1847

Continuation of the voting on the questions of the penalty to be inflicted on General Cubières.

The penalty of civic degradation is carried by 130 votes to 48.

He is also condemned to a fine of 10,000 francs.

No imprisonment.

It seems that the decision in favour of inflicting the penalty of civic degradation on General Cubières which has just been arrived at has already been made public and has reached the prison. Just now I heard in the street the dreadful cries of Madame de Cubières and her sister, Madame de Sampays, who were with the General when the news was communicated to him.

17 July 1847

Sentence on Parmentier.

On the question of civic degradation, I said:

'As the Court is aware, in order that a great example might be made, I would have preferred President Teste to be left in his degrading isolation, alone under the burden of civic degradation. The Court did not agree with me; it thought proper to associate General Cubières with him. I cannot do otherwise than associate Parmentier with him. I vote for civic degradation, while profoundly regretting that after this great social and public penalty has been inflicted on two ex-Ministers, on two peers of France, to whom it is everything, I am obliged to inflict it on this wretch, to whom it is nothing.'

Parmentier is condemned to civic degradation and a fine of 10,000 francs. No imprisonment.

As we were about to leave, and were in the cloakroom, Anatole de Monsequiou, who had consistently voted in the most lenient sense, pointed out to me, in the second compartment of the cloakroom, near the one where I always change, an old peer's robe hanging next to the Minister of Public Instruction's robe. This robe was worn at the elbows, the gilt of the buttons was rubbed off, the embroidery faded; an old ribbon of the Legion of Honour is in the button-hole, more yellow than red, and half undone. Above this robe, was written, according to custom, the name of its owner: *M. Teste.*

My opinion is that the public will consider the judgement of the Court of Peers just in the case of Teste, harsh in that of Cubières, and lenient in that of Parmentier.

At half-past four the doors were thrown open to the public. A huge crowd had been waiting since the morning. In a moment the galleries were noisily filled. It was like a wave. Then there was profound silence when the calling of names began. The peers replied, generally speaking, in a barely audible and weary tone of voice.

Then the Chancellor put on his mortar-board of black velvet lined with ermine and read out the judgement. The Public Prosecutor was at his post. The Chancellor read out the judgement in a firm tone, very remarkable in an old man of eighty. Whatever may have been said by certain newspapers, he did not shed any 'silent tears'.

The judgement will be read presently by the Chief Clerk of the Court, Cauchy, to the condemned men.

It will be just a month ago tomorrow, the 18th, that Teste was arraigned by the judicial committee of the peers and that he said to them: 'I thank you for placing me in a position which gives me the precious privilege of defending myself.'

21 July 1847

It is a curious fact that Monsieur Teste, who, as Minister of Public Works, had this Luxembourg prison built, is the first Minister who has been confined in it. This reminds one of the gibbet of Montfaucon, and of Enguerrand de Marigny.

In this prison Monsieur Teste occupies a room separated only by a partition from General Cubières's room. The partition is so thin that, as Monsieur Teste speaks loudly, Madame de Cubières was obliged on the first day to knock on the wall to warn Monsieur Teste that she could hear everything he said. The pistol-shot, too, made General Cubières start as if it had been fired in his own room.

The sitting of the 12th had been so decisive that it was feared that some act of desperation might be committed. During the sitting itself, the Duc Decazes had had iron bars fitted in the prisoners' windows. They found these bars in the windows on their return, but did not feel any surprise at seeing them. They also had their razors taken from them and had to dine without knives.

Policemen were detailed to remain by their side day and night. However, it was thought that Monsieur Teste might be left alone with his son and the counsel who were defending him. He dined with them, almost in silence: a remarkable fact, for he was a great talker. The little he did say was concerning matters foreign to the trial.

At nine o'clock the son and the barristers retired. The policeman who was to watch Monsieur Teste received orders to go up to his room at once; it was during the few minutes which elapsed between the departure of his son and the entrance of the policeman that Monsieur Teste made his attempt to commit suicide.

Many people doubted whether this attempt was seriously intended. This was the tenor of the comments in the Chamber. Monsieur Delessert, the Prefect of Police, whom I questioned on this subject, told me there could be no doubt that Monsieur Teste had tried to kill himself in earnest. But he believes that only one pistol-shot was fired.

After his condemnation, General Cubières received a great many visits; the sentence of the Court missed its mark by its excessive severity. The General's visitors, on their way to his cell, passed Parmentier's, which had a door with a glass panel and a white curtain, through which he could be seen. All of them as they passed by heaped Parmentier with terms of contempt, which obliged the man to hide in a corner where he was no longer visible.

During the trial the heat was intense. The Chancellor was continually obliged to call back the peers, who went off to the refreshment bars or the lobbies.

Lord Normanby did not miss a single sitting.

22 July 1847

Teste's name has already been removed from his seat in the House of Peers. It is General Achard who now occupies his chair.

Yesterday, Tuesday, 21 July, as I was walking from the Académie to the House of Peers, about four o'clock, I met, near the exit of the Institut, in the most deserted part of the Rue Mazarin, Parmentier coming out of prison. He was going towards the quay. His son was with him.

Parmentier, dressed in black, was holding his hat in his hand, behind his back; with his other arm he was leaning on his son. The son looked sad. Parmentier seemed completely overwhelmed. He had the exhausted appearance of a man who has just been for a long walk. His bald head seemed to be bowed beneath his shame. They were walking slowly.

It was stated today at the Chamber that Madame de Cubières gave a *soirée* two days after the condemnation. It seems that in reality she simply refrained from shutting her door.

She has just written a letter to the newspapers, which will not do her husband much good, but in which there is none the less this fine passage: 'He has had his peerage, his rank, everything, even his dignity as a citizen, taken from him. He retains his scars.'

The Chancellor offered to let Monsieur de Cubières leave the prison by one of the private gates of the Chancellor's official residence in the Luxembourg. A cab would have waited there for Monsieur de Cubières, and he would have got in without being seen by anyone in the street. Monsieur de Cubières refused.

An open carriage, drawn by two horses, came and took up its position at the Rue de Vaugirard gate in the midst of the crowd. Monsieur de Cubières got into it, accompanied by his wife and Madame de Sampayo, and that is how he left prison.

Since then he has had over a hundred visitors every evening. There are always some forty carriages at his door.

THE PRISON OF THE CONDEMNED

1847

THE prison of the condemned, built by the side of, and as a counterpart to, the prison for juvenile offenders, is a living and striking antithesis. It is not just the beginning and the ending of the evil-doer facing each other; it is also the perpetual confrontation of the two penal systems—solitary confinement and imprisonment in common. This *vis-à-vis* is almost enough to decide the question. It is a dark and silent duel between the dungeon and the cell, between the old prison and the new.

On one side are all the condemned, pell-mell; the child of seventeen with the old man of seventy; the prisoner of thirteen months with the convict for life; the beardless lad who has filched some apples, and the highway murderer rescued from the Place Saint-Jacques, and sent to Toulon in view of 'extenuating circumstances'; the almost innocent and the virtually damned; blue eyes and grey beards; hideous, pestilential workshops, where working side by side in semi-darkness, at dirty, foetid tasks, without air, daylight, speech, without looking at each other, without interest, there are horrible, mournful spectres, some of whom inspire terror by reason of their age, others by reason of their youth.

On the other side there is a cloister, a hive; each worker in his cell, each soul in its *alvéole*: a huge three-storeyed building inhabited by neighbours who have never seen each other: a town composed of a host of small hermitages; nothing but children, and children who do not know each other; who live for years close to each other without ever hearing the noise of each other's steps or the sound of their voices—separated by a wall, by an abyss: work, study, tools, books, eight hours' sleep, one hour's rest, one hour's play in a small walled court, prayers morning and evening, thought all the time.

On one side a sewer, on the other a garden.

You enter a cell; you find a child standing at a bench lighted by a frosted glass window, of which one pane at the top can be opened. The child is dressed in coarse serge; he is clean, grave, quiet. He stops working and greets you. You question him; he replies with a serious gaze, and in subdued tones. Some of them make locks, a dozen a day; others carve furniture, and so on. There are as many occupations as storeys; as many workshops as corridors. The child can read and write besides. He has a master in prison for his brain as well as for his body.

You must not think however that, because of its mildness, this prison is insufficient chastisement. No; it is profoundly sad. All the prisoners have a punished appearance which is characteristic.

There are still many more criticisms to be made; the solitary system is just beginning. It has almost all its improvements to come; but, incomplete and imperfect as it is at present, it is admirable when compared with the system of imprisonment in common.

The prisoner—a captive on all sides, and free only on the working side—takes an interest in what he makes, whatever it may be. The idle boy who hated all occupations, becomes an enthusiastic worker.

When one is in solitary confinement one manages to find light in the darkest dungeon.

5 August 1847

The other day, I was visiting the prison of the condemned, and I said to the Governor, who was accompanying me:

'You have a man condemned to death here now, haven't you?'

'Yes, a man called Marquis, who murdered a prostitute, Térisse, with intent to rob her.'

'I should like to speak to that man,' I said.

'Sir,' replied the Governor, 'I am here to take your orders, but I cannot admit you to the condemned cell.'

'Why not?'

'The police regulations forbid us to allow anybody into the cell of a person condemned to death.'

I replied:

'I am not acquainted with the terms of the police regulations, Monsieur le Directeur de la Prison, but I know what the law permits. The law places the prisons under the supervision of the Chambers, and the officials under the supervision of the Peers of France, who can be called upon to judge them. Wherever it is possible that an abuse may exist, the law-giver must go in and look. Abuses may exist in the cell of a man condemned to death. It is, therefore, my duty to enter, and yours to admit.'

The Governor made no reply and led the way.

We skirted a small courtyard in which there are some flowers, and which is surrounded by a gallery. This is the exercise-ground of the prisoners condemned to death. It is surrounded by four lofty buildings. In the middle of one of the sides of the gallery there is a heavy door bound with iron. A wicket opened and I found myself in a kind of gloomy ante-chamber, paved with stone. In front of me there were three doors, one directly opposite me, the others on either hand: three heavy doors, each pierced with a grating, and plated with iron. These three doors open into three cells intended for the condemned criminals awaiting their fate after the double appeal to the judge and to the Supreme Court. This generally means a respite of two months.

'We have never had more than two of these cells occupied at the same time,' said the Governor.

The door of the centre one was opened. It was that of the condemned cell occupied at the time.

I went in.

As I crossed the threshold a man rose quickly and remained on his feet.

This man was at the other end of the cell. It was he whom I saw first. A pale shaft of light coming from a deep-set window above his head lit him up from behind. His head was bare, his neck was bare; he was wearing shoes, brown woollen trousers, and a strait-waistcoat. The sleeves of this waistcoat of coarse grey canvas were tied together in front. Through a gap in the canvas I could see a pipe already filled. He had been about to light this pipe at the moment when the door had opened. This was the condemned man.

Nothing could be seen through the window but a glimpse of the rainy sky.

There was a moment's silence. I was stirred by too many emotions at once to be able to speak.

He was a young man, obviously not more than twenty-two or twenty-three years old. His chestnut hair, which was naturally curly, was cut short; his beard had not been trimmed. He had beautiful big eyes, but his expression was mean and ugly, his nose broken, his temples prominent, the bones behind the ears broad, which is a bad sign, the forehead low, the mouth coarse, and at the bottom of his left cheek there was that peculiar swelling produced by anguish. He was pale. His whole face was downcast; nevertheless, at our entry he forced a smile.

He was standing with his bed on his left, an untidy truckle-bed on which he had probably been lying just before; and on his right a small wooden table, painted a crude yellow colour, and having as a top a plank painted to imitate St. Anne marble. On this table there were some glazed earthenware dishes containing some boiled vegetables and a little meat, a piece of bread, and a leather pouch full of tobacco. A straw-bottomed chair stood beside the table.

This was not like the horrible condemned cell at the Conciergerie. It was a good-sized room, fairly light, painted yellow, furnished with the bed, table, and chair I have already mentioned, a china stove on our left, and a shelf fitted in the corner opposite the window, laden with old clothes and crockery. In another corner there was a square chair, which took the place of the ignoble tub of the old prisons. Everything was clean, or nearly so, and in good order, being swept and aired and tidied up, and had that indescribable homeliness about it which deprives things of their unpleasantness as well as of their beauty. The window, which was fitted with double bars, was open. Two small chains for supporting the sashes hung from a couple of nails above the condemned man's head. Near the stove there stood two men, a soldier, armed only with his sword, and a warder. Condemned criminals always have this escort of two men, who do not leave them night or day. These men are relieved every three hours.

I did not take in all these details at once. The condemned man absorbed all my attention.

Monsieur Paillard de Villeneuve was with me. The Governor was the first to break the silence.

'Marquis,' he said, pointing to me, 'this gentleman is here in your interest.'

'If you have any complaint to make,' I said, 'I am here to listen to it.'

The condemned man bowed and replied with a smile which caused me a pang:

'I have no complaints, sir; I am quite comfortable here. These gentlemen' (indicating the two warders) 'are very kind and are good enough to talk to me. The Governor comes to see me now and then.'

'Are you well fed?' I asked.

'Very well, sir; I have double rations.' Then he added after a pause:

'*We* are entitled to double rations; and then I have white bread too.'

I glanced at the piece of bread, which was indeed very white. He added:

'Prison bread is the only thing to which I would have been unable to accustom myself. At Sainte-Pélagie, where I was detained, we formed a society of young men to keep to ourselves and not to mix with the others, and also to have white bread.'

L

I asked:

'Were you better off at Sainte-Pélagie than here?'

'I was very comfortable at Sainte-Pélagie, and I am very comfortable here.'

I continued:

'You said that you did not wish to mix with the others. What do you mean by "the others"?'

'There were a great many common people there,' he replied.

The condemned man was the son of a porter in the Rue Chabanais.

'Is your bed comfortable?' I asked.

The Governor lifted the coverings, and said:

'Look, sir. A hair mattress, two mattresses, and two blankets.'

'And two bolsters,' added Marquis.

'Do you sleep well?' I asked.

He replied without hesitation:

'Very well.'

There was a book lying open on the bed.

'You read?'

'Yes, sir.'

I picked up the book. It was a *Short Geography and History*, printed in the last century. The first pages and half the binding were missing. The book was open at a description of the Lake of Constance.

'I lent him that book,' said the Governor.

I turned to Marquis.

'Does this book interest you?'

'Yes, sir,' he replied. 'The Governor has also lent me some books about the voyages of La Pérouse and Captain Cook. I am very fond of the adventures of our great navigators. I have read them already, but I like reading them again, and I shall read them again with pleasure in another year or another ten years.'

He did not say *I would* read them, but *I shall* read them. The poor young man was a good talker, and was fond of hearing himself speak. 'Our great navigators' is literally his own expression. He talked like a newspaper. In all his other remarks I noticed this absence of naturalness. Everything disappears in the face of death except affectation. Goodness vanishes, wickedness disappears, the benevolent man becomes bitter, the blunt man gentle, the affected man remains affected. It is a strange thing that death touches you, but does not give you simplicity.

He was a poor conceited workman; a bit of an artist, too much and too little, who had been destroyed by vanity. He liked to cut a figure and enjoy himself. He had stolen a hundred francs one morning from his father's chest of drawers, and the next day, after a few hours of pleasure, good meals, entertainments, debauchery, and so on, had killed a prostitute in order to rob her.

This terrible ladder, which has so many rungs, which leads from domestic robbery to murder, from the paternal reprimand to the scaffold, criminals like Lacenaire and Poulmann take twenty years to descend; he, this young man who was a child only yesterday, had hurtled down it. In twenty-four hours he had, as an old convict, a former schoolmaster, said in the courtyard, taken all his degrees.

What an abyss a destiny like that is!

He turned over the pages for a few minutes, and I continued:

'Did you have no means of existence?'

He raised his head, and replied with some pride:

'Why, yes, sir.'

Then he went on, without any interruption from me.

'I was a furniture designer. I have even studied to be an architect. My name is Marquis. I was a pupil of Monsieur Le Duc.'

He was referring to Monsieur Viollet le Duc, the architect of the Louvre. I noticed that he pronounced the words *Marquis* and *Monsieur Le Duc* with a certain satisfaction. But he had not finished speaking.

'I had started planning a Journal of Designs for cabinet-

makers. I had already prepared a few plates. I wanted to provide upholsterers with designs in the Renaissance style made
according to the rules of the trade, which they never have.
They are forced to content themselves with engravings of
very incorrect styles.'

'That was a good idea. Why didn't you carry it out?'

'Nothing came of it, sir.'

He said this quietly, and added:

'However, I cannot say that I was short of money. I had
talent, I sold my designs, I should have certainly ended up by
selling them at my own price.'

I could not help asking him:

'Then, why . . .?'

He understood, and answered:

'I really cannot say. It was an idea which crossed my mind.
I would not have thought myself capable of it until that fatal
day.'

At the words 'fatal day' he stopped, then continued, with
a sort of nonchalance:

'I am sorry I have no designs here; I would have shown
them to you. I also painted landscapes. Monsieur Le Duc had
taught me water-colour painting. I succeeded in the Cicéri
style. I have done things which anybody would have sworn
were Cicéri's. I am very fond of drawing. At Sainte-Pélagie I
drew the portraits of several of my companions, but only in
crayons. They would not let me have my box of water-colours.'

'Why not?' I asked, without thinking.

He hesitated. I was sorry I had put the question, for I
guessed the reason.

'Sir,' he said, 'it was because they fancied there might be
some poison in the colours. They were wrong. They are water
colours.'

'But,' remarked the Governor, 'surely there is some red lead
in the vermilion?'

'Possibly,' he replied. 'The fact is, they did not allow it, and
I had to content myself with the crayons. The portraits were
good likenesses, though.'

'And what do you do here?'

'I keep busy.'

He remained deep in thought after this reply, then he added:

'I would like to draw. This' (indicating the strait-waistcoat) 'would not interfere with me. At a pinch I could manage to draw.' He moved his hand about under his sleeve as he spoke. 'And then these gentlemen are very kind' (indicating the warders). 'They have already offered to let me raise the sleeves. But I do something else. I read.'

'You see the chaplain, I suppose?'

'Yes, sir; he comes to see me.'

Here he turned to the Governor, and said:

'But I have not seen the Abbé Montès yet.'

That name in his mouth had a sinister effect on me. I had seen the Abbé Montès once in my life, one summer day on the Pont-au-Change, in the cart which was carrying Louvel to the scaffold.

Nevertheless the Governor replied:

'Dammit all, he's an old man; he is nearly eighty-six. The poor old fellow attends when he can.'

'Eighty-six!' I said. 'That is just what is wanted, provided he has a little strength. At his age one is so near to God that one ought to say some very beautiful things.'

'I shall be glad to see him,' said Marquis, calmly.

'You must live in hope,' I said.

'Oh!' he said, 'I am not discouraged. First, I have my appeal to the Court of Appeal, and then I have my petition for a pardon. The sentence which has been pronounced may be quashed. I do not say that it is not just, but it is a little severe. They could have taken my age into account, and given me the benefit of extenuating circumstances. And then I have signed my petition to the King. My father, who comes to see me, has told me not to be alarmed. It is Monsieur Le Duc himself who will submit the petition to His Majesty. Monsieur Le Duc knows me well; he knows his pupil Marquis. The King is not in the habit of refusing him anything. It is impossible that I should be refused a pardon—I do not say a free pardon but . . .'

He fell silent.

'Yes,' I said, 'be of good cheer; here on earth you have your judges on one side, and your father on the other. But above, you have also your Father and your Judge who is God, who cannot feel the need to condemn you without, at the same time, experiencing the desire to pardon you. So you must not give up hope.'

'Thank you, sir,' replied Marquis.

Again silence fell.

Then I asked: 'Do you require anything?'

'I should like to go out and walk in the yard a little oftener. That is all, sir. I am allowed out for only a quarter of an hour a day.'

'That is not sufficient,' I said to the Governor. 'Why is this?'

'Because of our great responsibilities,' he replied.

'Well,' I said, 'put four guards on duty if two are not enough. But don't refuse this young man a little air and sunlight. A court in the centre of a prison, bolts and bars everywhere, four high walls all around, four guards always there, the strait-waistcoat, sentries at every wicket, two sentry rounds, and two ramparts sixty feet high, what have you to fear? The prisoner ought to be allowed to walk in the courtyard when he asks permission.'

The Governor bowed and said:

'You are right, sir. I shall carry out your suggestions.'

The condemned man thanked me effusively.

'It is time for me to leave you,' I said. 'Turn to God, and keep your spirits up.'

'I shall remain in good spirits, sir.'

He accompanied me to the door, which was then shut on him.

The Governor led me into the next cell on the right.

It was longer than the other. It contained only a bed and a coarse earthenware vessel under the bed.

'It was here,' the Governor told me, 'that Poulmann was confined. In the six weeks which he spent here he wore out three pairs of shoes walking up and down. He even wore down the planks. He never stopped walking, and managed to cover fifteen leagues a day in his cell. He was a terrible man.'

'Did you have Joseph Henri too?' I asked.

'Yes, sir; but in the infirmary. He was ill. He was always writing to the Keeper of the Seals, to the Public Prosecutor, to the Chancellor, to the Great Referendary—four-page letters to everybody, and in small close writing, too. One day, I said to him, jocularly: "It is lucky that you are not compelled to read what you have written." Obviously nobody ever read those letters. He was a lunatic.'

As I was leaving the prison the Governor showed me the two encircling paths: high walls, thin patches of grass, a sentry-box every thirty paces. All this has a chilling effect.

He pointed out to me, under the very windows of the condemned cells, a place where two soldiers on duty blew their brains out last year. They put the muzzles of their rifles in their mouths and blew their heads open. You can still see the two bullet-holes in the sentry-box. The rain has washed away the blood-stains on the wall. One man killed himself because the orderly officer, seeing him without his rifle which he had left in the sentry-box, said to him in passing, 'Fifteen days in the cells.' The motive in the case of the other man was never discovered.

THE DUC DE PRASLIN[1]

18 August 1847, 4 p.m.

I HAVE just learnt that the Duchesse de Praslin was murdered last night in her mansion, No. 55, Faubourg Saint-Honoré.

20 August 1847

The Court of Peers has been convened for tomorrow to arraign Monsieur de Praslin.

Saturday, 21 August 1847. Written at the sitting

At seven minutes past two the public sitting opens. The Keeper of the Seals, Hébert, mounts the tribune, and reads the ordinance which constitutes the Court of Peers.

There are some women in the galleries; a man, stout, bald, and white-haired, with a ruddy face, closely resembling Parmentier, is in the west tribune, and for a moment attracts the attention of the peers.

The Chancellor has the galleries cleared; the Public Prosecutor, Delangle, is admitted, and the Advocate-General, Bresson, both in red robes. The Chancellor notices that the galleries, including that of the reporters, have not been com-

---

[1] The Duc de Choiseul-Praslin had married the daughter of Marshal Sébastiani in 1824, when he was nineteen and his bride sixteen. The marriage appeared to be a happy one until the arrival in the Praslins' house of a governess, Mademoiselle Deluzy, who became the Duke's mistress. Sébastiani threatened to obtain a separation and thus ruin his son-in-law unless Mademoiselle Deluzy was dismissed; and Praslin obeyed. But on 18 August 1847 the Duchess was found stabbed to death. The Duke was promptly arrested, and on the 20th was transferred to the Luxembourg, where he died on the 24th: a phial which had contained arsenic was found in his possession. [Tr.]

pletely cleared; he becomes angry, and gives orders to the
ushers. The galleries are cleared with some difficulty.

Monsieur de Praslin was arrested yesterday, and transferred
to the prison of the Chamber on the Chancellor's warrant. He
was committed this morning at daybreak. He is in the cell
where Monsieur Teste was.

It was Monsieur de Praslin who, on 17 July, passed me the
pen to sign the warrant for the arrest of Messieurs Teste and
Cubières. Exactly a month after, on 17 August, he signed
his own warrant with a dagger.

The Duc de Praslin is a man of middle height, and of
commonplace appearance. He has a very gentle, but false,
manner. He has an ugly mouth and a horribly forced smile.
He is a fair, pallid man; pale, livid, like an Englishman. He
is neither fat nor thin, neither handsome nor ugly. He has no
signs of breeding in his hands, which are big and ugly. He
always looks as if he is about to say something which he never
does say.

I have only spoken to him three or four times in my life.
The last time we were coming up the great staircase together.
I told him that I was going to interrogate the Minister of War
if they did not pardon Dubois de Gennes, whose brother had
been the duke's secretary; he said he would support me.

He had behaved rather badly towards this Dubois de
Gennes. He dismissed him for some trifling matter. The duke
undertook to present his petitions to the King with his own
hands, and he put them in the post.

Monsieur de Praslin did not speak in the Chamber. He
used to vote severely in trials. He decided very harshly in the
Teste case.

In 1830 I occasionally met him at the house of the Marquis
de Marmier, since the Duke. He was then the Marquis de
Praslin, as his father was alive. I had noticed the Marquise, a
good-looking, stout woman, in contrast to the Marquis, who
was then very thin.

The poor duchess was literally hacked to pieces with a knife
and brained with the butt of the pistol. Allard, Vidocq's

successor at the Sûreté, said: 'It was clumsily done; pro-
fessional murderers work better than that; a man of the
world is responsible!'

The Comte de Nocé came up to me in the cloakroom and
said: 'Can you understand it? He lit a fire to burn his
dressing-gown.'

I replied: 'He should have saved his energy to blow his
brains out.'

A month ago the army received a blow in the case of
General Cubières; the magistrature with President Teste; now
it is the turn of the old nobility with the Duc de Praslin.

Yet this must come to an end.

Sunday, 22 August 1847

At the moment one can still see, in Mademoiselle de Luzzy's
window, in Madame Lemaire's house in the Rue du Harlay,
overlooking the courtyard, the melon, the bouquet, and the
basket of fruit which the duke brought from the country the
very evening before the murder.

The duke is seriously ill. People say he has been poisoned.
Just now I heard a flower-girl say: *'Mon Dieu*, I hope they
don't kill him! It amuses me so much to read the details in
the paper every morning.'

In his address to the Court, in secret session, the Chancellor
said that the duty which devolved upon the Court was the
saddest the peers had ever been called upon to perform and
the most painful in his experience. His voice literally changed
while he spoke these words. Before the sitting began he had
come into the reading-room. I had bid him good morning,
and we had shaken hands. The old Chancellor was overcome
with emotion.

The Chancellor also said: 'There have been rumours of
suicide and escape. The peers may set their minds at rest. No
precaution will be spared to ensure that the accused, if he

should be found guilty, will not escape in any way the public and legal punishment which he would have incurred and deserved.'

They say that the Public Prosecutor is already telling his friends his 'party piece'—the description of the room after the murder; here the sumptuous furniture, the gold fringes, the silken hangings, and so on; there, a pool of blood; here, the open window, the rising sun, the trees, the gardens stretching away as far as the eye could reach, the song of the birds, the sunlight, and so on; there the corpse of the murdered duchess. Delangle is impressed by the contrast, and is dazzled by himself!

On the 17th, Mademoiselle de Luzzy had dined at Madame Lemaire's, at the under-teacher's table. She was pale and appeared to be unwell. 'What is the matter with you?' asked Mademoiselle Julie Rivière, one of her companions. Mademoiselle de Luzzy replied that she did not feel very well; that she had fainted that day in the Rue Saint-Jacques, but that the doctor had not thought it necessary to bleed her.

Doctor Louis is the Praslin family practitioner. They sent for him to see the duke. The Prefect of Police made the doctor promise that he would not speak to the duke about anything but his health. The precaution turned out to be absolutely superfluous. The duke scarcely responded, even by signs, to the doctor's questions. He was in a strange torpor. Monsieur Louis saw that he had tried to poison himself by swallowing a narcotic.

Monsieur Lous did not think that he ought to be moved on the 20th. He thought that if the Chancellor had him moved to the Luxembourg in spite of his advice, it was in the hope that the duke would die on the way. I do not think so.

The people are exasperated against the duke; the family is even more indignant than the people. If he were to be judged by his family he would be more severely condemned than by the Court of Peers, and more cruelly tortured than by the people.

27 August 1847

On Wednesday, coming from the Académie with Cousin and
the Comte de Saint-Aulaire, Cousin said:

'You will see this Mademoiselle de Luzzy, she is a rare
woman. Her letters are masterpieces of wit and style. Her
interrogation is admirable; even so, you will read it only as
translated by Cauchy. If you had heard her you would have
been astonished. No one could have more grace, more tact,
more intelligence. If she is kind enough to write some day for
us, we will give her the Prix Montyon. She is wilful and im-
perious too; she is a woman at once wicked and charming.'

I said to Cousin: 'Ah! You aren't in love with her, are
you?'

To which he replied: 'Hee!'

'What do you think of the case?' Monsieur de Saint-Aulaire
asked me.

'There must have been some motive. If not, the duke is a
madman. The cause is in the duchess or in the mistress; but it
must exist, otherwise the thing is an impossibility. At the
bottom of a crime such as this there is either a powerful
motive or a great folly.'

That is, in fact, my opinion. As for the duke's ferocity, it
can be explained by his stupidity: he was an animal—and a
wild animal at that.

The populace have already coined the verb *prasliner*—to
prasliner your wife.

The examining peers visited the Praslin mansions the day
before yesterday.

The bedroom is still in the state in which it was found on
the morning of the murder. The blood has turned from red
to black. That is the only difference. This room gives one the
horrors. One can see the terrible struggle and resistance put
up by the duchess as they actually occurred. Everywhere are
the prints of bloody hands going from one wall to another,

from one door to another, from one bell-pull to another. The unhappy woman, like a wild animal caught in a snare, must have rushed round and round the room, screaming and looking for a way out while the murderer was stabbing her.

From the Rue de Vaugirard gate one can see three windows in the prison which have projecting shafts. They are the only ones. Three months ago they had neither bars nor shafts. The bars were fitted for President Teste, and the shafts for the Duc de Praslin.

Doctor Louis told me: 'The day after the murder, at half-past ten in the morning, I was called to Monsieur de Praslin's house. I knew nothing. Imagine my utter stupefaction: I found the duke in bed; he was already in custody. Eight people, who relieved each other every hour, never took their eyes off him. Four policemen were sitting on chairs in corners of the room. I studied his condition, which was terrible. The symptoms indicated cholera or poison. People accuse me of not having said at once, "He has taken poison." That would have been tantamount to denouncing him and would have done for him. Poisoning is a tacit confession of guilt. "You should have stated your opinion," the Chancellor told me. I replied: *"Monsieur le Chancelier*, where an opinion is a denunciation, a doctor will not give an opinion." '

'Besides,' continued Monsieur Louis, 'the duke was very gentle: he worshipped his children, and spent his life with one of them on his knee, and sometimes another on his back at the same time. The duchess was beautiful and intelligent: she had become a huge size. The duke suffered terribly, but showed the greatest fortitude. Not a word, not a complaint in the midst of the tortures produced by the arsenic.'

It would seem that Monsieur de Praslin was a very well-made man. At the post-mortem the doctors were greatly impressed. One of them exclaimed: 'What a handsome corpse!' He was a fine athlete, Doctor Louis told me.

The coffin in which they buried him bears a lead plate, on

which there is the number 1054. A number after his death, such as convicts have in life, is the only epitaph of the Duc de Choiseul-Praslin.

Mademoiselle Deluzy—not de Luzzy—is still in the Conciergerie. She goes for a walk every day at two o'clock in the courtyard. Sometimes she wears a nankeen dress, sometimes a silk gown with broad stripes. She knows that many gazes are levelled at her from all the windows. People who watch her say she strikes attitudes. She is a source of entertainment to Monsieur Teste, whose window overlooks that courtyard. She was still in confinement on the 31st.

Granier de Cassagnac, who has seen her, has given me this description of her. She has a very low forehead, her nose is turned up, her hair is very light-coloured. None the less, all considered, she is a pretty woman. She looks straight at everybody who passes her, trying to inspect them, and perhaps to fascinate them.

She is one of those women who have too much intelligence to have much feeling. She is capable of committing follies, not out of passion but out of selfishness.

30 August 1847

A sitting in which the Court is dissolved.

At a quarter past one I entered the Chamber; there were only a few peers present. Monsieur Villemain, Monsieur Cousin, Monsieur Thénard; a few generals, including General Fabvier; a few former presidents, including Monsieur Barthe; there was also Monsieur le Comte de Bondy, who bears a singular resemblance to the Duc de Praslin, although he is much more handsome.

I chatted with General Fabvier, then for a long time with Monsieur Barthe, about everything in general and the House of Peers in particular. It was necessary, we agreed, to raise its reputation, to make the people sympathetic towards it, by making it sympathetic towards the people. We spoke about the suicide of Alfred de Montesquiou. In the cloakroom it was the general topic, as well as another sad incident: the Prince d'Eckmuhl was arrested last night and put in a lunatic asylum after having stabbed his mistress.

At two o'clock the Chancellor rose; he had on his right the Duc Decazes, and on his left the Vicomte de Pontécoulant. He spoke for twenty minutes.

The Public Prosecutor was admitted.

There were about sixty peers. The Duc de Brancas and the Marquis de Fontis were beside me.

Monsieur Delangle laid down his brief for the prosecution, holding that the Court was dissolved by reason of the duke's death.

The Public Prosecutor went out. The Chancellor said:

'Does anyone wish to address the Court?'

Monsieur de Boissy rose. He partly approved of what the Chancellor had said. The poison had been taken before the Court of Peers had been convened: consequently no responsibility rested on the Court. Public opinion accused the peers charged with the investigation of having connived at the poisoning.

Comte Lajuinais: 'An opinion without any grounds.'

Boissy: 'But generally held. (*No! No!*) I insist that it should be established that no responsibility for the poisoning rests upon the Chancellor, the investigating peers, or the Court.'

The Chancellor: 'No one can possibly entertain such an opinion: the post-mortem report completely settles the question.'

Monsieur Cousin agreed with the Chancellor, and while sharing Monsieur de Boissy's anxiety, believed that there was no foundation for the rumour.

Monsieur de Boissy persisted. He believed there had been complicity. He did not accuse any of the officers of the Court.

Monsieur Barthe rose, and gave way to the Duc Decazes, who related the circumstances of his interview with Monsieur de Praslin on the Tuesday he died, at ten o'clock in the morning.

This is the interview:

'You are in great pain, my dear fellow?' asked Monsieur Decazes.

'Yes.'

'It is your own fault. Why did you take poison?'

Silence.

'Did you take laudanum?'

'No.'

'Then did you take arsenic?'

The sick man looked up and said: 'Yes.'

'Who procured the arsenic for you?'

'No one.'

'What do you mean? Did you buy it yourself at the chemist's?'

'I brought it from Praslin.'

Silence. The Duc Decazes continued:

'This is the time—for the sake of your family, your memory, your children—to speak. To take poison is to confess one's guilt. It is inconceivable that an innocent person would deprive his nine children of their father when they are already mother-less. You are guilty, then?'

Silence.

'Do you regret your crime, at least? I beg of you to say if you deplore it.'

The accused raised his eyes and hands to heaven, and said, with an agonized expression: 'You ask if I deplore it!'

'Then confess. Don't you wish to see the Chancellor?'

The accused made an effort, and said: 'I am ready.'

'Well, then,' said the duke, 'I will go and inform him.'

'No,' replied the sick man, after a pause, 'I am too weak today. Tomorrow. Tell him to come tomorrow.'

At half-past four that afternoon he was dead.

This could not be officially recorded as it was a private conversation which Monsieur Decazes repeated because the Court was, in a sense, informal.

Monsieur Barthe drew attention to the fact that the poisoning had taken place on Wednesday the 19th, and had not been renewed.

Monsieur de Boissy wished to punish those who had guarded the duke so carelessly. He poisoned himself on Wednesday, at ten in the evening.

The Chancellor said that Monsieur de Boissy was mistaken: it was four in the afternoon. Besides, such things happen frequently in ordinary cases, and in the best-guarded prisons.

The decree dissolving the Court was voted unanimously.

The Duc de Massa, after the vote, asked that the words 'his wife' should be inserted in the decree. There was a Dowager Duchesse de Praslin. This was allowed.

The Public Prosecutor was recalled, and the decree was read to him. The sitting broke up at five minutes to three.

Many peers remained to chat in the hall. Monsieur Cousin said to Monsieur de Boissy: 'You were right to ask for information. It was excellent.'

Monsieur Decazes added to his statement the following details. When the duke was taken to the Luxembourg he was clad in a dressing-gown and trousers. During the journey he did not vomit. He only complained of a consuming thirst. When he arrived, at five in the morning, they undressed him, and put him to bed at once. They did not give him back his dressing-gown and his trousers until the next day, when they moved him into the next room, to be examined by the Chancellor. After this interrogation they undressed him again and put him back to bed. Therefore, even if he had some poison in his pockets, he could not have taken it.

It is true that they did not search him, but that would have been futile. They watched his movements closely.

M

THE PLEASURES OF SPA

18 September 1847

HERE are, in this year 1847, the pleasures of the rich, noble, fashionable, intelligent, generous, and distinguished visitors taking the waters at Spa:

(1) Fill a bucket with water, throw into it a twenty-sou piece, call a poor child, and say to him: 'I will give you that coin if you can pick it up with your teeth.' The child plunges his head into the water, chokes, suffocates, and comes up all dishevelled and shivering with the piece of silver between his teeth—and everybody laughs. It is such good fun.

(2) Take a pig, grease its tail, and bet who will keep hold of the tail longest; the pig pulls one way, the gentleman the other. Ten, twenty, a hundred louis, are staked on this. Whole days are passed in such amusements.

In the meantime old Europe is falling to pieces, revolutions germinate between the chinks and crevices of the old social order; the future is gloomy, and the rich are on trial in this century as the nobles were in the last.

BÉRANGER

4 November 1847

TODAY the École Normale, in the Rue d'Ulm, was opened. Monsieur Dubois had asked me to be present. As I was coming out I saw approaching me, in the corridor which leads to the staircase, a man whom I did not recognize at first. He had a round, red face, bright, clear eyes, and long greyish hair. He was over sixty, with a good-natured, smiling mouth, an old frock-coat, carelessly buttoned up, a big quaker hat, with a broad brim, and, apart from his paunch, a certain resemblance to my brother Abel.

It was Béranger.

'Ah! Good day, Hugo!'

'Ah! Good day, Béranger.'

He took my arm. We walked along together.

'I will accompany you a little way. Have you a carriage?'

'My legs!'

'Well, I have the same.'

We went along the Estrapade. In the Rue Saint-Jacques two men, dressed in black, approached us.

'Dammit all,' said Béranger, 'here are two pedants—one a product of Sainte-Barbe, the other a member of the Académie des Sciences. Do you know them?'

'No.'

'Happy man. Hugo, you have always been a lucky fellow.'

The two pedants left us after bidding us good day. We went up the Rue Saint-Hyacinthe.

Béranger continued:

'So you were compelled last month to eulogize a great man of the quarter-hour, who died between his confessor, his mistress, and his cuckold.'

'Ah!' I said, 'you deserve to be something better than a Puritan. Don't speak like that of Frédéric Soulié, who had real talent, and a heart with no malice in it.'

'The fact is,' replied Béranger, 'I said a foolish thing for the sake of being clever. I am not a Puritan, I hate the breed. A Puritan is a man of spite.'

'And above all a fool. True virtue, true morality, and true greatness are intelligent and indulgent.'

In the meantime we crossed the Place Saint-Michel, still arm in arm, and turned up the Rue Monsieur-le-Prince.

'You have done well,' Béranger said to me, 'to be content with that popularity which one can dominate. I have a great deal of trouble to escape from that popularity which carries you with it. What a slave the man is who has the misfortune to win that sort of popularity! Take the Reformist banquets. They wear me out, and I have the greatest difficulty in the world to avoid them. I make excuses: I am old; I have a bad digestion; I no longer dine out; I don't move about, etc. All in vain! They tell me that I owe it to myself, that a man like myself must pay that forfeit—and a hundred others like it. I am furious, but I have to smile and put a good face on it! What is that but the old profession of a Court jester? To amuse a prince and to amuse the people is the same thing. What difference is there between a poet following the Court and a poet following the crowd? Marot in the sixteenth century, Béranger in the nineteenth—my dear fellow, it might be the same man! I am against it. I lend myself to it as little as possible. They are wrong about me. I am a man of opinion, and not of party. Oh, I hate their popularity. I am very much afraid that our poor Lamartine is going in for that sort of popularity. I pity him. He will see what it is! Hugo, I have some common sense. I tell you, be content with the popularity you have; it is the right sort. Let me tell you about another experience of mine. In 1829, when I was in prison on account of my songs, how popular I was! There was not a hosier, a pastry-cook, or a reader of the *Constitutionnel*, who did not consider himself entitled to come to console me in my cell. "Let us go and see Béranger!" They came! And I, who was musing over our poetic trivialities or looking for a refrain or a rhyme between the bars of my window, was obliged, instead of finding my rhyme, to receive my hosier! Poor popular devil that I was, I was not at liberty in my prison. Oh! If it were to happen again! How they did bore me!'

Chatting thus, we reached the Rue Mazarin and the door of the Institut, which was my destination. It was the Académie's day.

'Are you coming in?' I asked him.

'Good heavens, no! I leave that to you!'

And he fled.

THE DEATH OF
MADAME ADÉLAÏDE

31 December 1847

THIS dismal year, which opened on a Friday, finishes on a Friday.

When I awoke, I was informed of the death of Madame Adélaïde.

At three o'clock the peers went to the Palace to offer the King their sympathy. We were a large assembly.

The Chancellor was there in his robes, with the antique three-cornered hat of the Chancellors embellished with a huge gold tassel. Lagrenée, Mornay, Villemain, Barante; Generals Sébastiani, Lagrange, and others; the Duc de Broglie and Monsieur de Mackau, just appointed Admiral of France, were all present.

The King received the peers in the Throne-room; he was dressed in black, without any decorations, and was in tears. The Duc de Nemours, Monsieur de Joinville, and Monsieur de Montpensier were in black, without star or ribbon, like the King. The Queen, the Duchesse d'Orléans, and Mesdames de Joinville and Montpensier, were in deep mourning.

The King came over to me and said: 'I thank Monsieur Victor Hugo; he always comes to me on sad occasions.' Tears prevented him from saying any more.

What a blow this is for the King! His sister was a friend to him. She was a woman of intelligence and good counsel, who tended to share the King's views without necessarily doing so always. Madame Adélaïde had something manly and cordial about her, with considerable tact. She had great conversational powers. I remember one evening, she conversed with me for a long time, and intelligently at that, on the subject of Monsieur de Chateaubriand's *Rancé*, which had just been published.

My dear little Didine went with her mother one day to see her. Madame Adélaïde gave her a doll. My daughter, who was then seven years old, came back delighted. Some days afterwards, she happened to hear a great discussion in the drawing-room about the Philippists and the Carlists. Playing with her doll, she said in a low voice :

'I am an Adélaïdist.'

I have been an Adélaïdist too. The death of this likeable old princess has caused me real grief.

She died in three days from inflammation of the lungs, which followed an attack of influenza. On Monday she attended the Royal reception. Who could have guessed that she would never see 1848?

Almost every morning the King had a long conversation, principally on political matters, with Madame Adélaïde. He consulted her about everything, and never embarked on any serious matter against her advice. He regards the Queen as his guardian angel; one might say that Madame Adélaïde was his guiding spirit. What a loss this is for an old man! A void in his heart, in his house, in his habits. It pained me to see him weeping. One felt that the sobs came from the bottom of his heart.

His sister had never left him. She had shared his exile, she shared to some extent his throne; she was devoted to her brother, wrapped up in him; her selfishness was the *I* of Louis-Philippe.

She made Monsieur de Joinville her heir, Odilon Barrot and Dupin her executors.

The peers left the Tuileries upset by all this sorrow, and uneasy about the shock the King had received.

This evening all the theatres are closed.

Thus ends the year 1847.

THE FEBRUARY DAYS

23 February 1848

As I arrived at the Chamber of Peers—it was exactly three
o'clock—General Rapatel came into the cloakroom and said:
'The session is over.'

I went to the Chamber of Deputies. As my cab was turning
into the Rue de Lille a serried and endless column of men
wearing jackets, smocks, and caps, and marching arm-in-arm,
three by three, came out of the Rue Bellechasse and headed for
the Chamber. I could see that the other end of the street
was blocked by rows of infantry of the line, with their arms
at the ready. I drove on past the men in smocks, who were
accompanied by some women who were shouting: 'Up with
the line! Down with Guizot!'

They stopped when they arrived within rifle-shot of the
infantry. The soldiers opened their ranks to let me through.
They were talking and laughing. A very young man was
shrugging his shoulders.

I did not go any farther than the lobby. It was filled with
busy, anxious groups. In one corner were Monsieur Thiers,
Monsieur de Rémusat, Monsieur Vivien, and Monsieur Mer-
ruau (of the *Constitutionnel*); in another Monsieur Émile de
Girardin, Monsieur d'Alton-Shée, and Monsieur de Boissy,
Monsieur Franck-Carré, Monsieur d'Houdetot, and Monsieur
de Lagrenée. Monsieur Armand Marrast had taken Monsieur
d'Alton aside. Monsieur de Girardin stopped me; then France
d'Houdetot and Lagrenée. Messieurs Franck-Carré and Vigier
joined us. We talked. I said to them:

'The Cabinet is seriously at fault. It has forgotten that in
times like ours there are precipices right and left and that it
does not do to govern too near the edge. It says to itself: "It

is only a riot," and it almost congratulates itself on the out-break. It believes it has been strengthened by it; yesterday it was falling, today it is up again! But, in the first place, who can tell where a riot will end? Riots, it is true, strengthen the hands of Cabinets, but revolutions overthrow dynasties. And what a rash game, risking the dynasty to save the ministry! What is to be done? The tension of the situation draws the knot tighter, and now it is impossible to undo it. The hawser may break and then everything will go adrift. The Left has manœuvred imprudently and the Cabinet wildly. Both sides are responsible. But what madness for this Cabinet to mix a police question with a question of liberty and to oppose the spirit of chicanery to the spirit of revolution! It is like sending process-servers with stamped paper to serve upon a lion. Monsieur Hébert splitting hairs in the face of a riot! What an idea! Unfortunately it is too late to break up the elements of the crisis. Blood is going to flow.'

As I was saying this a deputy passed us and said:

'The Ministry of Marine has been taken.'

'Let us go and see!' France d'Houdetot said to me.

We went out. We passed through a regiment of infantry guarding the head of the Pont de la Concorde. Another regiment barred the other end of it. On the Place Louis XV,[1] cavalry was charging dark, immobile groups, which at the approach of the riders fled like swarms of bees. Nobody was on the bridge except a general in uniform and on horseback, with the cross of a commander of the Legion of Honour hung around his neck—General Prévot. As he galloped past us he shouted: 'They are attacking!'

As we reached the troops at the other end of the bridge, a major on horseback, in a burnous with gold braid on it, a stout man with a kind, pleasant face, saluted Monsieur d'Houdetot.

'Is there any news?' France asked him.

[1] Now the Place de la Concorde. [Tr.]

'The news is that I got there just in time!' replied the major.

It was this major who cleared the Palace of the Chamber, which the rioters had invaded at six o'clock this morning.

We walked on to the Place. Charging cavalry was whirling around us. At the corner of the bridge a dragoon raised his sword against a man in a smock. I do not think he struck him. Besides, the Ministry of Marine had not been 'taken'. A crowd had thrown a stone at one of the windows and wounded a man who was looking out. Nothing more.

We could see a number of vehicles lined up like a barricade in the broad avenue of the Champs-Élysées, on a level with the *rond-point*.

'They are firing over there,' Houdetot said to me. 'Can you see the smoke?'

'Nonsense!' I replied. 'It is the spray from the fountain. That fire is water.'

And we burst out laughing.

There was some fighting going on there, however. The people had constructed three barricades with chairs. The guard at the main square of the Champs-Élysées had turned out to pull the barricades down. The people had driven the soldiers back to the guardhouse with volleys of stones. General Prévot had sent a squad of Municipal Guards to relieve the soldiers. The squad had been surrounded and compelled to take refuge in the guardhouse with the others. The crowd had hemmed in the guardhouse. A man had taken a ladder, climbed on to the roof, pulled down the flag, torn it up and thrown it to the people. A battalion had to be sent to free the guard.

'Well, I'll be damned,' France d'Houdetot said to General Prévot, who had told us all this. 'A flag taken!'

'Taken, no! Stolen, yes!' snapped the general.

We returned to the bridge. Monsieur Vivien was passing and came up to us. He was extremely calm, and even jovial; though this did not stop him from having untidy hair, a dirty shirt, and black fingernails. With his big, old, wide-brimmed hat and his coat buttoned up to his cravat, the former Keeper of the Seals looked like a policeman. The two of us agreed about the situation. Undoubtedly at this moment one can feel the whole constitutional machine rocking. It no longer rests squarely on the ground. One can hear it cracking. The crisis is complicated by the disturbed condition of the whole of Europe.

Monsieur Pèdre Lacaze came up arm-in-arm with Napoleon Duchâtel. Both of them were in high spirits. They lighted their cigars from France d'Houdetot's cigar and said:

'Have you heard? Genoude is going to bring an impeachment on his own account. They would not allow him to sign the impeachment made by the Left. He would not admit defeat, and now the Ministry is caught between two fires. On the left, the whole of the Left; on the right, Monsieur de Genoude.'

Then Napoleon Duchâtel went on:

'They say that Duvergier de Hauranne has been carried about in triumph on the shoulders of the crowd.'

'They won't have found that very hard,' said France d'Houdetot.

'It is true that he doesn't carry much weight,' said Pèdre Lacaze.

And these gentlemen went off.

Vivien told me that the King had thrown an electoral reform bill into his drawer, saying as he did so: 'That is for my successor!' That is Louis XV's *mot*, with reform taking the place of the deluge.

It appears to be true that the King interrupted Monsieur Sallandrouze when he was laying before him the grievances of the 'Progressives', and asked him curtly: 'Do you sell many carpets?'[2]

At this same meeting with the Progressives, the King noticed Monsieur Blanqui, and going up to him, asked affably:

'Well, Monsieur Blanqui, what are people saying? What is going on?'

'Sire,' replied Monsieur Blanqui, 'I ought to tell the King

[2] Sallandrouze was a carpet-manufacturer. [Tr.]

that in the departments, and especially at Bordeaux, there is a great deal of agitation.'

'Ah,' interrupted the King. 'More agitation!' and he turned his back on Monsieur Blanqui.

While we were talking, Vivien said: 'Listen! I think I can hear firing!'

A young staff officer, addressing General d'Houdetot with a smile, asked: 'Are we going to stay here long?'

'Why?' asked France d'Houdetot.

'Well, I am dining out this evening,' said the officer.

At that moment a group of women in mourning and children dressed in black passed rapidly along the other pavement of the bridge. A man was holding the eldest child by the hand. I looked at him and recognized the Duc de Montebello.

'Hullo!' exclaimed Houdetot. 'The Minister of Marine!' He ran over and chatted for a moment with Monsieur de Montebello. The duchess had taken fright and the whole family was taking refuge on the Left Bank.

Vivien and I returned to the Palace of the Chamber. Houdetot left us. The next moment we were surrounded. Boissy said to me:

'You weren't at the Luxembourg, were you? I tried to speak about the situation in Paris. I was booed. At the words "The capital in danger", I was interrupted, and the Chancellor, who had come to preside just for that purpose, called me to order. And do you know what General Gourgaud said to me? "Monsieur de Boissy, I have sixty guns with their powderchests full of grapeshot. I filled them myself." I replied: "General, I am delighted to know what the Palace really thinks." And do you know what Marshal Bugeaud, who has been in command of Paris for the past two hours, said? "If I had fifty thousand women and children in front of me, I would open fire." Some pretty things are going to happen before tomorrow morning.'

At that moment Duvergier de Hauranne, hatless, his hair dishevelled, and looking pale but pleased, passed by and stopped to shake hands with me.

I left Duvergier and went into the Chamber. There were not as many as a hundred deputies there. A bill about the Bank of Bordeaux was being debated. A man who was talking through his nose occupied the tribune, and Monsieur Sauzet was reading the articles of the bill with a sleepy air. Monsieur de Belleyme, who was coming out, shook hands with me as he passed, and said: 'Alas!'

Several deputies came up to me, among them Monsieur Marie, Monsieur Roger (of the Loiret), Monsieur de Rémusat, and Monsieur Chambolle. I told them the story of the tearing down of the flag, which was serious in view of the audacity of an attack on a guardhouse in the open.

'What is even more serious,' said one of them, 'is that there is something very bad behind all this. During the night the doors of more than fifteen mansions in Paris were marked with a cross, including the Princesse de Liéven's house in the Rue Saint-Florentin, and Madame de Talhouët's mansion.'

'Are you sure of this?' I asked.

'With my own eyes I saw the cross on the door of Madame de Liéven's house,' he replied.

President Franck-Carré met Monsieur Duchâtel this morning and said: 'Well, how is everything?'

'All is well,' answered the Minister.

'What are you doing about the riot?'

'I am letting it be. What can they do in the Place Louis XV and the Champs-Élysées? It is raining. They will tramp about there all day. Tonight they will be tired out and will go home to bed.'

Monsieur Étienne Arago came in and without stopping told us: 'There are seven wounded and two killed already. Barricades have been set up in the Rue Sainte-Avoye.'

The session ended. I went out with the deputies and returned by way of the quays.

On the Place de la Concorde the cavalry was still charging. An attempt to erect two barricades had been made in the Rue Saint-Honoré. The paving-stones in the Marché Saint-Honoré

were being torn up. The omnibuses which had been overturned to make the barricades had been righted by the troops.
In the Rue Saint-Honoré the crowd let the Municipal Guards
go by, and then stoned them from behind. A multitude was
swarming along the quays, making a din like an angry ant-
heap. I saw a very pretty woman in a green velvet hat and a
large cashmere shawl pass by, in the midst of a group of bare-
armed men in smocks. She had raised her skirt very high on
account of the mud, with which she was spattered, for it was
raining off and on. The Tuileries were closed. At the Carrousel gates the crowd had stopped and was gazing through
the arcades at the cavalry lined up in battle array in front of
the palace.

Near the Pont du Carrousel I met Monsieur Jules San-
deau.

'What do you think of all this?' he asked.

'That the riot will be suppressed, but that the revolution will
triumph.'

Patrols were marching all the way along the quay, while the
crowd shouted: 'Hurray for the line!' The shops were closed
and the windows of the houses open.

In the Place du Châtelet I heard a man say to a group: 'It
is 1830 all over again!'

No. In 1830 there was the Duc d'Orléans behind Charles X.
In 1848 there is a void behind Louis-Philippe. It is a sad thing
to descend from Louis-Philippe to Ledru-Rollin.

I passed by the Hôtel de Ville and along the Rue Saint-
Avoye. At the Hôtel de Ville all was quiet. Two National
Guards were walking to and fro in front of the gate, and
there were no barricades in the Rue Sainte-Avoye. In the Rue
Rambuteau a few National Guards, in uniform, and wearing
their swords, came and went. In the Temple quarter they
were beating to arms.

Up to now the powers that be have made a show of doing
without the National Guard this time. This is perhaps prudent.
This morning the National Guards on duty at the Chamber
refused to obey orders.

The King is said to be extremely calm and even merry. But this game must not be played too long. Every trick which is won at it only adds up to the trick which is lost.

The Molé Ministry was certainly not a Reform Government, but the Guizot Ministry had been an obstacle to reform for so long! This obstacle had been removed; this was enough to pacify and content the childlike heart of the generous people. In the evening Paris gave itself up to rejoicing; the population turned out into the street; everywhere one could hear the popular refrain: 'Lights! Lights!' In the twinkling of an eye the city was illuminated as for a fête.

In the Place Royale, in front of the *mairie*, a few yards from my house, a crowd had collected which was growing denser and noisier every moment. Some officers and National Guards from the guardhouse there, in order to get them away from the *mairie*, shouted: 'To the Bastille!' and, arm-in-arm, put themselves at the head of a column which, repeating: 'To the Bastille!' set off joyfully behind them. Hat in hand, the procession marched round the July Column to the shout of: 'Up with Reform!' greeted the troops massed in the square with the cry of: 'Up with the line!' and went off into the Faubourg Saint-Antoine. An hour later the procession returned, its ranks greatly swollen, with torches and flags, and made its way to the main boulevards, with the intention of going home by way of the quays, so as to share the joy of its victory with the whole city.

Midnight is striking at this moment. There are ten guns on the Place de Grève. The appearance of the Marais quarter is lugubrious. I have just returned from a stroll there. The street lamps are broken and extinguished on the boulevard so well named the 'dark boulevard'. The only shops open tonight were those in the Rue Saint-Antoine. The Théâtre Beaumarchais was closed. The Place Royale is guarded like a place of arms.

Troops are concealed in the arcades. In the Rue Saint-Louis, a battalion is leaning silently against the walls in the shadows.

Just now, as the clock struck the hour, we got up and went on to the balcony, saying: 'It is the tocsin!'

I could not have slept in a bed. I spent the night in my drawing-room writing, thinking, and listening. Now and then I went out on to my balcony and strained my ears to listen, then I came back into the room and paced to and fro, or dropped into an arm-chair and dozed. But my sleep was disturbed by feverish dreams. I dreamed that I could hear the murmur of angry crowds, and the sound of distant firing; the tocsin was clanging from the church towers. I awoke. It was the tocsin.

The reality has been more horrible than the dream. That crowd which I had seen marching and singing so gaily on the boulevards had at first continued on its peaceful way without let or hindrance. The infantry regiments, the artillery, and the cuirassiers had everywhere opened their ranks to let the procession pass through. But on the Boulevard des Capucines a mass of troops, infantry and cavalry, who were guarding the Ministry of Foreign Affairs and its unpopular Minister, Monsieur Guizot, blocked both pavements and the roadway. Faced by this insurmountable obstacle, the head of the column tried to stop and turn; but the irresistible pressure of the huge crowd behind pushed the front ranks on. At that moment a shot was fired, on which side is not known. A panic ensued, followed by a volley. Eighty people fell dead or wounded. There arose a general cry of horror and fury: 'Vengeance!' The corpses of the victims were placed in a tumbril lighted by torches. The crowd faced about and, in the midst of curses, resumed its march, which had now taken on the character of a funeral procession. In a few hours Paris was covered with barricades.

24 February 1848

At daybreak, from my balcony, I see a noisy column of people, including a number of National Guards, arrive in front of the *mairie*. The building is guarded by about thirty Municipal Guards. The mob loudly demands the soldiers' arms. Flat refusal by the Municipal Guards and a menacing roar from the crowd. Two National Guard officers intervene: 'What is the use of further bloodshed? Resistance would be useless.' The Municipal Guards lay down their rifles and ammunition and withdraw without being molested.

The Mayor of the Eighth Arrondissement, Monsieur Ernest Moreau, sends a message asking me to come to the *mairie*. He tells me the appalling news of the massacre on the Boulevard des Capucines. And at brief intervals further news of increasing seriousness arrives. The National Guard this time has definitely turned against the Government, and is shouting: 'Up with Reform!' The army, frightened at what it did yesterday, seems determined not to take any further part in this fratricidal struggle. In the Rue Sainte-Croix-la-Bretonnerie the troops have fallen back before the National Guard. At the neighbouring *mairie* of the Ninth Arrondissement, we are informed, the soldiers are fraternizing and patrolling with the National Guard. Two other messengers in smocks arrive one after the other; 'The Neuilly Barracks has been taken.' 'The Minimes Barracks has surrendered.'

'And from the Government I have received neither instructions nor news!' says Monsieur Ernest Moreau. 'What Government, if any, is there? Is the Molé Ministry still in existence? What is to be done?'

'Go to the Prefecture of the Seine,' says Monsieur Perret, a member of the General Council. 'It isn't far to the Hôtel de Ville.'

'Well, then, come along with me.'

They go. I reconnoitre the Place Royale. Everywhere there is agitation, anxiety, and feverish expectation. Everywhere work is being pushed forward on barricades which are already formidable. This time it is more than a riot, it is an insurrection. I return home. A soldier of the line, on sentry duty at the entrance to the Place Royale, is chatting amicably with the sentry of a barricade constructed twenty paces from him.

At a quarter-past eight Monsieur Ernest Moreau returns from the Hôtel de Ville. He has seen Monsieur de Rambuteau and brings slightly better news. The King has entrusted the formation of a Cabinet to Thiers and Odilon Barrot. Thiers is not very popular, but Odilon Barrot stands for reform. Unfortunately the concession is coupled with a threat: Marshal Bugeaud has been invested with the overall command of the National Guard and of the army. Odilon Barrot stands for Reform, but Bugeaud stands for repression. The King is holding out his right hand and clenching his left fist.

The Prefect asked Monsieur Moreau to spread and proclaim this news in his district and in the Faubourg Saint-Antoine.

'That is what I am going to do,' says the Mayor.

'Good,' I say, 'but believe me, you will be well advised to announce the Thiers–Barrot Ministry and say nothing about Marshal Bugeaud.'

'You are right.'

The Mayor requisitions a squad of National Guards, takes with him his two deputies and the Municipal Councillors present, and goes down on to the Place Royale. A roll of drums attracts the crowd. He announces the new Cabinet. The people applaud to repeated shouts of 'Up with Reform!' The Mayor adds a few words recommending order and unity, and is universally applauded.

'The situation is saved!' he says, grasping my hand.

'Yes,' I say, 'If Bugeaud will give up the idea of being the saviour.'

Monsieur Ernest Moreau, followed by his escort, goes off to repeat his proclamation on the Place de la Bastille and in the faubourg, and I return home to reassure my family.

N

Half an hour later the Mayor and his cortege return to the *mairie* in considerable agitation. This is what had happened:

The Place de la Bastille was occupied at its two extremities by troops, motionless, with their arms at the ready. The people moved freely and peaceably between the two lines. The Mayor, arriving at the foot of the July Column, made his proclamation, and once again the crowd applauded vigorously. Monsieur Moreau then made off in the direction of the Faubourg Saint-Antoine. At that moment a number of workers accosted the soldiers amicably and said: 'Your arms, give up your arms.' In obedience to a sharp order from their captain the soldiers refused. Suddenly a shot rang out, followed by other shots. The terrible panic which had occurred the previous day on the Boulevard des Capucines was perhaps about to be renewed. Monsieur Moreau and his escort were pushed about, knocked over. The firing on both sides lasted over a minute, and five or six people were killed or wounded.

Fortunately, this time the incident occurred in broad daylight. At the sight of the blood they had shed there was a sudden revulsion of feeling on the part of the troops, and after a moment of surprise and horror the soldiers, prompted by an irresistible impulse, raised the butts of their rifles in the air and shouted: 'Long live the National Guard!' The general in command, being powerless to control his men, retreated to Vincennes by way of the quays. The people remain in control of the Bastille and of the faubourg.

'It is a result that might have cost more dear, in my case especially,' remarks Monsieur Moreau. And he shows us his hat which has been pierced by a bullet. 'A brand new hat!' he adds with a laugh.

Half-past ten. Three students from the École Polytechnique have arrived at the *mairie*. They report that the students have broken out of the school and placed themselves at the disposal of the people. A certain number have distributed themselves like this among the *mairies* of Paris.

The insurrection is making progress every hour. It is now reported to be demanding that Marshal Bugeaud be replaced and the Chamber dissolved. The pupils of the École Polytechnique go further and talk about the abdication of the King.

What is happening at the Tuileries? There is no news, either, from the Ministry, no order from the General Staff. I decide to go to the Chamber of Deputies, by way of the Hôtel de Ville, and Monsieur Ernest Moreau is kind enough to accompany me.

We find the Rue Saint-Antoine bristling with barricades. We make ourselves known and the insurgents help us to clamber over the heaps of paving stones. Approaching the Hôtel de Ville, from which the roar of a great crowd reaches our ears, and crossing a building site, we see Monsieur de Rambuteau, the Prefect of the Seine, hurrying towards us.

'Why, *Monsieur le Préfet,* what are you doing here?' I ask.

'Prefect! How do I know whether I am still Prefect?' he replies with a surly air.

A crowd, which looks anything but benevolent, has already begun to gather. Monsieur Moreau notices a new house which is to let. We go inside, and Monsieur de Rambuteau recounts his misadventure.

'I was in my office, with two or three Municipal Councillors, when we heard a lot of noise in the corridor. The door was thrown open and a big fellow, a captain of the National Guard, came in at the head of an excited body of troops.

' "Monsieur," said the man, "you must get out of here."

' "Pardon me, Monsieur, here at the Hôtel de Ville I am at home, and here I stay."

' "Yesterday you may have been at home in the Hôtel de Ville; today the people are at home here."

' "Oh! But . . ."

' "Go to the window and look at the square."

'The square had been invaded by a huge noisy crowd in which workers, National Guards, and soldiers were mingled pell-mell. And the soldiers' rifles were in the hands of the men of the people. I turned to the intruders and said :

' "You are right, gentlemen, you are the masters here."

' "In that case," said the captain, "tell your employees to recognize my authority."

'That was too much. I retorted: "What do you take me for?" I picked up a few papers, issued a few orders, and here I am. Since you are going to the Chamber, if there is still a Chamber, tell the Minister of the Interior, if there is still a Ministry, that at the Hôtel de Ville there is no longer either a Prefect or a Prefecture.'

It is with great difficulty that we make our way through the human ocean which, with a noise like that of a storm, covers the Place de l'Hôtel de Ville. At the Quai de la Mégisserie there is a huge barricade; thanks to the Mayor's sash we are allowed to clamber over it. Beyond this the quays are almost deserted. We reach the Chamber of Deputies by way of the Left Bank.

The Palais Bourbon is filled with a buzzing crowd of deputies, peers, and high officials. From a rather large group comes the shrill voice of Monsieur Thiers: 'Ah! here is Victor Hugo!' And Monsieur Thiers comes to us and asks for news about the Faubourg Saint-Antoine. We add the news about the Hôtel de Ville. He shakes his head gloomily.

'And how are things here?' I ask. 'First of all, are you still a Minister?'

'I? Oh, I was left behind long ago! At the moment Odilon Barrot is President of the Council and Minister of the Interior.'

'And Marshal Bugeaud?'

'He, too, has been replaced, by Marshal Gérard. But that is nothing. The Chamber has been dissolved, the King has abdicated and is on his way to Saint-Cloud, and the Duchesse d'Orléans is Regent. Ah! the tide is rising, rising, rising!'

Monsieur Thiers advises us, Monsieur Ernest Moreau and me, to come to an understanding with Monsieur Odilon Barrot. Action by us in our district, which is such an important

THE FEBRUARY DAYS 185

one, could be extremely useful. We therefore set out for the Ministry of the Interior.

The people have invaded the Ministry and even penetrated into the Minister's office, where a not over-respectful crowd comes and goes. At a large table in the middle of the huge room secretaries are writing. Monsieur Odilon Barrot, red-faced and tight-lipped, with his hands behind his back, is leaning against the mantelpiece.

'You know the situation, don't you?' he says when he sees us. 'The King has abdicated and the Duchesse d'Orléans is Regent.'

'If the people agrees,' says a man in a smock who is passing.

The Minister takes us into a window recess, looking uneasily about him as he does so.

'What are you going to do? What are you doing?' I ask him.

'I am sending telegrams to the departments.'

'Is that very urgent?'

'France must be informed of the events.'

'Yes, but meanwhile Paris is making those events. And has it finished making them? The Regency is all very well, but it has got to be sanctioned.'

'Yes, by the Chamber. The Duchesse d'Orléans ought to take the Comte de Paris to the Chamber.'

'No, since the Chamber has been dissolved. If the duchess has to go anywhere, it is to the Hôtel de Ville.'

'How can you think of such a thing? What about the danger?'

'There is no danger. A mother and child! I will answer for the people. They will respect the woman in the princess.'

'Well, then, go to the Tuileries, see the Duchesse d'Orléans, advise her, explain the situation to her.'

'Why don't you go yourself?'

'I have just come from there. Nobody knew where the duchess was; I could not speak to her. But if you see her tell her that I am at her disposal, that I await her orders. Oh, Monsieur Victor Hugo, I would give my life for that woman and for that child!'

Odilon Barrot is the most honest and the most devoted man in the world, but he is the opposite of a man of action; one can feel uncertainty and indecision in his words, in his gaze, in his whole person.

'Listen,' he goes on, 'what matters, what is urgent, is that the people should be made acquainted with these grave changes, the abdication and Regency. Promise me that you will go and proclaim them at your *mairie*, in the faubourg, and wherever you can.'

'I promise.'

I set off with Monsieur Moreau in the direction of the Tuileries.

In the Rue Bellechasse there are galloping horses. A squadron of dragoons flashes by and seems to be fleeing from a man with bare arms who is running behind them brandishing a sword.

The Tuileries are still guarded by troops. The Mayor shows his sash and they let us pass. At the gate the concierge, to whom I make myself known, informs us that the Duchesse d'Orléans, accompanied by the Duc de Nemours, has just left the palace with the Comte de Paris, no doubt to go to the Chamber of Deputies. We have, therefore, no other course than to continue on our way.

At the entrance to the Pont du Carrousel bullets whistle past our ears. Insurgents in the Place du Carrousel are firing at the court carriages leaving the stables. One of the coachmen has been killed on his box.

'It would be stupid of us to stay here as spectators and get ourselves killed,' says Monsieur Ernest Moreau. 'Let us cross the bridge.'

We skirt the Institut and the Quai de la Monnaie. At the Pont Neuf we pass a band of men armed with pikes, axes, and rifles, headed by a drummer, and led by a man waving a sword and wearing a long coat in the King's livery. It is the

coat of the coachman who has just been killed in the Rue
Saint-Thomas-du-Louvre.

When we arrive, Monsieur Moreau and I, at the Place
Royale we find it filled with an anxious crowd. We are
promptly surrounded and questioned, and it is not without
some difficulty that we reach the *mairie*. The mass of people
is too compact to allow us to address them in the Place. With
the Mayor, a few officers of the National Guard, and two
students of the École Polytechnique, I go up to the balcony of
the *mairie*. I raise my hand, silence falls as if by magic, and I say:

'My friends, you are waiting for news. This is what we
know: Monsieur Thiers is no longer Minister and Marshal
Bugeaud is no longer in command (*Applause*). They have
been replaced by Marshal Gérard and Monsieur Odilon Barrot
(*Applause, but less general*). The Chamber has been dissolved.
The King has abdicated. (*Universal cheering*). The Duchesse
d'Orléans is Regent (*A few isolated cheers, mingled with low
murmurs*).'

I continue:

'The name of Odilon Barrot is a guarantee that the widest
possible appeal will be made to the nation; and that you will
have a truly representative government.'

My declaration is greeted with applause at several points,
but it seems obvious that the great bulk of the crowd is un-
certain and dissatisfied.

We go back into the hall of the *mairie*.

'Now,' I say to Monsieur Ernest Moreau, 'I must go and
make the proclamation in the Place de la Bastille.'

But the Mayor is disheartened.

'You can see that it is useless,' he says sadly. 'The Regency
is not accepted. And you have spoken here in a district where
you are known and loved. At the Bastille you will be faced
with the revolutionary people of the faubourg who may give
you a rough reception.'

'I must go,' I say. 'I promised Odilon Barrot that I would.'

'I have changed my hat,' the Mayor goes on with a smile, 'but remember my hat this morning.'

'This morning the army and the people were face to face, and there was some danger of a conflict; now, however, the people are alone, the people are the masters.'

'Masters—and hostile; be careful how you go!'

'Never mind, I have promised, and I will keep my promise.'

I tell the Mayor that his place is at the *mairie* and that he ought to stay there. But several National Guard officers come forward spontaneously and offer to accompany me, among them the worthy Monsieur Launaye, my former captain. I accept their friendly offer, and we form a little procession which goes by way of the Rue du Pas-de-la-Mule and the Boulevard Beaumarchais towards the Place de la Bastille.

There, there was a restless, excited crowd in which workers predominated, many of them armed with rifles taken from the barracks or given up to them by the soldiers. There were shouts and the song of the Girondins: '*Die for the fatherland!*' There were countless groups talking and arguing passionately. They turned round, they looked at us, they questioned us, 'What's the news? What's going on?' And they followed us. I heard my name murmured with different intonations: 'Victor Hugo! It's Victor Hugo!' A few people greeted me. When we reach the July Column we were surrounded by a considerable crowd. In order to make myself heard I climbed up on to the base of the column.

I will only repeat the words which it was possible for me to make my turbulent audience hear. It was much less a speech than a dialogue, but the dialogue of one voice with ten, twenty, a hundred more or less hostile voices.

I began by announcing at once the abdication of Louis-Philippe, and, as in the Place Royale, applause that was practically unanimous greeted the news. But there were also shouts of 'No! No abdication! Deposition! Deposition!' I was obviously going to have a difficult time.

When I announced the Regency of the Duchesse d'Orléans, violent protests arose; 'No! No! No Regency! Down with the Bourbons! Neither King nor Queen! No masters!'

I repeated: 'No masters! I don't want them any more than you do. I have defended liberty all my life.'

'Then why do you proclaim the Regency?'

'Because a Regent is not a master. Besides, I have no right whatever to proclaim the Regency; I am merely announcing it.'

'No! No! No Regency!'

A man in a smock shouted: 'Let the peer of France be silent. Down with the peer of France!' And he levelled his rifle at me. I looked him in the eyes and raised my voice so loudly that the crowd fell silent: 'Yes, I am a peer of France, and I speak as a peer of France. I swore fidelity, not to a royal person, but to the Consitutional Monarchy. As long as no other government has been established it is my duty to be faithful to this one. And I have always thought that the people approved of a man who did his duty, whatever that duty might be.'

There was a murmur of approval around me and here and there a few cheers. But when I endeavoured to continue: 'If the Regency . . .' the protests redoubled. I was allowed to take up only one of these protests. A workman had shouted: 'We don't want to be governed by a woman.' I retorted sharply:

'I don't want to be governed by a woman either, nor even by a man. It was because Louis-Philippe wanted to govern that his abdication today is necessary and just. But a woman who reigns in the name of a child! Isn't that a guarantee against any thought of personal government? Look at Queen Victoria in England. . . .'

'We are French, we are!' shouted the crowd. 'No Regency!'

'No Regency? What then? Nothing is ready, nothing. There would be a total upheaval, ruin, distress, civil war, perhaps; the unknown in any case.'

One voice, a single voice, cried: 'Long live the Republic!'

Not a single other voice echoed it. Poor, great people,

irresponsible and blind! They know what they do not want, but they do not know what they want.

From that point the noise, the shouts, the threats became such that I gave up the attempt to make myself heard. The worthy Launaye said: 'You have done what you wanted to, what you promised to do; the only thing that remains for us to do is to withdraw.'

The crowd opened before us, curious and inoffensive. But twenty paces from the column the man who had threatened me with his rifle caught up with me and once again levelled his weapon at me, shouting: 'Down with the peer of France!' 'No! Respect for the great man!' cried a young workman, pushing the rifle downwards. I thanked this unknown friend with a wave of the hand and passed on.

At the *mairie*, Monsieur Ernest Moreau, who it seems had been very anxious about us, greeted us joyfully and warmly congratulated me. But I knew that even when their passions are aroused the people are just; and not the slightest credit was due to me, for I had not felt the slightest anxiety.

While these things were happening in the Place de la Bastille, this was what was happening at the Palais Bourbon.

There is at this moment a man whose name is on everybody's lips and the thought of whom is in everybody's mind; that man is Lamartine. His eloquent and vivid *History of the Girondins* has just taught France something about the Revolution for the first time. Hitherto he had only been illustrious; he has become popular and may be said to hold Paris in his hand.

In the universal confusion his influence could be decisive. This is what they said to themselves in the offices of the *National*, where the chances of the Republic had been weighed, and where a scheme for a provisional government had been drawn up from which Lamartine had been left out. In 1842, at the time of the debate on the Regency which resulted in the choice of the Duc de Nemours, Lamartine had spoken warmly in favour of the Duchesse d'Orléans. Did he hold the same opinion today? What did he want? What would he do? It was essential to find the answer to these questions. Monsieur Armand Marrast, the editor of the *National*, took with him three notorious Republicans, Monsieur Bastide, Monsieur Hetzel, the publisher, and Monsieur Bocage, the eminent actor who created the part of Didier in *Marion de Lorme*. All four went to the Chamber of Deputies. They found Lamartine there and held a conference with him in the offices.

They all spoke in turn, and expressed their convictions and hopes. They said that they would be happy to think that Lamartine was with them in wanting the immediate realization of the Republic. If, however, he considered that the transition of the Regency was necessary they asked him to help them at least to obtain serious guarantees against any retrogression. They anxiously awaited his decision in this great matter.

Lamartine listened to them in silence, then asked them to allow him a few minutes for reflection. He sat down at a table apart from them, leaned his head on his hands, and thought. His four visitors, standing and silent, gazed at him respectfully. It was a solemn moment. 'We listened to history passing,' Bocage told me later.

Lamartine raised his head and said: 'I will oppose the Regency.'

A quarter of an hour later the Duchesse d'Orléans arrived at the Chamber holding by the hand her two sons, the Comte de Paris and the Duc de Chartres. Monsieur Odilon Barrot was not with her. The Duc de Nemours accompanied her.

She was acclaimed by the deputies. But since the Chamber had been dissolved, were there any deputies?

Monsieur Crémieux ascended the tribune and flatly proposed a provisional government. Monsieur Odilon Barrot, who had been fetched from the Ministry, arrived eventually and pleaded for the Regency, but without either enthusiasm or energy. Suddenly a mob of people and National Guards with arms and flags invaded the chamber. The Duchesse d'Orléans, on the advice of her friends, withdrew with her children.

The Chamber of Deputies then vanished, submerged by a sort of revolutionary assembly. Ledru-Rollin harangued this crowd. Then came Lamartine, who was awaited and acclaimed. He opposed the Regency, as he had promised.

That settled it. The names of candidates for a provisional government were thrown to the people. And by shouts of 'Yes' or 'No' the people elected successively: Lamartine, Dupont de l'Eure, Arago, and Ledru-Rollin unanimously; Crémieux, Garnier-Pagès, and Marie by a majority.

The new ministers at once set out for the Hôtel de Ville.

At the Chamber of Deputies the word 'Republic' had not been uttered once in any of the speeches of the orators, not even in that of Ledru-Rollin. But now, outside, in the street, the elect of the people heard this word, this shout, everywhere. It flew from mouth to mouth and filled the air of Paris.

The few men who, in these supreme and anxious days, held the destiny of France in their hands were themselves at once tools and playthings in the hands of the mob, which is not the people; and of chance, which is not providence. Under the pressure of the multitude, in the splendour and terror of their triumph, which overwhelmed them, they decreed the Republic without knowing that they were doing anything so momentous.

They took half a sheet of paper, at the head of which were printed the words: 'Prefecture of the Seine. The Prefect's Office.' Monsieur de Rambuteau had perhaps used the other half of the sheet that very morning to write a love-letter to one of his 'little bourgeoises', as he called them.

At the dictation of the terrible roar of shouting outside Lamartine wrote this sentence:

'The Provisional Government declares that the Provisional Government of France is the Republican Government, and that the nation shall be immediately called upon to ratify the decision of the Provisional Government and of the people of Paris.'

I have held this paper, this dirty sheet smeared and blotted with ink, in my hands. It was still stamped, still palpitating, so to speak, with the fever of the moment. The words hurriedly written on it were scarcely formed. 'Called' was misspelt.

When these half-dozen lines had been written, Lamartine signed his name and handed the pen to Ledru-Rollin.

Ledru-Rollin read aloud the phrase: 'The Provisional Government declares that the Provisional Government of France is the Republican Government . . .'

'The word "Provisional" occurs twice,' he said.

'That is true,' said the others.

'It must be crossed out once at least,' said Ledru-Rollin.

Lamartine understood the significance of this grammatical observation, which was quite simply a revolution by omission.

'But we must await the sanction of France,' he said.

'I can do without the sanction of France,' cried Ledru-Rollin, 'when I have the sanction of the people.'

'But who knows at present what the people want?' observed Lamartine.

'I do,' said Ledru-Rollin.

There was a moment's silence. The noise of the crowd outside sounded like the roar of the ocean. Ledru-Rollin went on:

'What the people want is the Republic at once, the Republic without waiting.'

'The Republic without any delay,' said Lamartine, concealing an objection in this interpretation of Ledru-Rollin's words.

'We are provisional,' said Ledru-Rollin, 'but the Republic is not!'

Monsieur Crémieux took the pen from Lamartine's hands, crossed out the word 'provisional' at the end of the third line and wrote beside it: 'present'.

'The present government?' said Ledru-Rollin. 'All right. I would prefer permanent, but I will sign all the same.'

The seal of the City of Paris was on the table. Since 1830 the ship sailing beneath a sky studded with fleurs-de-lis and with the device *Praelucent certius astris*, had disappeared from the seal of the City. The seal was merely a circle with just the words *Ville de Paris* in the centre. Ledru-Rollin took the seal and stamped the bottom of the paper so hastily with it that the words appeared upside down. Nobody thought of putting the date.

Next to Lamartine's signature, a scarcely legible signature in which one can distinguish all the hesitation affecting the poet's heart, Ledru-Rollin traced his calm signature decorated with that commonplace clerk's paraph which he shares with Proudhon. After and below Ledru-Rollin, Garnier-Pagès signed with the same assurance and the same paraph. Then Crémieux, then Marie, and finally Dupont de l'Eure, whose hand was trembling with old age and emotion.

Only these six men signed. At that moment the Provisional Government consisted only of these six deputies.

A few minutes later, this scrap of paper was a law, this scrap of paper was the future of the people, this scrap of paper was the future of the world. The Republic had been proclaimed. *Alea jacta*, as Lamartine later observed.

25 February 1848

During the morning everything at and around the *mairie* of the Eighth Arrondissement was relatively calm, and the steps to maintain order taken the previous day with the approval of Monsieur Ernest Moreau seemed to ensure the safety of the district.

I thought I might leave the Place Royale and make for the centre of the city with my son Victor. The excitement of a people (of the people of Paris!) on the day after a revolution was a sight that had an irresistible attraction for me.

The weather was cloudy and grey, but mild and dry. The streets were pulsating with a noisy, happy crowd. The people were continuing with incredible ardour to fortify the barri-

cades which had already been constructed, and to build new
ones. Groups with flags flying and drums beating marched
along shouting 'Long live the Republic!' and singing the
Marseillaise and *Die for the Fatherland!* The cafés were
crowded to overflowing, but many of the shops were closed
as on holidays; and indeed the whole city looked as if it were
on holiday.

I made my way along the quays of the Pont Neuf. There, at
the bottom of a proclamation, I read the name of Lamartine,
and having seen the people, I felt an inexplicable urge to go
and see my great friend. I therefore turned back with Victor
towards the Hôtel de Ville.

As on the previous day, the square in front of the building
was filled with a crowd, and the crowd was so dense that it
immobilized itself. It was impossible to approach the steps at
the front of the building. After several attempts to get near
them, I was about to retire when I was noticed by Monsieur
Froment-Meurice, the artist-goldsmith, the brother of my
young friend Paul Meurice. He was a major in the National
Guard, and on duty with his battalion at the Hôtel de Ville. I
explained our problem to him. 'Make way!' he shouted
authoritatively. 'Make way for Victor Hugo!' and the human
wall opened, somehow or other, before his epaulets.

Once we had climbed the steps, Monsieur Froment-Meurice
led us up all sorts of stairways and through corridors and
rooms crowded with people. Seeing us go by, a man of the
people left one group and planted himself in front of me.

'Citizen Victor Hugo,' he said, 'shout: "Long live the Republic!" '

'I will shout nothing by order,' I said. 'Do you understand
what liberty is? For my part, I practise it. Today I will shout:
"Long live the people" because it pleases me to do so. The
day I shout: "Long live the Republic!" it will be because I
want to.'

'Hear, hear! He is right,' murmured several voices, and we
passed on.

After a good many detours Monsieur Froment-Meurice

showed us into a little room where he left us while he went to inform Lamartine that I wished to see him.

The glass door of the room where we were gave on to a gallery, along which I saw my friend David d'Angers, the great sculptor, passing. I called out to him. David, who was an old-time Republican, was beaming. 'Ah, my friend, what a wonderful day!' he exclaimed. He told me that the Provisional Government had appointed him Mayor of the Eleventh Arrondissement. 'They have sent for you for something of the same kind, I suppose?' he said. 'No,' I said, 'I have not been sent for. I came of my own accord just to shake Lamartine's hand.'

Monsieur Froment-Meurice returned and announced that Lamartine was expecting me. I left Victor in the room, telling him to wait there till I came back, and once again followed my obliging guide through more corridors which led to a big vestibule which was crowded with people. 'They are all office-seekers!' said Monsieur Froment-Meurice. The Provisional Government was installed in the adjoining room. The door was guarded by two armed grenadiers of the National Guard, who were impassive and deaf to both entreaties and threats. I had to force my way through this crowd. One of the grenadiers, who had been told that I was coming, opened the door a little way to let me in. The crowd tried to take advantage of this and rushed at the sentries, who, with the aid of Monsieur Froment-Meurice, forced them back and closed the door behind me.

I was in a spacious hall which formed the corner of one of the pavilions of the Hôtel de Ville, and was lighted on two sides by lofty windows. I would have preferred to find Lamartine alone, but there were with him, dispersed about the room and talking to friends or writing, three or four of his colleagues in the Provisional Government, Arago, Marie, and Armand Marrast. Lamartine rose as I entered. On his frock-coat, which was buttoned up as usual, he wore a broad tricolour sash, slung across his shoulder. He came forward to meet me, and holding out his hand, exclaimed: 'Ah! You have come over to us, Victor Hugo! What a recruit for the Republic!'

'Not so fast!' I said with a laugh. 'I have come simply to see my friend Lamartine. Perhaps you don't know that yesterday while you were opposing the Regency in the Chamber I was defending it in the Place de la Bastille.'

'Yesterday, that was all right; but today! Today there is neither Regency nor Royalty. It is impossible that Victor Hugo should not be a Republican at heart.'

'Theoretically, yes, I am. The Republic is, in my opinion, the only rational form of government, the only one worthy of the nations. The universal Republic will be the ultimate achievement of progress. But has its hour struck in France? It is because I want the Republic that I want it to be viable and definitive. You are going to consult the nation, aren't you—the whole nation?'

'The whole nation? Certainly. We of the Provisional Government have all spoken in favour of universal suffrage.'

At that moment Arago came up to us with Monsieur Armand Marrast, who held a paper in his hand.

'My dear friend,' Lamartine said to me, 'this morning we chose you to be Mayor of your arrondissement.'

'And here is the patent signed by us all,' said Armand Marrast.

'I thank you,' I said, 'but I cannot accept it.'

'Why not?' continued Arago. 'This is a non-political and purely honorary post.'

'We were informed just now about the attempted revolt at La Force,' added Lamartine. 'You did better than suppress it, you forestalled it. You are loved and respected in your arrondissement.'

'My authority is wholly moral,' I said. 'It could only lose weight by becoming official. Besides, on no account would I dispossess Monsieur Ernest Moreau, who has acted loyally and valiantly these last few days.'

Lamartine and Arago insisted: 'Do not refuse our patent.'

'Very well,' I said, 'I will take it—for the sake of the

o

autographs; but it is understood that I shall keep it in my pocket.'

'Yes, keep it,' said Armand Marrast laughingly, 'so that you can say that one day you were *pair* and the next day *maire*.'

Lamartine took me into a window-recess.

'It is not a *mairie* I would like you to have,' he said, 'but a ministry. Victor Hugo, the Republic's Minister of Instruction! Come now, since you say that you are a Republican!'

'A Republican . . . in theory. But in fact, yesterday I was a peer of France, yesterday I was for the Regency, and believing the Republic to be premature, I would still be for the Regency today.'

'Nations are above dynasties,' Lamartine went on. 'I too have been a Royalist.'

'Yes, but you were a deputy, elected by the nation. I was a peer, appointed by the King.'

'The King, in choosing you, under the terms of the Constitution, in one of the categories from which the Upper House was recruited, only honoured the peerage and himself.'

'Thank you,' I said, 'but you look at things from the outside; I consult my conscience.'

We were interrupted by the noise of a prolonged fusillade which suddenly broke out on the square. A bullet smashed a window-pane above our heads.

'What is the matter now?' exclaimed Lamartine in sorrowful tones.

Monsieur Armand Marrast and Monsieur Marie went out to see what was happening.

'Ah, my friend,' continued Lamartine, 'how hard this revolutionary power is to bear! One has such heavy and unexpected responsibilities to assume before one's conscience and in the presence of history! I don't know how I have been living during the past two days. Yesterday I had a few grey hairs; tomorrow they will all be white.'

'Yes, but you are doing your duty as a man of genius magnificently,' I told him.

After a few minutes Monsieur Armand Marrast returned.

'It was not against us,' he said. 'Nobody could explain to me how the wretched incident occurred. There was a collision and the rifles went off, but why? Was it a misunderstanding? Was it a quarrel between Socialists and Republicans? Nobody knows.'

'Are there any wounded?'

'Yes, and even a few dead.'

A gloomy silence followed. I rose. 'You probably have some measures to take?' I said.

'What measures?' answered Lamartine. 'This morning we resolved to decree what you have already been able to do on a small scale in your district; the organization of a militia— every Frenchman a soldier as well as a voter. But we need time, and meanwhile . . .' He pointed to the waves and eddies of the thousands of heads in the square outside. 'Look, it is the sea!'

A boy wearing an apron came in and spoke to him in low tones.

'Ah! Good!' said Lamartine. 'It is my luncheon. Will you share it with me, Hugo?'

'Thank you, I have already lunched.'

'I haven't and I am dying of hunger. At least come and watch the feast; I will let you go afterwards.'

He took me into a room which gave on to an interior courtyard. A gentle-faced young man who was writing at a table rose and made as if to withdraw. He was the young workman whom Louis Blanc had had attached to the Provisional Government.

'Stay here, Albert,' said Lamartine. 'I have nothing of a private nature to say to Victor Hugo.'

We greeted each other, Monsieur Albert and I.

The little waiter showed Lamartine a table on which there were some mutton chops in an earthenware dish, a loaf of bread, a bottle of wine, and a glass. All this came from a wine-shop in the neighbourhood.

'Well,' said Lamartine, 'what about a knife and fork?'

'I thought you had knives and forks here,' said the boy. 'I had enough trouble to bring this here, and if I've got to go and fetch knives and forks. . . .'

'Never mind!' said Lamartine. 'I'll manage.'

He broke the bread, took a chop by the bone and tore the meat off with his teeth. When he had finished he threw the bone into the fireplace. He disposed of three cutlets in this way, and drank two glasses of wine.

'You must admit that this is a primitive meal!' he said. 'But it is an improvement on our supper last night. We had only a little bread and cheese among us, and we all drank water from the same chipped sugar-basin. Which didn't, it seems, prevent a newspaper this morning from denouncing the great orgy of the Provisional Government!'

I did not find Victor in the room where he was supposed to have waited for me. I assumed that he had grown tired of waiting and had returned home alone.

When I came out on to the Place de Grève the crowd was still excited and dismayed at the inexplicable affray which had occurred an hour before. The body of a wounded man who had just died was carried past me. They told me it was the fifth. It was being taken, like the other bodies, to the Salle Saint-Jean, where the dead of the previous day, who numbered over a hundred, were already exposed.

Before returning to the Place Royale I went on a tour of our guardhouses. Outside the Minimes Barracks a boy of about fifteen, armed with the rifle of a soldier of the line, was proudly mounting guard. It seemed to me that I had already seen him in the morning or even the day before.

'Are you on sentry duty again?' I asked him.

'No, not again—still. I haven't been relieved.'

'Why, how long have you been here?'

'Oh, a good seventeen hours!'

'What, haven't you had any sleep? Haven't you had anything to eat?'

'Yes, I've had something to eat.'

'You went to get it, I suppose?'

'No, I didn't! A sentry doesn't leave his post! This morning I shouted to the people in the shop across the road that I was hungry, and they brought me some bread.'

I hastened to have the good child relieved.

Arriving at the Place Royale, I asked for Victor. He had not returned. I was seized with a shudder of fear. For some reason the vision of the dead who had been taken to the Salle Saint-Jean crossed my mind. What if my Victor had been caught in that bloody affray? I gave some pretext for going out again. Vacquerie was there; I told him of my anxiety in a whisper, and he offered to accompany me.

First of all we went to see Monsieur Froment-Meurice, whose establishment was in the Rue Lobau, next to the Hôtel de Ville, and I asked him to have me admitted to the Salle Saint-Jean. At first he tried to dissuade me from seeing the hideous sight; he had seen it the previous day and was still filled with the horror it had inspired in him. I thought that his reluctance was an attempt to keep something from me. I insisted all the more, and we set off.

In the large Salle Saint-Jean, transformed into a vast mortuary, the long line of corpses lay on camp beds. For the most part they were unrecognizable. And I carried out the dreadful review, shuddering when one of the dead was young and slim with dark brown hair. Yes, the sight of those poor blood-stained corpses was indeed horrible. But I could not describe it; all that I saw of each body was that it was not that of my child. Finally I reached the last one, and breathed freely once more.

As I was coming out of the lugubrious place I saw Victor, very much alive, running towards me. When he had heard the firing he had left the room where he was waiting for me, and not being able to find his way back, he had been to see a friend.

THE FLIGHT OF LOUIS-PHILIPPE

1848

IT was Monsieur Crémieux who said to King Louis-Philippe these sad words: 'Sire, you must leave.'

The King had already abdicated. The fateful signature had been written. He looked fixedly at Monsieur Crémieux.

The sharp firing in the Place du Palais Royal could be heard outside; it was the moment when the Municipal Guards of the Château d'Eau were attacking the barricades in the Rue de Valois and the Rue Saint-Honoré.

Every few moments huge shouts arose and drowned the noise of the musketry. It was obvious that the populace was drawing near. From the Palais Royal to the Tuileries it is only a step for the Giant called Revolt.

Monsieur Crémieux stretched his hand out in the direction of the ominous noise coming from outside and repeated:

'Sire, you must leave.'

The King, without saying a word in reply, and without taking his staring eyes off Monsieur Crémieux, took off his general's hat which he handed at random to someone beside him, doffed his uniform with its heavy silver epaulets, and said, without rising from the big arm-chair in which he had been slumped for several hours:

'A round hat, a frock-coat.'

They brought him a frock-coat and a round hat. In an instant he was nothing but an elderly tradesman.

Then he cried in an urgent tone of voice:

'My keys, my keys!'

The keys were not forthcoming.

Meanwhile the noise grew louder; the firing seemed to be approaching, the terrible uproar increased.

The King kept repeating: 'My keys, my keys!'

At last the keys were found and brought to him. He locked a portfolio which he put under his arm, and a larger portfolio which a valet took charge of. He displayed a kind of feverish agitation. There was a general hustle around him. The princes and the valets could be heard calling out: 'Quick, quick!' The Queen alone was calm and proud.

They set off. They crossed the Tuileries. The King gave his arm to the Queen, or, to be more accurate, the Queen gave her arm to the King. The Duchesse de Montpensier was supported by Monsieur Jules de Lasteyrie, the Duc de Montpensier by Monsieur Crémieux.

The Duc de Montpensier said to Monsieur Crémieux:

'Stay with us, Monsieur Crémieux; do not leave us. Your name may be useful to us.'

In this way they reached the Place de la Révolution. There the King turned pale.

He looked around for the four carriages which he had ordered from his stables. They were not there.

Coming out of the stables the driver of the first carriage had been shot. And at the time the King was looking for them in the Place Louis XV,[1] the people were burning them in the Place du Palais Royal.

At the foot of the obelisk there was a small hackney carriage with one horse.

The King walked rapidly up to it, followed by the Queen.

In the cab there were four women holding four children on their knees.

The four women were Mesdames de Nemours and de Joinville, and two ladies of the Court. The four children were the King's grandsons.

The King threw open the door, and said to the four women: 'Get out! All of you! All of you!'

He said nothing but these few words.

The firing became more and more alarming. The mob could be heard surging into the Tuileries.

[1] Now the Place de la Concorde. [Tr.]

In the twinkling of an eye the four women were standing on the pavement—the same pavement on which Louis XVI's scaffold had been erected.

The King got into, or rather plunged into, the empty cab; the Queen followed him. Madame de Nemours climbed up in front. The King was still carrying his portfolio under his arm. The bigger one, which was green, was put into the cab with some difficulty, Monsieur Crémieux pushed it in with his fist.

'Go on!' said the King.

The cab started up. They took the Neuilly road.

Thuret, the King's valet, climbed up behind. But he could not stand on the bracket-seat. He then attempted to get on to the horse, and ended up by running along. The carriage passed him.

Thuret ran as far as Saint-Cloud, thinking he would find the King there. But there he was told that the King had left for Trianon.

At that moment the Princess Clementine and her husband, the Duke of Saxe-Coburg, arrived by railway.

'Quick, Madame,' said Thuret: 'let us take the train and go to Trianon. The King is there.'

It was in this way that Thuret managed to rejoin the King.

Meanwhile, at Versailles, the King had obtained a berline and a kind of omnibus. He occupied the carriage with the Queen; his suite took the omnibus. They harnessed post-horses and set out for Dreux.

As he continued his journey, the King took off his wig and put on a black silk cap, which he pulled down to his eyes. He had not shaved since the previous day. He had had no sleep. He was unrecognizable. He turned to the Queen, who said: 'You look a hundred years old!'

There are two roads to Dreux; the one on the right is the better, being well-paved, and is the road generally taken; the other is full of ruts and is longer.

The King said: 'Postilion, take the road on the left.'

He did well; he was hated at Dreux. Some of the towns-people were waiting on the high road with hostile intentions.

In this way he escaped the danger.

The sub-prefect of Dreux, who had been notified of his approach, joined him and handed him twelve thousand francs—half in notes, and half in silver in bags.

The berline left the omnibus behind to do the best it could, and made for Évreux. The King knew a country house about two miles from the town which belonged to a loyal subject, Monsieur de ——.

It was pitch-dark when the carriage reached this mansion. It drew up.

Thuret got out, and rang the bell for a long time; at last someone appeared.

Thuret asked: 'Monsieur de ——?'

He was away. It was winter. Monsieur de —— was in town.

His farmer, a man called Renard who had opened the door, explained this to Thuret.

'It doesn't matter,' replied Thuret. 'I have here an old lady and gentleman, friends of his, who are very tired. Just open the house for us.'

'I haven't got the keys,' said Renard.

The King was worn out by fatigue, suffering and hunger. Renard looked at the old man, and felt sorry for him.

'Monsieur and Madame,' he said. 'Come in, all the same. I can't open the château for you; but I can offer you the hospitality of the farm-house. Come in. Meanwhile I will send someone to Évreux to fetch my master.'

The King and Queen alighted. Renard took them into the main room in the farm. There was a fine fire in it. The King was chilled to the bones.

'I am very cold,' he said. Then he continued: 'I am very hungry.'

Renard said:

'Monsieur, do you like onion-soup?'

'Very much,' said the King.

They made some onion-soup, and produced the remains of the farm dinner, some sort of cold stew, and an omelette.

The King and Queen sat down at table and everyone with

them—Renard the farmer, his ploughman, and Thuret the valet. The King ate greedily everything he was given. The Queen did not eat anything.

In the middle of the meal the door opened. It was Monsieur de ——, who had just arrived in a hurry from Évreux.

He saw Louis-Philippe, and exclaimed: 'The King!'

'Silence!' cried the King.

But it was too late.

Monsieur de —— reassured him. Renard was a good fellow. They could trust him. Everyone at the farm could be trusted.

'Well,' said the King. 'I must be on my way at once. What shall I do?'

'Where do you wish to go?' asked Renard.

'Which is the nearest seaport?'

'Honfleur.'

'Well, then, I will make for Honfleur.'

'All right,' said Renard.

'How far is it from here?'

'Twenty-two leagues.'

The King exclaimed in horror:

'Twenty-two leagues!'

'You will be at Honfleur tomorrow morning,' said Renard.

Renard had a trap which he used to go the round of the markets. He was a breeder and seller of horses. He harnessed a pair of strong horses to his trap.

The King settled himself in one corner, Thuret in the other, Renard, as coachman, in the middle; a bag of oats was placed across the apron, and they set off.

It was seven o'clock in the evening.

The Queen did not leave until two hours later in the berline, with some post-horses.

The King had put the bank-notes in his pocket. As for the money-bags, they worried him.

'More than once I could see that the King was on the point of telling me to throw them away,' said Thuret to me later, when telling me this story.

They passed through Évreux, but not without some trouble.

At the end of the town, near the church of Saint-Taurin, there was a crowd of people who stopped the carriage.

A man seized the bridle, and said:

'They say the King is escaping this way.'

Another man held a lantern to the King's face.

Finally a sort of officer of the National Guard, who for some moments had been handling the harness in a suspicious way, cried out:

'Why, it's old Renard! I know him, citizens.'

He added, in a low voice, turning to Thuret:

'I recognize your companion in the corner. Get away quickly.'

Thuret has told me since:

'He spoke just in time, for I thought that he had just cut the traces of one of the horses and I was about to stab him. I already had my knife open in my hand.'

Renard whipped his horses, and they left Évreux behind them.

They kept on all night. From time to time they halted at roadside inns and Renard fed the oats to his horses.

He said to Thuret: 'Get down. Be as much at your ease as you can. Talk familiarly to me.' He also *'tutoyer-ed'* the King.

The King pressed his black cap down to his nose, and maintained a profound silence.

At seven o'clock in the morning they reached Honfleur. The horses had covered twenty-two leagues, without rest, in twelve hours. They were exhausted.

'It is time,' said the King.

From Honfleur the King travelled to Trouville. He hoped to hide himself in a house formerly occupied by Monsieur Duchâtel when he came sea-bathing in the holidays. But the house was shut up. They were obliged to take shelter with a fisherman.

General Rumigny arrived during the morning, and nearly ruined everything. An officer recognized him on the quay.

At last the King managed to embark. The Provisional Government did its best to help.

Nevertheless, at the last moment, a police commissioner proved rather over-zealous. He presented himself on board the vessel, in sight of Honfleur, and searched it from stem to stern.

Between decks he looked closely at the old gentleman and lady who were sitting in a corner, looking as if they were keeping an eye on their luggage.

However, he showed no sign of leaving.

Suddenly the captain took out his watch, and said:

'*Monsieur le Commissaire de Police*, do you intend to remain on board or go ashore?'

'Why do you ask?' said the commissioner.

'Because if you are not in France in fifteen minutes you will be in England in the morning.'

'You are about to sail, then?'

'Immediately.'

The commissioner made up his mind to leave, very discontented, and after vainly scenting a prey.

The vessel sailed.

It nearly foundered within sight of Le Havre. The weather being bad and the night dark, it collided with a large ship which carried away part of its masts and bulwarks. The damage was repaired as well as possible, and the next morning the King and Queen were in England.

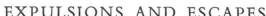

EXPULSIONS AND ESCAPES

1848

On 24 February the Duc and Duchesse Decazes were literally driven out of the Luxembourg. And by whom? By the very denizens of the palace, all employees of the Chamber of Peers, all appointed by the Grand Referendary. It was rumoured in the district that during the night the peers were going to meet, commit some anti-revolutionary act, publish a proclamation, etc. The entire Faubourg Saint-Jacques prepared to march against the Luxembourg. There was a panic. The duke and duchess were first begged, then urged, then forced to leave the palace.

'We will leave tomorrow. We do not know where to go. Let us spend the night here,' they said.

They were driven out.

They slept in a lodging-house. Next day they took up residence at No. 9, Rue Verneuil.

Monsieur Decazes was very ill. A week before he had undergone an operation. Madame Decazes bore it all with cheerfulness and courage. This is a trait of character which women often display in situations brought about by the stupidity of men.

The ministers escaped, but not without difficulty. Monsieur Duchâtel in particular had a bad fright.

Monsieur Guizot, three days before, had left the Hôtel des Capucines and installed himself at the Ministry of the Interior. He lived there *en famille* with Monsieur Duchâtel.

On 24 February, Monsieur Duchâtel and Monsieur Guizot were about to sit down to luncheon when an usher rushed in looking terrified. The head of the column of rioters was coming out of the Rue de Bourgogne. The two ministers left the table and managed to escape just in time by way of the garden. Their families followed them: Monsieur Duchâtel's young wife, Monsieur Guizot's aged mother, and the children.

It is interesting to note that Monsieur Guizot's luncheon became Monsieur Ledru-Rollin's supper. This is not the first time that the Republic has eaten what was originally served to the Monarchy.

Meanwhile the fugitives had gone down the Rue Bellechasse. Monsieur Guizot walked first, giving his arm to Madame Duchâtel. His fur-lined overcoat was buttoned up, and his hat was stuck on the back of his head as usual. He was easily recognizable. In the Rue Hillerin-Bertin, Madame Duchâtel noticed that some men in smocks were staring hard at Monsieur Guizot. She drew him into a doorway. It so happened

that she knew the concierge. They took Monsieur Guizot up
to an empty room on the fifth floor and hid him there.

Monsieur Guizot spent the day in this hiding-place, but he
could not stay there. One of his friends remembered a bookseller, a great admirer of Monsieur Guizot, who in better days
had often declared that he would gladly devote himself to and
give his life for him whom he called 'a great man', and that
he only hoped that the opportunity to do so might present
itself. (I have not been told the name of this bookseller.) The
friend called on him, reminded him of what he had said, and
told him that the hour had come. The good bookseller did not
fail in what was expected of him. He placed his house at Monsieur Guizot's disposal and hid him there for ten whole
days. At the end of that time the eight seats in one compartment of a carriage on the Northern Railway were hired. Monsieur Guizot made his way to the station at nightfall. The
seven people who were helping in his escape entered the compartment with him. They reached Lille, then Ostend, and
from Ostend Monsieur Guizot crossed over to England.

Monsieur Duchâtel's escape was more complicated.

He managed to obtain a passport as an agent of the Republic on a mission. He disguised himself, dyed his eyebrows,
put on blue spectacles, and left Paris in a post-chaise. Twice he
was stopped by National Guards in the towns through which
he passed. With great audacity he declared that he would
hold responsible before the Republic those who delayed him
on his mission. The word 'Republic' produced its effect. The
Minister was allowed to pass. The Republic saved Monsieur
Duchâtel.

In this way he reached a seaport (Boulogne, I think), under
the impression that he was being hotly pursued, and very nervous as a result. A Channel steamer was about to leave for
England. He went on board at night. He was installing himself for the voyage when he was informed that the steamer
would not leave that night. He thought that he had been
discovered and that he was done for. The steamer had merely
been detained by the British Consul, probably to facilitate, if

necessary, the flight of Louis-Philippe. Monsieur Duchâtel landed again and spent that night and the following day in the studio of a woman painter who was devoted to him.

The next day he embarked on another steamer. He went below at once and waited for the boat to leave. He scarcely dared to breathe, fearing that at any moment he might be recognized and arrested. At last the steamer got under way. Hardly had the paddle wheels begun to revolve, however, when shouts of 'Stop! Stop!' were raised on the quay and on the boat, which stopped short. This time the poor devil of a Minister thought it was all up with him.

The din was caused by an officer of the National Guard, who had lingered too long over his farewells on deck, and did not want to be taken to England against his will. When he found that the vessel had cast off he had shouted: 'Stop!' and his family on the quay had taken up the shout. The officer was put ashore and the steamer started.

This was how Monsieur Duchâtel left France and travelled to England.

KING JEROME

1848

ONE morning in March 1848 there entered my drawing-room in the Place Royale a man of medium height, about sixty-five or sixty-six years of age, dressed in black, with a red and blue ribbon in his buttonhole, and wearing trousers with under-straps, patent leather boots, and white gloves. He was Jerome Napoleon, King of Westphalia.

He had a very gentle voice, a charming though somewhat timid smile, straight hair turning grey, and something of the Emperor's profile.

He had come to thank me for the permission which had

been given to him to return to France, which he attributed to me, and to ask me to get him appointed Governor of the Invalides. He told me that Monsieur Crémieux, a member of the Provisional Government, had said to him the previous day:

'If Victor Hugo asks Lamartine to do it, it will be done. Formerly everything depended upon an interview between two emperors; now everything depends upon an interview between two poets.'

'Tell Monsieur Crémieux that it is he who is the poet,' I said to King Jerome.

In November 1848, the King of Westphalia lived on the first floor above the entresol at No. 3, Rue d'Alger. It was a small apartment with mahogany furniture and woollen velvet upholstering.

The wallpaper of the drawing-room was grey. The room was lighted by two lamps and adorned with a heavy clock in the Empire style and two pictures, of doubtful authenticity, although the frame of one bore the name 'Titian', and the frame of the other the name 'Rembrandt'. On the mantelpiece was a bronze bust of Napoleon, the traditional bust which the Empire bequeathed to us.

The only vestiges of his royal existence which remained to the prince were his silverware and dinner service, which were decorated with royal crowns richly engraved and gilded.

Jerome at that time was only sixty-four years old, and did not look his age. His eyes were bright, his smile kindly and charming, and his hands small and still shapely. He usually dressed in black with a gold chain in his buttonhole from which hung three crosses: the Legion of Honour, the Iron Crown, and the Order of Westphalia, created by him in imitation of the Iron Crown.

Jerome talked well, always with grace and often with wit. He was full of reminiscences and spoke of the Emperor with a mixture of respect and brotherly affection which was touching. A little vanity was perceptible; I would have preferred pride.

For the rest, he accepted all the varied qualifications which were brought upon him by his strange position as a man who was no longer a king, no longer an outlaw, and yet not a citizen. Everybody addressed him as he pleased. Louis-Philippe called him 'Highness', Monsieur Boulay de la Meurthe 'Sire' or 'Your Majesty', Alexandre Dumas 'Monseigneur'. I addressed him as 'Prince', and my wife called him 'Monsieur'. On his card he wrote 'General Bonaparte'. In his place I would have taken a different view of my position. King or nothing.

In 1847, the day following that on which Jerome, recalled from exile, had returned to Paris, as evening was drawing on and he had vainly waited for his secretary, he felt bored and lonely and went out. It was at the end of summer. He was staying at the house of his daughter, Princess Demidoff, which was just off the Champs-Élysées.

He crossed the Place de la Concorde, looking about him at the statues, the obelisk, the fountains, all those things which were new to the exile who had not seen Paris for thirty-two years. He continued along the Quai des Tuileries. Some day-dream or other gradually took hold of him. When he reached the Pavillon de Flore, he went through the gate, turned to the left, and started climbing a flight of stairs under the arch. He had gone up two or three steps when he felt himself seized by the arm. It was the porter who had run after him.

'Hi! Monsieur, monsieur, where are you going?'

Jerome gazed at him in astonishment and replied:

'Why, to my apartments, of course!'

Hardly had he uttered these words when he awoke from his dreams. The past had bewitched him for a moment. Recounting the incident to me, he added:

'I went away shamefacedly, apologizing to the porter.'

P

LOUIS-PHILIPPE IN EXILE

3 May 1848

THE Orléans family in England are literally poverty-stricken; they are twenty-two at table and drink water. There is not the slightest exaggeration in this. Absolutely all they have to live on is an income of about 40,000 francs made up as follows: 24,000 francs a year from Naples, which comes from Queen Marie-Amélie, and the interest on a sum of 340,000 francs which Louis-Philippe had left in England in the following circumstances. During his last triumphal voyage, made in October 1844 with the Prince de Joinville, he had a credit of 500,000 francs opened for him with a London banker. Of this sum he spent only 160,000 francs. He was greatly amazed and very agreeably surprised on arriving in London to find that the balance of the 500,000 francs remained at his disposal.

Monsieur Vatout is with the Royal Family. For them all there are only three servants, of whom one, and one only, came with them from the Tuileries. In this state of destitution they asked Paris for restitution of what belongs to them in France. But their property is under seizure, for different reasons, and has remained so in spite of their claims. One of the motives put forward by the Provisional Government is the debt of the civil list, which amounts to thirty million francs. Strange ideas have been entertained about Louis-Philippe. He may have been covetous, but he was certainly not miserly; he was the most prodigal, the most extravagant, and the least careful of men: he had debts, accounts, and arrears everywhere. He owed 700,000 francs to a cabinet-maker; to his market gardener he owed 70,000 francs for *butter*.

Consequently none of the seals placed on the property could be broken and everything is held to secure the creditors—

everything, even down to the personal property of the Prince and Princesse de Joinville, rents, diamonds, etc., even down to a sum of 198,000 francs which belongs in her own right to the Duchesse d'Orléans.

All that the Royal Family was able to obtain was their clothing and personal effects, or rather what could be found of these. Three long tables were set up in the theatre at the Tuileries, and on these were laid out all that the revolutionaries of February had turned over to the Governor of the Tuileries, Monsieur Durand Saint-Armand. It formed a queer collection—court costumes stained and torn, grand cordons of the Legion of Honour that had been trailed through the mud, stars of foreign orders, swords, diamond tiaras, pearl necklaces, a collar of the Golden Fleece, etc. Each of the princes' legal representatives, an aide-de-camp or a secretary, took what he recognized. It seems that on the whole very little was recovered. The Duc de Nemours merely asked for some linen and in particular his heavy-soled shoes.

The Prince de Joinville, meeting the Duc de Montpensier, greeted him thus: 'Ah! So here you are, Monsieur; you were not killed. Bad luck!'

Gudin, the marine painter, who has just come back from England, saw Louis-Philippe. The King is greatly depressed. He said to Gudin: 'I don't understand. What happened in Paris? What got into the Parisians? I haven't any idea. One of these days they will recognize that I did not do a single thing wrong.' He did not, indeed, do a single thing wrong; he did everything wrong.

He had moreover reached an incredible degree of optimism; he believed himself to be more of a King than Louis XIV and more of an Emperor than Napoleon. On Tuesday the 22nd he was exuberantly gay, and that very day he was still occupied solely with his own affairs, and those of the pettiest character. At two o'clock, when the first shots were being fired, he was conferring with his lawyers and business agents, Messieurs de Gérante, Scribe, and Denormandie, as to how to turn Madame Adélaïde's will to the best account. On Wednesday, at one o'clock, at the very moment that the National Guard was declaring against the Government, which meant revolution, the King sent for Monsieur Hersent to commission a picture of some kind.

Charles X was a lynx in comparison.

Louis-Philippe in England, however, bears his misfortunes worthily. The English aristocracy acted nobly; eight or ten of the wealthiest peers wrote to Louis-Philippe to offer him their *châteaux* and their purses. The King replied: 'I accept and keep only your letters.'

At this time of writing (May 1848) the Tuileries has already been repaired, and Monsieur Empis remarked to me this morning: 'After the polishers have finished there will be no sign of any damage.' Neuilly and the Palais-Royal, however, have been devastated. The picture gallery of the Palais-Royal, a rather poor one incidentally, has been practically destroyed. Only a single picture remains perfect and intact, and that is the portrait of Philippe Égalité. Was it deliberately respected by the rioters or is its preservation an irony of chance? The National Guards amused themselves, and are still amusing themselves, by cutting faces to which they take a fancy out of those canvases which were not entirely destroyed by fire.

THE FIFTEENTH OF MAY

1848

THE invasion of 15 May was a curious sight.

Let the reader imagine the market mingled with the Senate. Swarms of ragged individuals descending, or rather streaming, down the pillars of the lower galleries, and even the upper ones, into the hall; thousands of flags waving in all directions;

the women frightened and raising their hands in the air; the rioters perched in the reporters' gallery; the corridors crowded; heads, shoulders, howling mouths, outstretched arms, clenched fists everywhere; no one speaking, everybody yelling; the representatives motionless—and this going on for three hours.

The President's desk, the secretary's platform, the tribune, had disappeared, and were nothing but a heap of men. Men were sitting on the back of the President's chair, straddling the brass griffins of his arm-chair, standing on the secretary's table, on the shorthand-writers' desks, on the banisters of the double staircase, on the velvet of the tribune; most of them were barefoot, but to make up for this they kept their heads covered.

One of them seized and pocketed one of the two small clocks which were on either side of the tribune for the use of the *Moniteur* reporters.

A terrifying din. The dust hung about like smoke; the noise was like thunder. It took half-an-hour to make half a sentence audible.

Blanqui remained pale and cold in the midst of it all.

The rioters in the galleries struck the bonnets of the ladies with their flag-staffs; torn between curiosity and terror, the ladies stood firm for three-quarters of an hour, but they ended up by taking flight and disappeared. One remained for some time; she was pretty, well dressed, and wore a pink bonnet; she looked terrified, as if she were ready to throw herself into the hall to escape from the mob which was stifling her.

One member, Monsieur Duchaffaut, was taken by the throat and threatened with a dagger. Many other representatives were ill-treated.

One of the ringleaders, who was not a man of the people, a fellow of sinister appearance with bloodshot eyes and a nose resembling the beak of a bird of prey, exclaimed:

'Tomorrow we will set up in Paris as many guillotines as we have planted trees of liberty.'

THE NATIONAL ASSEMBLY

20 June 1848

I WENT to the National Assembly today for the first time.

The hall is of a rare ugliness. Beams instead of columns; partitions instead of walls; distemper instead of marble; something like the theatre at Carpentras enormously magnified.

The tribune, which bears the date of the February days, resembles the musicians' platform at the Café des Aveugles. The members sit on planks covered with green baize, and write on a bare board. In the midst of all this stands the old mahogany desk of the Chamber of Peers, with its four lacquered brass caryatids, and its scales represented inside crowns.

I found several ushers from the Chamber of Peers there. One of them gazed at me for a long time with a melancholy air.

The three first representatives who greeted me, and with whom I shook hands, were Messieurs Boulay da la Meurthe, Edgar Quinet, and Altaroche.

I went and sat in the place of Dupont de l'Eure, who is ill just now.

July 1848

Lamennais, with the face of a pole-cat and the eye of an eagle, a coloured cotton cravat badly tied; a saffron-brown frock-coat; very short, baggy nankeen trousers; blue socks, heavy shoes. The badge of a representative was in his button-hole. His voice is so weak that those present had to gather round the tribune in order to hear what he was saying, and even then they could scarcely hear him.

After the June days, Blaise, Lamennais's nephew, went to see his uncle to tell him: 'I am quite all right.' Blaise was an officer of the National Guard. As soon as Lamennais caught sight of him in the distance, he shouted to him, without even giving Blaise a chance to open his mouth:

'Go away; you horrify me; you have just fired at the poor!'

It is a good story.

Lamennais occupies the third place on the third bench on the Radical side, in the second bay to the left of the President, beside Jean Reynaud. He has his hat in front of him, and as he is small his hat hides him. He spends his time trimming his nails with a penknife.

He lived for a long while in the Quartier Beaujon, quite near to Théophile Gautier. Delage often called on them both in turn. Gautier used to say to him, speaking of Lamennais: 'Go and see your old man in his clouds.'

Proudhon is the son of a Besançon cooper. He was born in 1805. Lately he has lived in the Rue Dauphine, and published his journal, the *Représentant du Peuple*, there. Those who had business with the editor went up to see him there in a sort of window-frame, and found Proudhon writing in a smock and wooden clogs.

The Assembly today heard the details of the Proudhon proposal expounded by the author.

They saw appear in the tribune a man about forty-five years of age, fair, with little hair but bushy whiskers. He wore a black frock-coat and black waistcoat. He did not speak; he read. He held his hands clenched on the red velvet of the tribune, his manuscript between them. His voice was vulgar; his accent was common and hoarse; and he wore spectacles.

The beginning was listened to with anxiety; then the Assembly started laughing and murmuring; then everyone began to chatter. The Chamber began to empty, and the orator ended in the midst of general indifference the speech he had begun in a sort of terror.

Proudhon lacked neither talent nor power. Nevertheless he

wilted visibly at his failure, and displayed none of the sublime impudence of great innovators.

Lamennais listened to the end of Proudhon's speech with his red handkerchief pressed to his eyes, as if he were in tears.

3 August 1848

Reading the Report of the Commission of Inquiry concerning the May days.

Caussidière, who was absent at first, arrived at half-past two, and sat down in his place on the top-most benches. He was wearing a white waistcoat and a black frock-coat.

Louis Blanc was sitting on the top benches next to Ferdinand Gambon, and kept running his hand through his hair.

Pierre Leroux was on the third bench, below Louis Blanc, and next to Lamennais. Pierre Leroux and Lamennais had opera-glasses. Leroux directed his at the public galleries. Lamennais lowered his head and seemed to be reading. From time to time he cleaned his nails and plunged his thumb into his snuff-box.

Cavaignac arrived later, and sat down with folded arms near Monsieur Marie, on the Ministerial benches.

Lamartine was in his usual place at the end of the lower bench of the second bay on the left, separated from Garnier-Pagès by Pagnerre. Lamartine folded his arms like Cavaignac; he was pale and calm in comparison with Ledru-Rollin, who was above him, red and agitated.

Ledru-Rollin is a fat man with good teeth, the ideal of Anne of Austria. He has fat white hands, with which he caresses his fringe of beard.

Proudhon was sitting beside Lagrange, in the last triangular bay on the left at the end of the hall. The ladies in the diplomatic gallery above his head gazed at him with a kind of horror, and remarked audibly: 'What a monster!' Proudhon, dressed in grey trousers and a brown frock-coat, had his legs crossed, and was half reclining on his bench, so that his head was scarcely visible over the back of the seat.

Lagrange, beside him, sat bolt upright, his black coat tightly buttoned. People noted his angular features, honest and bewildered. He had a turned-down collar and white cuffs.

Caussidière kept stirring in his seat during the reading of the Report. Louis Blanc asked in indignant tones to be allowed to speak. Caussidière cried: 'It is shameful!' At the words 'stupid bourgeois' which the Report attributed to him, he cried: 'Calumny!' During the reading of the second part of the Report Ledru-Rollin took a pen and made notes. The reading of the first part lasted an hour.

The *rapporteur*, Bauchart, a lawyer from Saint-Quentin, talks and gesticulates like a Public Prosecutor.

During the reading of the Report it was impossible for me not to believe that I was listening to Franck-Carré in the Court of Peers.

Odilon Barrot climbed the stairs and left the Assembly. The galleries noted his bottle-green coat and his crown of white hair, like a bishop's tonsure.

25 August 1848

Did Louis Blanc and Caussidière take part in the events of 15 May and 24 June? That is the grave question which the Assembly, acting as a Court, had to decide in this night sitting.

The galleries were filled to overflowing; every member was in his place. The eight lamps and the seven chandeliers were lighted. There was a rumour of rioting on the boulevards. There have been gatherings lately in the Palais-Royal gardens. 'Why didn't they shut the gates?' exclaimed Monsieur de Champvans. The troops were said to be tired out.

The Assembly had a sombre appearance. Eight o'clock struck with the mournful sound of a tocsin. The hall was insufficiently lighted. I could make out beneath the first chandelier the venerable, bowed head of Arago; and, near to him, the gentle, calm, and stern profile of Lamartine.

As I was crossing the floor Lamartine called to me. He was sitting talking to Vivien, who was standing. He said to me:

'What do you advise me to do? Should I speak or should I keep silent?'

I replied: 'Do not speak. Keep silent. You have very little to do with it. It is all beneath you. Remain above it.'

He replied: 'That is my own opinion.'

'It is also mine,' said Vivien.

'So,' replied Lamartine, 'I will say nothing.' Then, after a pause, he added:

'Unless the discussion turns to me and damages me.'

I replied: 'Not even in that case, believe me. Let us keep our cries of pain for the woes of France and not for our little worries.'

'Thank you,' said Lamartine. 'You are right.'

And I returned to my place.

Cavaignac was in his place, the first on the left of the Ministerial bench, separated from Goudchaux and Marie by his hat, placed on the Ministerial bench. Caussidière and Ledru-Rollin had not yet arrived.

Louis Blanc began to speak.

During an interruption, caused by Louis Blanc comparing himself to Lamartine, Caussidière arrived, stepped up to the desk of the President, and chatted with Marrast. Then he went to his seat.

There was a man in shirt-sleeves, a spectator, who was perched up in the very roof of the hall, near the opening of a chandelier, and who listened and watched from there.

The Abbé Fayat, the Bishop of Orleans, and General Lamoricière, the Minister of War, came in and sat down on the Ministerial bench beside Messieurs Goudchaux and Marie. Towards the conclusion of Louis Blanc's speech, Colonel de Ludre, who had come and sat beside me, and my other neighbour, Monsieur Archambaut, fell asleep, in the midst of the agitation of the Assembly.

At ten o'clock the Prefect of Police, Ducoux, arrived, and sat down beside Cavaignac.

Louis Blanc spoke for an hour and forty minutes. He closed with an eloquent peroration, and with a protest which came from the heart.

It was nearly midnight when Caussidière appeared in the tribune with a huge roll of papers, which he announced that it was his intention to read. A murmur of apprehension ran round the Assembly. In fact the manuscript had a great many pages but, as the writing was large, each page contained only a few words: the reason for this was that Caussidière reads with difficulty, and he must have big letters like a child.

Caussidière wore a single-breasted frock-coat buttoned up to his necktie. His Tartar face, his broad shoulders, and his enormous height were in curious contrast with his hesitating accents and his awkward attitude. There is both a giant and a child in this man. Nevertheless, I believe he was mixed up in that May business—nothing has been proved as regards June.

He read, among other documents, a letter from Ledru-Rollin, addressed to him on 23 April: to him as Prefect—Ledru-Rollin being Minister. This letter warned him of a conspiracy to slit his throat, and ended with these words: 'Goodnight as usual, but keep wide awake!'

At another moment Caussidière, refusing to explain himself, exclaimed: 'The National Tribune was not instituted for the purpose of retailing tittle-tattle.'

At one o'clock in the morning, in the midst of a profound silence which fell suddenly on the noisy assembly, the President, Marrast, read a demand to authorize the Public Prosecutor, Cornu, to proceed against Louis Blanc and Caussidière.

This brought Louis Blanc to the tribune with a violent protest. His protest was energetic, but his voice had changed.

At times shouts arose from all parts of the Chamber; the spectators stood up in the galleries. The chandeliers went out several times, and they had to be relighted during the sitting.

At half-past two in the morning Lamartine left, with bent head, and with his hands in his pockets. He crossed the hall with a downcast air. He returned an hour later.

Just as the votes were about to be taken, Caussidière, who could see how the Assembly felt, approached the Ministerial bench, and said to General Cavaignac: 'Is it decided then?'

Cavaignac replied: 'It is my duty.'

'General,' said Caussidière, 'are you going to have me arrested here like that? My mother and sisters are over there, dammit!'

'What do you wish me to do?' asked General Cavaignac.

'Give me forty-eight hours. I have things to attend to. I must have time to breathe!'

'Very well,' replied Cavaignac; 'only arrange it with Marie.'

The Minister of Justice agreed to the forty-eight hours, and Caussidière took advantage of them to make his escape.

At daybreak the Assembly was still sitting. The chandeliers turned pale. Through the windows the grey and dismal dawn was visible. The white curtains fluttered in the morning breeze. It was very cold in the Chamber.

From my seat I could make out the figures of men perched on the outside sills, silhouetted against the light.

The voting was carried out with blue and white tickets. The white ones were for the accusation, the blue ones against. Each ticket, as usual, bore the name of the member voting.

At the last ballot I got nearly all my neighbours to put in blue tickets, even Monsieur Isambert, who was very indignant against the accused representatives.

A state of emergency was voted by 493 to 292. The majority was 393—93 thus occurring twice.

The Assembly afterwards approved of the proceedings being taken.

At six o'clock in the morning it was all over; the ladies came crowding down from the galleries by the single staircase, most of them looking for their husbands. Journalists called to each other in the corridors, the ushers chatted on business. It was said that gendarmes had been seen in the entrance hall.

Eyes were dull, faces were pale, and a magnificent sunrise bathed the Place de la Concorde in its light.

21 September 1848

Two bishops spoke today, the Abbé Parisis, Bishop of Langres, and the Abbé Fayat, Bishop of Orleans. The question was the freedom of education.

The Abbé Parisis, a man with a ruddy face and big, round, blue, protuberant eyes, carries his fifty-five years with an air which savours more of ecclesiastical gravity and official humility than of gravity and humility pure and simple. He spoke from memory, with some pomposity, a few sentences which were received with cries of 'Well said!' The effect of the cassock in the tribune varies: with the Abbé Parisis it inspires respect; with the Abbé Fayat it arouses laughter.

The Abbé Fayat is an easy-going man, a regular ladybird, more like a cockchafer than a bishop. In the Assembly, he goes from bench to bench, sitting on the ushers' chairs, laughing with the blues, with the whites, with the reds; laughing with everyone, and getting laughed at by everyone. He wears a skull-cap of black velvet; his white hair makes him venerable in spite of himself. He has a Gascon accent, and ascends the tribune blowing his nose into an enormous coloured handkerchief, which looks like a sick man's handkerchief. Everyone laughs at him. He says bombastically that the great danger of the age is the Romantic school. (Laughter.) He proposes an amendment. (Laughter.) 'Is it supported?'—'No, no.' He descends and blows his nose. (Laughter.)

Such are our two bishops!

October 1848

Monsieur Armand Marrast, who is, by the way, a man of sense, and I believe a brave man, had been a schoolmaster before he edited the *Tribune*, then the *National*. I do not know at which school: Louis le Grand, I believe. On the day he was elected President of the Assembly, people said to him: 'Poor Marrast! Him President of the National Assembly! With his shrill little voice and his mean air! Him, that sometime usher! He will soon go under.' But not a bit of it! Monsieur Marrast proved a remarkable President.

Why? Precisely because he had been a schoolmaster. He found that the habits of an usher served the President of an Assembly admirably. 'Silence, gentlemen.'—'Monsieur So-and-So, go to your seat.'—'Bang, bang, bang' (the paper-knife slapping the table.—'Monsieur de la Rochejacquelein, I can hear nobody but you!'—'Messieurs les Ministres, you are talking so loudly that people cannot hear one another!'

And so on.

It is all very simple. Controlling schoolboys and controlling men comes to the same thing; because there is already something of the man in the schoolboy, and there remains something of the schoolboy in the man.

THE JUNE DAYS

June 1848

THE June insurrection presented peculiar features from the outset.[1] It suddenly manifested itself to terrified society in monstrous and unknown forms.

The first barricade was erected in the morning of Friday

[1] At the end of June, four months after the proclamation of the Republic, regular work had come to a standstill and the useless workshops known as the 'national workshops' had just been abolished by the National Assembly.

Then the prevailing poverty caused the outbreak of one of the most terrible insurrections recorded in history. The power at that time was in the hands of an Executive Council of five members, Lamartine, Arago, Ledru-Rollin, Garnier-Pagès, and Marie. General Cavaignac was the Minister of War. V.H the 23rd, at the Porte Saint-Denis. It was attacked the same day. The National Guard marched resolutely against it. The attacking force was made up of battalions of the First and Second Legions, which arrived by way of the boulevards. When the assailants got within range a tremendous volley was fired from the barricade and littered the ground with National Guards. The National Guard, more irritated than intimidated, charged the barricade.

At that moment a woman appeared on the top of the barricade, a young woman, beautiful, dishevelled, terrible. This woman, who was a prostitute, pulled her dress up to her waist and screamed to the guards in that frightful language of the brothel that one is always compelled to translate:

'Cowards! Fire, if you dare, at a woman's belly!'

Here the affair took an appalling turn. The National Guard did not hesitate. A volley brought the wretched creature down, and with a piercing shriek she toppled off the barricade. A horrified silence fell on both besiegers and besieged.

Suddenly another woman appeared. This one was even younger and more beautiful: she was almost a child, barely seventeen years old. Oh, the pity of it! She too, was a prostitute. Like the other she lifted her skirt, bared her belly, and screamed: 'Fire, you swine!' They fired. Riddled with bullets, she fell on to the body of the other woman.

It was thus that this war began.

Nothing could be more chilling and more sinister. It is a hideous thing, this abject heroism in which there bursts forth all the strength contained in weakness; this civilization attacked by cynicism and defending itself by barbarity. On one side the despair of the people, on the other the despair of society.

On Saturday the 24th, at four o'clock in the morning, I was at the barricade in the Place Baudoyer that was defended by the troops, as a representative of the people.

The barricade was a low one. Another barricade, narrow and high, protected it in the street. The sun was shining on the chimney-tops. The tortuous Rue Saint-Antoine wound before us in sinister solitude.

The soldiers were lying on the barricade, which was little more than three feet high. Their rifles were aimed between the paving-stones as if between crenallations. Now and then bullets whistled overhead and struck the walls of the houses around us, bringing down a shower of stone and plaster. Occasionally a smock, sometimes a head wearing a cap, appeared at the corner of a street. The soldiers promptly fired at it. When they hit their mark they congratulated themselves. 'Good! Well aimed! Capital!'

They laughed and chatted gaily. At intervals there was an explosion, and a hail of bullets rained on the barricade from roofs and windows. A very tall captain with a grey moustache stood erect at the centre of the barrier, above which half his body towered. The bullets rattled about him as about a target. He was impassive and serene and shouted:

'There, boys, they are firing. Lie down. Look out, Laripaud, you are showing your head. Reload!'

All at once a woman turned the corner of a street. She came slowly towards the barricade. The soldiers swore and shouted to her to get out of the way:

'Ah! the bitch! Get out of here, you whore! Get a move on, damn you! She's coming to reconnoitre. She's a spy! Let's bring her down! Down with the nark!'

The captain restrained them:

'Don't shoot! It's a woman!'

After advancing about twenty paces the woman, who really did seem to be observing us, disappeared through a low door which closed behind her.

That one was saved.

At eleven o'clock I returned from the barricade in the Place Baudoyer and took my usual place in the Assembly. A representative whom I did not know but who I have since learned to be Monsieur Belley, an engineer who lives in the Rue des Tournelles, came and sat beside me and said:

'Monsieur Victor Hugo, they have set fire to your house. The insurgents entered by the little door opening into the Cul-de-sac Guéménée.'

'And my family?' I asked.

'They are safe.'

'How do you know?'

'I have just come from there. Not being known, I was able to get over the barricades and make my way here. Your family had taken refuge to begin with in the *mairie*. I was there, too. Seeing that the danger was growing I advised Madame Victor Hugo to seek some other refuge. She found shelter with her children in the home of a chimney-sweep named Martignon who lives near your house, under the arcades.'

I knew the worthy Martignon family. This reassured me.

'And how about the riot?' I asked.

'It is a revolution,' replied Monsieur Belley. 'The insurgents are in control of Paris at this moment.'

I left Monsieur Belley and hurriedly made my way through the few rooms that separated the hall in which we held our sessions and the office occupied by the Executive Committee.

It was a small drawing-room belonging to the presidency, and was reached through two rooms which were smaller still. In these ante-chambers there was a buzzing crowd of distracted officers and National Guards. This frightened mob made no attempt to prevent anyone from entering.

I opened the door of the Executive Committee's office. Ledru-Rollin, very red, was half-sitting on the table. Monsieur Garnier-Pagès, very pale, and half-reclining in an arm-chair, formed an antithesis to him. The contrast was complete: Garnier-Pagès thin and bushy-haired, Ledru-Rollin stout and close-cropped. Two or three colonels, among them Representative Charras, were conversing in a corner. I recall Arago only vaguely. I do not remember whether Monsieur Marie was there. The sun was shining brightly.

Lamartine, standing in the window-recess on the left, was talking to a general in full uniform, whom I saw at that moment for the first and last time, and who was Négrier. Négrier was killed that same evening in front of a barricade.

I hurried over to Lamartine, who came forward to meet me. He was wan and agitated, his chin unshaven, his clothes dusty and unbrushed.

He held out his hand: 'Ah, good morning, Hugo!'

Here is the dialogue we had, every word of which is still fresh in my memory:

'What is the situation, Lamartine?'

'We are done for!'

'What do you mean by that?'

'I mean that a quarter of an hour from now the Assembly will be invaded.'

A column of insurgents was in fact coming down the Rue de Lille. A timely charge of cavalry dispersed it.

'Really? What about the troops?'

'There are no troops!'

'But you said on Wednesday, and again yesterday, that you had 60,000 men at your disposal!'

'So I thought.'

'But you mustn't give up like this. It is not only you who are at stake, but the Assembly, and not only the Assembly, but France, and not only France, but the whole of civilization. Why didn't you issue orders yesterday to bring in the garrisons of all the towns for forty leagues around Paris? That would have given you 30,000 men at once.'

'We gave the orders ...'

'Well?'

'The troops haven't come!'

Lamartine took my hand and said:

'I am not the Minister of War!'

At that moment a few representatives entered noisily. The

Assembly had just voted martial law. They told Ledru-Rolin and Garnier-Pagès so in a few words.

Lamartine half-turned towards them and said in a low voice:

'Martial law! Martial law! Well, declare it if you think fit. I have nothing to say!'

He dropped into a chair, repeating:

'I have nothing to say, neither yes nor no. Do what you like!'

Meanwhile General Négrier had come up to me.

'Monsieur Victor Hugo,' he said, 'I have come to reassure you; I have received news from the Place Royale.'

'Well, General?'

'Your family are safe.'

'Thank you! I have just been told so.'

'But your house has been burnt down.'

'What does that matter?' I said.

Négrier pressed my arm:

'I understand you. Let us think of only one thing. Let us save the country!'

As I was retiring Lamartine left a group and came to me.

'Good-bye,' he said. 'But don't forget this: don't judge me too hastily; I am not the Minister of War.'

The day before, as the riot was spreading, Cavaignac, after a few measures had been taken, had said to Lamartine:

'That's enough for today.'

It was five o'clock.

'What!' exclaimed Lamartine. 'Why, we still have four hours of daylight before us! And the riot will profit by them while we are wasting them!'

He could get nothing out of Cavaignac except:

'That's enough for today!'

On the 24th, about three o'clock, at the most critical moment, a representative of the people, wearing his sash, arrived at the *mairie* of the Second Arrondissement, in the

Rue Chauchat, behind the Opéra. He was recognized. It was Lagrange.

The National Guards surrounded him. In the twinkling of an eye the group became menacing:

'It is Lagrange! The man of the pistol shot![2] What are you doing here? You are a coward! Get behind the barricades—that's where you belong. Your friends are there—not with us! They say you are their leader—go and join them! They at any rate are brave! They are shedding their blood for your follies; and you, you are afraid! You have a dirty job to do, but at least do it! Get out of here! Off with you!'

Lagrange tried to speak. His voice was drowned by hooting.

That is how those madmen treated the honest man who, after fighting for the people, wanted to risk his life for society.

25 June 1848

The insurgents were firing all the way along the Boulevard Beaumarchais from the tops of the new houses. Many of them had installed themselves in the big house in the course of construction opposite the Galiote. At the windows they had stuck dummies—bundles of straw with smocks and caps on them.

I distinctly saw a man who had entrenched himself behind a little barricade of bricks in a corner of the balcony on the fourth floor of the house which faces the Rue du Pont-aux-Choux. The man took careful aim and killed a great many people.

It was three o'clock. The troops and mobiles lined the roofs of the Boulevard du Temple and returned the fire of the insurgents. A cannon had just been drawn up in front of the Gaîté to demolish the house of the Galiote and sweep the whole boulevard.

I thought I ought to make an effort to put a stop to the bloodshed, if possible, and advanced to the corner of the Rue

[2] It was generally believed that Lagrange fired the shot which led to the massacre in the Boulevard des Capucines on 23 February 1848. [Tr.]

d'Angoulême. As I was about to pass the little turret near
there I was greeted with a fusillade. The turret was riddled
with bullets behind me. It was covered with playbills which
were torn to pieces by the musketry. I detached a strip of
paper as a memento. The bill to which it belonged announced
for that very Sunday a fête at the Château des Fleurs, 'with
ten thousand lanterns'.

For four months we have been living in a furnace. What
consoles me is that the statue of the future will issue from it,
and it required such a brazier to melt such a bronze.

CHATEAUBRIAND

5 July 1848

CHATEAUBRIAND is dead. One of the splendours of this
century has passed away.

He was seventy-nine years old by his own reckoning; by the
reckoning of his old friend Monsieur Bertin the elder he was
eighty years of age. But he had a weakness, said Monsieur
Bertin, and that was that he insisted that he was born not
in 1768, but in 1769, because that was the year of Napoleon's
birth.

He died yesterday, 4 July, at eight o'clock in the morning.
For five or six months he had been suffering from a paralysis
which had almost destroyed his brain, and for five days from
inflammation of the lungs, which suddenly snuffed out his
life.

Monsieur Ampère announced the news to the Académie,
which decided to adjourn.

I left the National Assembly where a questor to succeed
General Négrier, who was killed in June, was being

nominated and went to Monsieur de Chateaubriand's house, No. 110, Rue du Bac.

I was received by Monsieur de Preuille, his nephew's son-in-law. I went into Chateaubriand's bedroom.

He was lying on his bed, a little iron bedstead with white curtains round it hanging from an iron ring in somewhat doubtful taste. The face was uncovered; the brow, the nose, the closed eyes, bore that noble expression which he wore in life, and which was enhanced by the grave majesty of death. The mouth and chin were hidden by a cambric handkerchief. On his head was a white cotton nightcap which, however, revealed the grey hair on his temples. A white cravat reached up to his ears. His dark face appeared more severe in the midst of all this whiteness. Under the sheet his narrow, sunken chest and his thin legs could be distinguished.

The shutters of the windows looking out on to the garden were closed. A little daylight was coming in through the half-opened door of the drawing-room. The bedroom and the dead man's face were illumined by four tapers burning at the corners of a table placed near the bed. On this table there were a silver crucifix, a vase full of holy water, and an aspergillum. Beside it a priest was praying.

Behind the priest a large brown-coloured screen hid the fireplace, above which a mirror and a few engravings of churches and cathedrals were partly visible.

At Monsieur de Chateaubriand's feet, in the angle formed by the bed and the bedroom wall, were two wooden boxes, placed one on top of the other. The larger, I was told, contained the complete manuscript of his memoirs, in forty-eight copybooks. Towards the end there had been such confusion in the house that one of the copybooks had been found that very morning by Monsieur de Preuille in a dark and dirty corner where the lamps were cleaned.

A few tables, a wardrobe, and some untidy blue and green arm-chairs encumbered rather than furnished the room.

The adjoining drawing-room, the furniture of which was hidden under unbleached covers, contained nothing remark-

able apart from a marble bust of Henri V[1] on the mantelpiece.
In front of this bust there was a full-length statuette of
Chateaubriand, and on each side of a window plaster busts of
Madame de Berri and her infant son.

Madame de Chateaubriand was charitable in public, which
did not prevent her from being a shrew at home. She founded
a hospice—the Marie-Thérèse Infirmary—visited the poor,
superintended crèches, succoured the sick, gave alms, and
prayed; at the same time she scolded her husband, her relatives,
her friends, and her servants, and was sour-tempered, stern,
prudish, spiteful, and bitter. God on high will weigh up all
these things.

She was ugly, pitted with small-pox, had a huge mouth,
little eyes, was insignificant in appearance, and played the
grande dame, although she was the wife of a great man rather
than of a great lord. By birth she was the only daughter of a
Saint-Malo shipowner. Monsieur de Chateaubriand feared her,
hated her, wheedled her, and cajoled her.

She took advantage of this to make herself unbearable to
mere human beings. I have never known anybody more shrew-
ish or more forbidding. I was a youth when I first used to call
on Monsieur de Chateaubriand. She received me very badly,
or rather she did not receive me at all. I entered and bowed,
but Madame de Chateaubriand did not see me. I was terrified.
This terror made my visits to Monsieur de Chateaubriand
veritable nightmares which tormented me for fifteen days and
fifteen nights in advance. Madame de Chateaubriand hated
anybody who came to see her husband except through the
doors that she opened. She had not presented me to him,
therefore she hated me. I was perfectly odious to her, and she
showed it.

Only once in my life and hers did Madame de Chateaubriand receive me graciously. One day I entered, a poor little

---

[1] The Duc de Chartres was always referred to by his supporters as Henri V,
which he would have become but for the 1830 Revolution. [Tr.]

devil, as unhappy as usual, looking like a frightened boy and twisting my hat about in my hands. At that time Monsieur de Chateaubriand was still living at No. 27, Rue Saint-Dominique.

I was frightened of everything there, even of the servant who opened the door. Well, I entered. Madame de Chateaubriand was in the drawing-room leading to her husband's study. It was a summer morning. There was a ray of sunshine on the floor, and—something which dazzled and astonished me much more than the ray of sunshine—a smile on Madame de Chateaubriand's face. 'Is that you, Monsieur Victor Hugo?' she said. I thought I was in the middle of a dream of the Arabian Nights. Madame de Chateaubriand smiling! Madame de Chateaubriand knowing my name, addressing me by my name! It was the first time that she had deigned to notice my existence. I bowed so low that my head nearly touched the floor. She went on: 'I am delighted to see you.' I could not believe my ears. 'I have been waiting for you,' she continued. 'It is a long time since you last called.' At this point I thought that there really must be something the matter either with her or myself. But then she pointed to a fairly large object of some kind on a little table, and added: 'I have been keeping this for you. I felt sure you would like to have it. You know what it is?' It was some chocolate made by a religious institution. She had taken the stuff under her patronage and the proceeds of its sale were destined for charitable works. I took it and paid for it. At that time I had to live for fifteen months on 800 francs. That Catholic chocolate and Madame de Chateaubriand's smile cost me 15 francs, that is to say, a fortnight's board. Fifteen francs meant as much to me then as 1,500 francs does now.

That was the most expensive smile of a woman that has ever been sold to me.

Towards the close of his life Chateaubriand was almost in his second childhood. His mind was lucid for only about two or three hours a day, or so Monsieur Pilorge, his former secretary, told me.

When, in February, he was told of the proclamation of the Republic he merely remarked: 'Will you be any the happier for it?'

When his wife died he came home from the funeral service roaring with laughter. Proof, said Pilorge, of softening of the brain. Proof, retorted Édouard Bertin, that he was of sound mind.

Monsieur de Chateaubriand, at the beginning of 1847, was a paralytic; Madame Récamier was blind. Every day at three o'clock Monsieur de Chateaubriand was carried to Madame Récamier's bedside. It was touching and sad. The woman who could no longer see stretched out her hands towards the man who could no longer feel; their hands met. God be praised! When life is fading away, love lives on.

LOUIS BONAPARTE

September 1848

On his arrival in Paris Louis Bonaparte took up his residence in the Place Vendôme. Mademoiselle George went to see him. They talked at some length. In the course of the conversation Louis Bonaparte led Mademoiselle George to a window looking out on to the column with the statue of Napoleon I on it, and said to her:

'I gaze at that all day long.'

'It's pretty high!' said Mademoiselle George.

24 September 1848

Louis-Napoleon appeared at the National Assembly today. He sat down on the seventh bench of the third bay on the left, between Monsieur Vieillard and Monsieur Havin.

He looks young, has a black moustache and goatee, and a parting in his hair, a black cravat, a black coat buttoned up, a turned-down collar, and white gloves. Perrin and Léon Faucher, sitting immediately below him, did not turn their heads. After a few moments the galleries started inspecting the prince through their opera glasses and the prince started inspecting the galleries through his own.

26 September 1848

Louis Bonaparte ascended the tribune at a quarter-past three. Black frock-coat, grey trousers. He read from a crumpled paper in his hand. He was listened to in complete silence. He pronounced the word 'compatriots' with a foreign accent. When he had finished a few voices replied: 'Long live the Republic!'

He slowly returned to his place. His cousin Napoleon, the son of Jerome, who resembles the Emperor so closely, leaned over Monsieur Vieillard to congratulate him.

Incidentally, he sat down without saying a word to his two neighbours. He is silent, but he seems to be embarrassed rather than taciturn.

9 October 1848

While the question of the presidency was being discussed Louis Bonaparte absented himself from the Assembly. But when the Antony Thouret amendment excluding members of the royal and imperial families was being debated he re-appeared. He sat down at the end of his bench next to his former tutor, Monsieur Vieillard, and listened in silence, now resting his chin on his hand, now twisting his moustache.

All of a sudden he rose and, in the midst of extraordinary agitation, walked slowly towards the tribune. One half of the Assembly shouted: 'The vote!' The other half shouted: 'Speak!'

Monsieur Sarrans was in the tribune. The president said:

'Monsieur Sarrans will allow Monsieur Louis-Napoleon Bonaparte to speak.'

He merely made a few insignificant remarks and descended from the tribune to the accompaniment of a roar of astonished laughter.

November 1848

On 19 November I dined at Odilon Barrot's at Bougival.

There were present Messieurs de Rémusat, de Tocqueville, Girardin, Léon Faucher, a member of the English Parliament and his wife, an ugly woman endowed with wit and beautiful teeth, Madame Odilon Barrot and her mother.

Towards the middle of the dinner Louis Bonaparte arrived with his cousin, Jerome's son, and Monsieur Abbatucci, the deputy.

Louis Bonaparte is distinguished, cold, gentle, intelligent, with a certain measure of deference and dignity, a German air and a black moustache; he bears no resemblance whatever to the Emperor.

He ate little, spoke little, and laughed little, although we were a merry party.

Madame Odilon Barrot seated him on her left. The Englishman was on her right.

Monsieur de Rémusat, who was sitting between the prince and myself, said to me loud enough for Louis Bonaparte to hear:

'I give my best wishes to Louis Bonaparte and my vote to Cavaignac.'

At that moment Louis Bonaparte was feeding Madame Odilon Barrot's greyhound with fried gudgeons.

December 1848

The proclamation of Louis Bonaparte as President of the Republic was made on 20 December.

The weather, which up to then had been admirable, and reminded one more of the approach of spring than of the beginning of winter, had suddenly changed. It was the first cold day of the year. Popular superstition could imagine that the sun of Austerlitz had clouded over.

This proclamation was made in a somewhat unexpected way. It had been announced for Friday. It was made suddenly on Wednesday.

About three o'clock the approaches to the Assembly were occupied by troops. A regiment of infantry was massed behind the Palais d'Orsay; a regiment of dragoons was echeloned along the quay. The troopers were shivering and looked gloomy. Crowds gathered anxiously, not knowing what it all meant. For some days there had been vague talk of a Bonapartist movement. The faubourgs, it was said, were going to turn out and march to the Assembly shouting: 'Long live the Emperor!' The day before, Government stocks had dropped 3 francs. Napoleon Bonaparte, Jerome's son, had come to see me, greatly alarmed.

The Assembly resembled a public square. It was a collection of groups rather than a parliament. In the tribune a very useful bill for regulating the publicity of the sessions and substituting the State Printing House, the former Royal Printing House, for the *Moniteur* press, was being discussed, but nobody was listening. Monsieur Bureau de Puzy, the questor, was speaking.

Suddenly there was a stir in the Assembly, which was invaded by a crowd of Deputies coming in by the door on the left. It was the committee appointed to count the votes and was returning to announce the name of the new President. It was four o'clock; the chandeliers were lighted; there was a huge crowd in the public galleries; all the ministers were present. Cavaignac, calm, dressed in a black frock-coat, and not wearing any decorations, was in his place. He kept his right hand thrust in the breast of his buttoned frock-coat, and made no reply to Monsieur Bastide, who whispered in his ear every now and then. Monsieur Fayet, the Bishop of Orleans, occupied the chair in front of the General. Which prompted the Bishop of Langres, the Abbé Parisis, to say: 'That is the place of a dog, not of a bishop.'

Lamartine was absent.

The *rapporteur*, Monsieur Waldeck-Rousseau, read out a cold speech which was given a cold reception. When he reached the enumeration of the votes cast and came to Lamartine's total, 17,910 votes, the Right burst out laughing. A petty revenge, the mean sarcasm of the unpopular men of yesterday for the unpopular man of today.

Cavaignac took his leave in a few brief, dignified words, which were applauded by the whole assembly. He announced that the Cabinet was resigning in a body, and that he, Cavaignac, was abandoning power. He thanked the Assembly in a voice filled with emotion. A few deputies wept.

Then President Marrast proclaimed 'Citizen Louis Bonaparte' President of the Republic.

A few deputies about the bench where Louis Bonaparte had sat applauded. The remainder of the Assembly preserved an icy silence. They were leaving the lover for the husband.

Armand Marrast called upon the nation's elect to take the oath of office. There was a stir.

Louis Bonaparte, buttoned up in a black frock-coat with the decoration of representative of the people and the star of the Legion of Honour on his breast, came in by the door on the right, ascended the tribune, repeated in a calm voice the words of the oath which President Marrast dictated to him, called God and men to witness, then read with that displeasing foreign accent of his a speech which was interrupted by a few rare murmurs of approval. He praised Cavaignac, and this was noted and applauded.

After a few minutes he came down from the tribune, not like Cavaignac, to the acclamations of the Chamber, but to an immense shout of 'Long live the Republic!' One voice shouted: 'Long live the Constitution!'

Before leaving, Louis Bonaparte went over to his former tutor, Monsieur Vieillard, who was sitting in the eighth bay on the left, and shook hands with him. Then the President of the Assembly invited the committee to accompany the President of the Republic to his palace and have rendered to him the honours due to his *rank*. The word caused the Mountain to murmur. I shouted from my bench: 'To his *position*!'

The President of the Assembly announced that the President of the Republic had charged Monsieur Odilon Barrot with the formation of a Cabinet, that the names of the new ministers would be announced to the Assembly in a message, and that a supplement to the *Moniteur* would also be distributed to the representatives that very evening.

It was noticed, for everything was noticed on that day which began a decisive phase, that President Marrast called Louis Bonaparte 'citizen' and Odilon Barrot 'monsieur'.

Meanwhile the ushers, with their chief Deponceau at their head, the officers of the Chamber, and the questors, among them General Lebreton in full uniform, had gathered together at the foot of the tribune; several representatives had joined them; there was a stir indicating that Louis Bonaparte was about to leave the enclosure. A few deputies stood up. There were shouts of 'Sit down! Sit down!'

Louis Bonaparte went out. The malcontents, to show their indifference, wanted to continue the debate on the Printing House Bill. But the Assembly was too agitated even to remain seated. It rose in a tumult and the Chamber emptied. It was half-past four. The entire proceedings had lasted half an hour.

As I left the Assembly, alone and shunned as a man who had missed or disdained the opportunity to be a Minister, I passed in the outer hall, at the foot of the staircase, a group in which I noticed Montalembert, and also Charngarnier in the uniform of a lieutenant-general of the National Guard. Charngarnier had just escorted Louis Bonaparte to the Élysée. I heard him say: 'Everything went off well.'

When I found myself in the Place de la Révolution,[1] there were no longer either troops or crowd; all had disappeared. A few passers-by were coming from the Champs-Élysées. The night was dark and cold. A bitter wind was blowing from the river, and at the same time a heavy storm-cloud moving slowly

[1] Place de la Concorde. [Tr.]

across the west covered the horizon with silent flashes of lightning. A December wind combined with August lightning—such were the omens of that day.

24 December 1848

Louis Bonaparte gave his first dinner last night, Saturday the 23rd, two days after his proclamation as President of the Republic.

The Chamber had adjourned for the Christmas holidays. I was at home in my new lodgings in the Rue de la Tour-d'Auvergne, occupied with some trifling matter, *totus in illis*, when a letter addressed to me was brought by a dragoon. I opened the envelope, and this is what I read:

'The orderly officer on duty has the honour to inform General Charngarnier that he is invited to dinner at the Élysée-National today, Saturday, at seven o'clock.'

I wrote underneath: 'Delivered by mistake to Monsieur Victor Hugo', and sent the letter back by the dragoon who had brought it. An hour later came another letter from Monsieur de Persigny, Prince Louis's former companion in conspiracy and now his private secretary. This letter contained profuse apologies for the error which had been made and informed me that I was among those invited. My letter had been addressed by mistake to Monsieur Conti, the representative for Corsica.

At the head of Monsieur de Persigny's letter were written the words: 'Household of the President'.

I noticed that the form of these invitations was exactly similar to the form employed by King Louis-Philippe. As I did not wish to do anything which might resemble intentional coldness, I dressed; it was half-past six, and I set out immediately for the Élysée.

Half-past seven was striking as I arrived there.

I glanced in passing at the sinister gateway of the Praslin mansion adjoining the Élysée. The large green carriage entrance, framed between two Doric pillars dating back to the

Empire, was closed, gloomy, and vaguely outlined by the light of a street lamp.

One of the double doors of the entrance to the Élysée was closed; two soldiers of the line were on sentry duty. The courtyard was scarcely lighted, and a mason in his working clothes was crossing it with a ladder on his shoulder; nearly all the windows of the outhouses on the right were broken and had been mended with paper.

I entered by the main door. Three servants in black coats received me; one opened the door, another took my mantle, the third said: 'The first floor, Monsieur.' I went up the grand staircase. There was a carpet and flowers, but also that chilly and unsettled atmosphere peculiar to places into which one is moving.

On the first floor an usher asked:

'Monsieur has come to dinner?'

'Yes,' I said. 'Are they at table?'

'Yes, Monsieur.'

'In that case, I am going.'

'But, Monsieur,' exclaimed the usher, 'nearly everybody arrived after the dinner had begun. Go in. Monsieur is expected.'

I noted this military and imperial punctuality, which was customary with Napoleon. With the Emperor seven o'clock meant seven o'clock.

I crossed the ante-chamber, then a drawing-room, and entered the dining-room. It was a square room wainscotted in the Empire style with white wood. On the walls there was an extremely mediocre collection of engravings and pictures, among them *Mary Stuart listening to Rizzio*, by the painter Ducis. Around the room there was a sideboard. In the middle there was a long table with round ends at which about fifteen guests were sitting. One end of the table, that at the back of the room, was raised, and there the President of the Republic was sitting between two women, the Marquise du Hallays-Coëtquen, *née* Princesse de Chimay (Tallien) on his right, and Madame Conti, the representative's mother, on his left.

The President stood up when I entered. I went up to him. We grasped each other's hand.

'I improvised this dinner,' he said. 'I invited only a few dear friends, and I hoped that I could count you among them. Thank you for coming. You have come to me, as I went to you, simply. Thank you.'

He again grasped my hand. The Prince de la Moskowa, who was next to General Charngarnier, made room for me beside him and I sat down at the table. I ate quickly, for the President had interrupted the dinner to give me 'time to catch up'. The second course had been reached.

Opposite me there was General Rulhières, a former peer, the representative Conti, and Lucien Murat. The other guests were unknown to me. Among them was a young cavalry major decorated with the Legion of Honour. This major was the only person in uniform; the others were in evening dress. The Prince had the rosette of the Legion of Honour in his buttonhole.

Everybody chatted with his neighbour. Louis Bonaparte seemed to prefer his neighbour on the right to his neighbour on the left. The Marquise du Hallays is thirty-six, and looks her age. Beautiful eyes, not much hair, an ugly mouth, white skin, splendid bosom, charming arms, the prettiest little hands in the world, admirable shoulders. At present she is separated from Monsieur du Hallays. She has had eight children, the first seven by her husband. She was married fifteen years ago. During the early period of their marriage she used to fetch her husband from the drawing-room in the daytime, say: 'Come along!' and take him off to bed. Sometimes a servant would come and say: 'Madame la Marquise is asking for Monsieur le Marquis.' The Marquis would obey the summons. This made the company who were present smile. Today the Marquis and the Marquise have fallen out.

'She was the mistress of Napoleon, Jerome's son, you know,' the Prince de la Moskowa said to me in a low voice. 'Now she is Louis's mistress.'

R

'Well,' I answered, 'changing a napoleon for a louis is an everyday occurrence.'

These bad puns did not prevent me from eating and watching.

The two women beside the President had square-topped chairs. The President's chair was surmounted with a little round top. Just as I was about to draw some conclusion from this I looked at the other chairs and saw that four or five guests, including myself, had chairs similar to that of the President. The chairs were covered with red velvet with gilt-headed nails. A more serious thing I noticed was that everybody addressed the President of the Republic as 'Monseigneur' and 'Your Highness'. I who called him 'Prince' sounded like a demagogue.

When we left the table the Prince asked after my wife, and then apologized profusely for the rusticity of the service.

'I am not properly installed as yet,' he said. 'The day before yesterday, when I arrived, there was hardly a mattress for me to sleep on.'

That was not surprising, seeing that Cavaignac had made Bonaparte's bed.

The dinner was a poor one, and the Prince did well to apologize. The service was of common white china and the silverware bourgeois, worn, and gross. In the middle of the table was a fairly fine crackle-ware vase, decorated with ormolu in the bad taste of the time of Louis XVI.

Suddenly we heard music in a nearby room.

'It is a surprise,' the President told us. 'It is the musicians from the Opéra.'

A minute later a hand-written programme was passed round which listed the five selections which were being played. They were:

1. Prière de *La Muette*.
2. Fantaisie sur des airs favoris de *La Reine Hortense*.
3. Finale de *Robert Bruce*.
4. *Marche Républicaine*.
5. *La Victoire*, pas redoublé.

In the rather uneasy state of mind which I, like the whole of France, was in at that moment I could not help noticing this *Victory* piece coming after the *Republican March*.

I rose from table still hungry.

We went into the main drawing-room which was separated from the dining-room by the smaller drawing-room through which I had passed on my way in.

This main drawing-room was extremely ugly. It was white, with figures after the fashion of Pompeii on the panels, and all the furniture was in the Empire style with the exception of the arm-chairs, which were in tapestry and gold and in fairly good rococo taste. There were three arched windows to which corresponded three large mirrors of the same shape on the other side of the salon, one of which, the middle one, was a door. The window curtains were of fine white satin with rich Persian flower patterns.

While the Prince de la Moskowa and I were talking about Socialism, the Mountain, Communism and so on, Louis Bonaparte came up and took me aside.

He asked me what I thought of the situation. I was guarded in my reply. I told him that things promised well, that the task was a difficult but noble one; that what he had to do was to reassure the bourgeoisie and satisfy the people, to give tranquility to the former, work to the latter, and life to all; that after three little governments, those of the elder Bourbons, Louis-Philippe and the Republic of February, a great one was required; that the Emperor had made a great government through war, and that he himself must make a great one through peace; that the French people, having been illustrious for three centuries, did not want to become ignoble; that it was his failure to appreciate the nobility of the people and the pride of the nation that was the chief cause of Louis-Philippe's downfall; that, in a word, he must decorate peace.

'How?' asked Louis-Napoleon.

'By all the glories of art, literature, and science, by the victories of industry and progress. Popular labour can work miracles. And then, France is a conquering nation; when she is not making conquests with the sword she wants to make them with the mind. Know this and go ahead. Ignore it and you will be lost.'

He looked thoughtful and moved away. Then he returned, thanked me warmly, and we continued our conversation.

We spoke about the press. I advised him to treat it with profound respect, and at the same time to establish a State press. 'The State without a newspaper, in the midst of newspapers,' I said, 'confining itself to governing while publicity and polemics are the rule, is like those fifteenth-century knights who obstinately went on fighting against guns with swords; they were always beaten. I admit that it was noble; you will admit that it was stupid.'

He spoke to me about the Emperor. 'It was here,' he said, 'that I saw him for the last time. I could not come back into this palace without feeling moved. The Emperor had me brought to him and laid his hand on my head. I was seven years old. It was in the main drawing-room downstairs.'

Then Louis Bonaparte talked to me about La Malmaison. He said:

'They have respected it. I visited the place about six weeks ago. This is how it happened. I had gone to see Monsieur Odilon Barrot at Bougival.

' "Dine with me," he said.

' "With pleasure." It was three o'clock. "What shall we do until dinner time?"

' "Let us go and see La Malmaison," suggested Monsieur Barrot.

'We set off, just the two of us. When we arrived at La Malmaison we rang the bell. A porter opened the gate. Monsieur Barrot spoke up.

' "We should like to see La Malmaison."

' "Impossible," replied the porter.

' "What do you mean, impossible?"

' "I have orders."

' "From whom?"

' "From Her Majesty Queen Christine, to whom the Château belongs at present."

' "But this gentleman is a stranger who has come expressly to see the place."

' "Impossible!"

' "Dammit all!" exclaimed Monsieur Odilon Barrot. "It's an odd thing that this door should be closed to the Emperor's nephew!"

'The porter gave a start and threw his cap on the ground. He was an old soldier who had been given this post as a pension.

' "The Emperor's nephew!" he cried. "Oh, Sire, come in!"

'He wanted to kiss my clothes.

'We went round the whole château. Everything is still more or less in its place. I recognized nearly everything, the First Consul's study, my mother's bedroom, my own. The furniture in many rooms is still the same. I found a little armchair I had when I was a child.'

I said to the Prince: 'You see! Thrones disappear and armchairs remain.'

While we were chatting a few people arrived, including Monsieur Duclerc, the former Minister of Finance on the Executive Committee, an old woman in black velvet whom I did not know, then Lord Normanby, the British Ambassador, whom the President quickly took into a nearby room. I had seen the same Lord Normanby taken aside in the same way by Louis-Philippe.

The President in his drawing-room had a timid air about him and did not seem at home. He came and went from one group to another more like an embarrassed stranger than the master of the house. But his remarks are to the point and sometimes witty.

He tried to get me to express an opinion about his Ministry, but in vain. I would not say either good or ill about it.

In any case the Ministry is just a mask, or to be more accurate, a screen. Thiers is behind it. This is beginning to annoy Louis Bonaparte. He has to contend with eight ministers who are all trying to reduce his power. Each is pulling the tablecloth his own way. Among these Ministers there are some avowed enemies. Nominations, promotions, lists arrive all made out from the Place Saint-Georges. They have to be accepted, signed, endorsed.

Yesterday Louis Bonaparte complained about all this to the Prince de la Moskowa, saying wittily: 'They want to turn me into the Prince Albert of the Republic.'

Odilon Barrot looked sad and discouraged. Today he left the Council with a dispirited expression. Monsieur de la Moskowa was there.

'Well,' he said, 'how goes it?'

'Pray for us!' replied Odilon Barrot.

'Dammit,' said Moskowa, 'that sounds serious!'

'What are we to do?' Odilon Barrot went on. 'How can we rebuild this old society in which everything is collapsing? Every effort you make to prop it up only helps to bring it down. If you touch it, it falls. Pray for us!'

And he raised his eyes to heaven.

I left the Élysée about ten o'clock. As I was going the President said to me: 'Wait a moment.' Then he went into a nearby room and came out again a moment later with some papers which he placed in my hand, saying: 'For Madame Victor Hugo.'

They were tickets of admission to see today's review from the gallery of the Garde-Meuble.

On my way home I thought a good deal. I thought about this abrupt moving-in, this attempt at etiquette, this bourgeois-republican-imperial mixture, this surface of a deep sea which for the moment is called the President of the Republic, the entourage, the person, the whole state of affairs. This man who can be, and is, addressed at one and the same time and from all sides at once as prince, highness, monsieur, monseigneur, and citizen, is not one of the least curious and characteristic elements of the situation.

Everything that is happening at present puts its mark on this all-purpose individual.

January 1849

The first month of Louis Bonaparte's presidency is drawing to a close. This is how things stand at the moment.

There are Bonapartists now of very recent vintage. Messieurs Jules Favre, Billault, and Carteret are paying court—politically speaking—to the Princesse Mathilde Demidoff. The Duchesse d'Orléans is residing with her two children in a little house at Ems, where she lives modestly yet royally. All the ideas of February are being questioned one after the other; 1849, disappointed, is turning its back on 1848. The generals want an amnesty, the wise want disarmament. The Constituent Assembly is furious because its term is expiring. Monsieur Guizot is publishing his book *On Democracy in France*. Louis-Philippe is in London; Pius IX is at Gaete. The bourgeoisie has lost Paris; Catholicism has lost Rome. Monsieur Barrot is in power. The sky is sad and rainy, with a ray of sunshine now and then. Mademoiselle Ozy is showing herself stark naked in the part of Eve at the Porte-Saint-Martin; Frédérick Lemaître is playing in *L'Auberge des Adrets* there. Five per cents are at 74, potatoes cost 8 sous the bushel, at the Central Market a pike can be bought for 20 sous. Monsieur Ledru-Rollin is trying to push the country into war. Monsieur Proudhon is trying to push it into bankruptcy. General Cavaignac attends the sessions of the Assembly in a grey waistcoat, and spends his time gazing at the women in the gallery through big ivory opera-glasses. Monsieur de Lamartine gets 25,000 francs for his *Toussaint L'Ouverture*. Louis Bonaparte gives grand dinners to Monsieur Thiers, who had him captured, and to Monsieur Molé who had him condemned. Vienna, Milan, and Berlin are calming down. The revolutionary fires are paling and seem to be dying out everywhere on the surface, but the peoples are still stirred by a profound impulse. The King of Prussia is getting ready to seize his sceptre again and the Emperor of Russia to draw his sword. There has been an earthquake at Le Havre; the cholera is at Fécamp; Arnal is leaving the Gymnase, and the Académie is nominating the Duc de Noailles as Chateaubriand's successor.

January 1849

At Odilon Barrot's ball on 28 January Monsieur Thiers went up to Monsieur Léon Faucher and said: 'Make So-and-So a prefect.' Monsieur Léon Faucher made a face, which is an easy thing for him to do, and said: 'Monsieur Thiers, there are objections.' 'That's odd!' replied Thiers. 'That's exactly the same answer the President of the Republic gave me the day I said: "Make Monsieur Faucher a Minister!"'

At this ball it was noticed that Louis Bonaparte sought Berryer's company, attached himself to him and led him into a quiet corner. The Prince looked as if he were following Berryer, and Berryer as if he were trying to avoid the Prince.

About eleven o'clock the President said to Berryer: 'Will you come to the Opéra with me?'

Berryer excused himself. 'Prince,' he said, 'it would make people talk. They would think I was having an affair.'

'Nonsense!' replied Louis Bonaparte with a laugh. 'Representatives are inviolable!'

The Prince went off alone, and the following quatrain was circulated:

> *In vain the Empire paints her face*
> *And tries to go too far.*
> *Berryer-Joseph flees the embrace*
> *Of Napoleon-Potiphar.*

February 1849

Although he is animated by the best intentions in the world and has a very obvious quantity of intelligence and ability, I fear that Louis Bonaparte will find his task too much for him. For him, France, the new age, the new spirit, the instincts peculiar to the soil and the period are so many closed books. He looks without understanding at the minds at work, at

Paris, events, men, things, and ideas. He belongs to that class of ignorant people who are called princes and to that category of foreigners who are called *émigrés*. Beneath nothing, outside everything.

To those who examine him closely he looks more like a subject than a ruler.

There is nothing of the Bonapartes about him, either in his face or his manner; he is probably not a Bonaparte. Everybody remembers the free and easy ways of Queen Hortense.

'He is a memento of Holland!' Alexis de Saint-Priest said to me yesterday. Louis Bonaparte has indeed something of the coldness of the Dutch.

Louis Bonaparte knows so little about Paris that the first time I saw him in the Rue de la Tour-d'Auvergne he said to me:

'I have been looking everywhere for you. I went to your old home. What is this Place des Vosges?'

'It is the Place Royale,' I said.

'Ah!' he continued. 'Is it an old square?'

He wanted to see Béranger. He went to Passy twice without being able to find him at home. His cousin Napoleon timed his visit better and found Béranger by his fireside. He asked him:

'What do you advise my cousin to do?'

'To observe the Constitution.'

'And what ought he to avoid doing?'

'Violating the Constitution.'

Béranger could not be persuaded to say anything more.

Yesterday, 5 December 1850, I was at the Français. Rachel was playing *Adrienne Lecouvreur*. Jerome Bonaparte was in the box next to mine. During one of the intervals I went to see him. We chatted. He said to me:

'Louis is mad. He distrusts his friends and delivers himself into the hands of his enemies. He distrusts his family and allows himself to be bound hand and foot by the old Royalist parties. On my return to France I was better received by Louis-Philippe at the Tuileries than I am at the Élysée by my nephew. I said to him the other day in front of one of his ministers (Fould): "Just remember! When you were a candidate for the presidency, this gentleman (I pointed to Fould) called on me in the Rue d'Alger, where I was living, and asked me on behalf of Messieurs Thiers, Molé, Duvergier de Hauranne, Berryer, and Bugead to enter the lists for the presidency. He told me that you would never get the support of the *Constitutionnel*; that in Molé's opinion you were an idiot, and that Thiers regarded you as a blockhead; that I alone could rally everybody to me and win against Cavaignac. I refused. I told them that you represented youth and the future, that you had a quarter of a century in front of you, whereas I could hardly count on eight or ten years; that I was an invalid and wanted to be left in peace. That is what these people were doing and that is what I did. And you forget all this! And you make these gentlemen the masters! And you throw out your cousin, my son, who defended you in the Assembly and did all he could to support your candidacy! And you are smashing universal suffrage, which made you what you are! Dammit all, I feel like saying like Molé that you are an idiot, and like Thiers that you are a blockhead!" '

The King of Westphalia paused for a moment, then continued:

'And do you know, Monsieur Victor Hugo, what he replied to me? "You will see!" No one knows what is at the bottom of that man!'

CHANCELLOR PASQUIER

9 February 1849

YESTERDAY, Thursday, as I was leaving the Académie where we had been discussing the word *accompagner*, I heard my name called out in the courtyard.

'Monsieur Hugo, Monsieur Hugo!'

I turned round. It was Monsieur Pasquier.

'Are you going to the Assembly?'

'Yes.'

'May I take you there?'

'With pleasure, *Monsieur le Chancelier*.'

I got into the carriage, which was a small brougham, lined with grey velvet. He made a big dog which was there lie down under his feet, and then we chatted.

'How are your eyes, *Monsieur le Chancelier*?'

'Bad, very bad.'

'Is it cataract?'

'Yes, and it's getting worse. But what can I do about it? I am like governments. I am going blind.'

I said, laughing:

'Perhaps that's as a result of having governed!'

He took the allusion in good part, and replied with a smile:

'It is not only myself who am going, it is everything. You are in a worse plight than I am. I am eighty-two years old, but you are a hundred. This Republic, born last February, is more decrepit than I, who am no more than an old fellow, and it will be dead before I who am about to die. I have seen so many things pass away! I shall see that go too.'

As he was in a mood for talking I let him go on. I listened to him thoughtfully. It seemed to me that I could hear the past judging the present. He continued:

'Who would have said that about universal suffrage? It is the scourge which has been our salvation. Our only fear a year ago, our only hope today. Providence has its own ways. I have never been a religious man, indeed I shared Voltaire's way of thinking, but seeing the things that have been happening, I feel like saying my *Credo* like an old woman.'

'And your *Confiteor* a little also,' I remarked.

'Oh, yes. You are right; *nostra culpa, nostral maxima culpa*! What a year 1847 was! How 1847 led up to 1848! Take just our Chamber of Peers for instance—Teste and Cubières condemned for corruption. The word "fraud" attached to the epaulets of a general, and the word "theft" to the robe of a President. And then the Comte Bresson cuts his throat. The Prince of Eckmühl stabs his mistress, an old whore who wasn't worth so much as a kick. The Comte Mortier tries to kill his children. The Duc de Praslin murders his wife. Isn't there the hand of Fate in all this? The upper class of society has shocked the lower. For example, we shall never rid the common people of the idea that we poisoned the Duc de Praslin. The accused a murderer and his judges poisoners— that is the impression it obtained of that case. Others believe that we saved that wretched duke and substituted some corpse or other in his place! There are people who declare that Praslin is in London, spending 100,000 francs a year with Mademoiselle de Luzzy. It is with that sort of thing, gossip, chatter, horrible talk, that the rotten old world was undermined. Now it has been toppled to the ground. Nobody has gained much as a result. Every sort of folly has been let loose at once. However, I believe that 1847 made an even sadder impression on me than 1848. All those horrible trials. The Teste case. My eyes were already failing at that time. I was obliged to have all the documents read to me, to have Monsieur de la Chauvinière to be my eyes when I could no longer use my own. You can't imagine how tiresome it is to have things read to you. Nothing remains in the mind. I don't know how I managed to preside over the case. And the Duc de Praslin's last six hours! What a sight! Ah, you, a tragic poet, who seeks for horror and for pity—you had them there! That unhappy man who lost everything at once, who was writhing in a dual agony, who had poison in his body and remorse in his soul! It was horrible. He refused everything, and he clung to everything. Occasionally he bit his hand in agony; he looked at us and watched us with a fixed stare; he seemed to be asking for life and demanding death at the one and the same time. I have never seen such frantic despair. The poison he had swallowed was such as to increase his strength towards the end, giving him extra vitality while it consumed him. As he was dying, I said to him: "Confess out of pity for yourself. Are you guilty?" He looked at me in terror and replied, faintly: "No!" That was a terrifying moment. He had a lie on his lips and truth in his eyes. Oh, I wish you had been there, Monsieur Hugo. But it is all over now. The other day I had a fancy to go and see the Luxembourg.'

He paused. I said:

'Well?'

'Well, they have spoiled it; rebuilt it all, that is to say, defaced it all. I didn't go into the palace; but I saw the garden. Everything is topsy-turvy. They have made walks in the nursery. English alleys in a nursery-ground! Can you understand that? It is folly!'

'Yes,' I said. 'That is characteristic of the time; small follies are mingled with great ones.'

We had got so far, when the carriage stopped at the entrance to the Assembly. I got out. We had just time to exchange our addresses.

'Where do you live now, Monsieur Hugo?'

'No. 37 Rue de la Tour d'Auvergne. And you, *Monsieur le Chancelier*?'

'No. 20 Rue Royale.'

'By the way,' he said, as he shut the door, 'it is still called the Rue Royale!'

MADEMOISELLE GEORGE

9 April 1849

MADEMOISELLE GEORGE came to see me the other day and said:

'I have come to you because I am in despair. What you said about Antonin Moyne upset me terribly. I assure you that one of these days something dreadful will happen to me. I went to see Boulay de la Meurthe, who used to lunch with me when I was living with Harel. He hid away and refused to see me. He is a miser. He is very rich, you know. Well, he would allow himself to be beaten for a crown piece, and afterwards cut it in four. I went to see Jerome. He received me. He said: "What do you want, Georgina?" I replied: "I want nothing. I believe I am richer than you, although I have nothing. But walk in front of me; hold yourself up; it seems to me that I can see something of the Emperor in you. That is all I wanted." He laughed and replied: "You are right; I am poorer than you. You have no money, but you can eat potatoes. I haven't a sou, but I have to treat people to truffles. Just imagine, tradesmen send me candles by dozens of pounds, and send me an account. What am I to do? People say: 'Ask for a pension.' "

'But I reply: "I am accustomed to command and not to beg." Monsieur Hugo, so much for Jerome! As for the President, he is a simpleton. I loathe him. In the first place, he is very ugly. He rides and drives well, and that's all. I went to call on him. He replied that he could not see me. When he was only poor Prince Louis, he received me in the Place Vendôme for two hours in succession, and the idiot made me look at the column. He has an English mistress, a pretty blonde, who deceives him in every possible way. I do not know

whether he is aware of it, but everybody else is. He goes to
the Champs-Élysées in a little Russian carriage, which he drives
himself. He will be upset one day by his horses, or by the
people. I told Jerome I detested that self-styled nephew of his.
Jerome put his hand over my mouth, and said: "Hold your
tongue, silly!" I said: "He speculates. Achille Fould goes and
sees him every day, and gets his news before everybody else,
then he goes and speculates for a rise or a fall. This is quite
certain with regard to the recent events in Piedmont. I know."
Jerome said to me: "Don't say things like that! It is that sort
of talk which ruined Louis-Philippe." What is Louis-Philippe
to me, Monsieur Hugo? He never did anything for Harel.
That is the truth. I am destitute. I plucked up my courage,
and went to call on Rachel—Mademoiselle Rachel—to ask her
to play *Rodogune* with me at my benefit. She did not admit
me, and asked me to write to her. Oh, no! I have not got to
that yet. I am a queen of the theatre as well as she, and one
day she will be a poor old pauper like me. No, I won't write
to her. I won't ask her for charity, I won't dance attendance
on her. She forgets that she was once a beggar. It doesn't occur
to her that she will come to that again. A beggar in the cafés,
Monsieur Hugo, that's what she was; she sang, and they threw
her coppers. Good. Now she plays *lansquenet* with Véron for
a louis, and wins or loses ten thousand francs a night. But in
thirty years she won't have six farthings, and she'll walk in
the mud with her shoes worn down at heel. In thirty years
she won't call herself Rachel with such an air as I call myself
George. She'll come up against some child with talent and
youth who will trample on her, and she'll grovel before her,
mark you. She'll grovel, and for this reason, that she is insolent. No, I won't go. No, I won't write to her. I have nothing
to eat, it is true. Tom earns nothing. He has a place in the
President's household which doesn't bring him anything. I
have a sister—you know Bébelle?—to take care of. Hostein
would not engage her at the Historique—the Théâtre-
Historique—for fifteen hundred francs. I have been to Boulay's
house, to the President's, to Rachel's; I haven't been able to

see anyone except you. I owe my porter ten francs, I have had
to pawn and sell the diamond buttons the Emperor gave me.
I play at the Théâtre Saint-Marcel; I play at the Batignolles;
I play in the suburbs; and I have not twenty-five sous to pay
for my cab. But I won't write to Rachel; I would rather drown
myself.'

AT THE ACADÉMIE

14 January 1850

ALFRED DE VIGNY and I have frustrated the election at the
Académie today.

Empis and Victor Leclerc were proposed. We would have
neither of them. We put in white tickets.

There were thirty-four voters; a majority was eighteen
votes. There were five ballots. Monsieur Empis had fifteen
votes, Monsieur Leclerc sixteen. There were votes given at
various times to Messieurs Émile Deschamps, Lamennais,
Alfred de Musset, and Béranger. With our two votes we could
decide the election. We stood firm. It had to be postponed,
and it is left over for a month.

At the first ballot, when the two white tickets were
announced, Monsieur Flourens said: 'There are two votes
lost.'

I replied: 'Lost? Say put out at interest!' My intention is
to make one of the two parties come to an arrangement with
us, who are the all-powerful make-weights, and to nominate
Balzac or Dumas in exchange for our votes.

It was in this way that I got Alfred de Vigny nominated
two years ago.

Today I was taking Dupin to task on the subject of Balzac.
He interrupted me:

'Well, I'll be damned! You would have Balzac enter the

Académie unopposed the first time just like that! You quote as examples Patin, Saint-Marc Girardin, Brifaut; but they prove nothing. Just imagine! Balzac in the Académie at the first attempt! A moment's thought will show you that it's impossible. You see, you have forgotten one thing : he deserves it.'

19 March 1850

At the Académie we are judging the Prose competition. This is how we do it.

Monsieur de Barante is reading a pamphlet. Monsieur Mérimée is writing. Messieurs Salvandy and Vitet are talking loudly. Messieurs Guizot and Pasquier are talking softly. Monsieur de Ségur is holding a newspaper. Messieurs Mignet, Ledrun, and Saint-Aulaire are laughing at some jest or other made by Monsieur Viennet. Monsieur Scribe is drawing with his pen on a paper-knife. Monsieur Flourens comes in and takes off his overcoat. Messieurs Patin, de Vigny, Pongerville, and Empis are looking at the ceiling or the carpet. Monsieur Sainte-Beuve utters an exclamation every now and then. Monsieur Villemain is reading the manuscript, while complaining of the sun coming in through the window opposite. Monsieur de Noailles is absorbed in a kind of directory which he is holding half-open. Monsieur Tissot is asleep. As for me, I am writing this. The other Academicians are absent.

The subject of the competition is a panegyric on Madame de Staël.

THE DEATH OF BALZAC

On 18 August 1850 my wife, who had been to see Madame de Balzac during the day, told me that Monsieur de Balzac was dying. I hurried round to his house.

Monsieur de Balzac had been suffering for eighteen months from an aneurism of the heart. After the February revolution

s

he had gone to Russia, where he had married. Some days before his departure I had met him on the boulevard. He was already complaining, and breathing noisily. In May 1850 he returned to France, married, rich, and dying! When he arrived his legs were already swollen. Four doctors who were consulted examined him. One of them, Monsieur Louis, told me on 6 July: 'He has not six weeks to live.' He was suffering from the same disease that Frédéric Soulié had.

On 18 August my uncle, General Louis Hugo, was dining with me. As soon as dinner was over I left him and took a cab to No. 14 Avenue Fortunée, in the Quartier Beaujon. It was there that Monsieur de Balzac lived. He had bought what remained of the mansion of Monsieur de Beaujon, a few rooms which had escaped demolition. He had furnished it magnificently, and turned it into a very pretty little house, having a carriage entrance in the Avenue Fortunée, and by way of a garden a long narrow courtyard, where the paving-stones were separated here and there by flowerbeds.

I rang. The moon was shining, but was obscured by clouds, The street was deserted. No one came. I rang again. The door opened. A maidservant appeared with a candle.

'What do you want, sir?' she asked.

She was crying.

I told her my name. She ushered me into a room on the ground floor in which, on a console table opposite the fireplace, there was a colossal bust of Balzac by David. A wax-candle was burning on a splendid table in the centre of the drawing-room, with six statuettes for legs, gilded in the most admirable taste.

Another woman, who was also crying, came and said:

'He is dying. Madame has gone to her own room. The doctors have not been here since yesterday. He has a wound in the left leg. Gangrene has set in. The doctors don't know what they are doing; they said that the dropsy was a buffy dropsy, an infiltration—that is what they called it—that the skin and the flesh were like fat, and that it was impossible to tap him. Last month, when he was going to bed, Monsieur bumped into a piece of ornamental furniture and tore the skin of his leg, and all the water in his body ran out. The doctors said: "Well, well!" They were greatly astonished, and since then they have made some punctures. They said: "Imitate Nature." But an abscess in the leg has appeared. It was Monsieur Roux who performed the operation. Yesterday they removed the dressing; the wound, instead of having suppurated, was red, dry, and angry. Then they said: "There is no hope for him," and have not been back since. Four or five have been sent for in vain. Each one said: "It is no use." He has had a bad night. This morning at nine o'clock Monsieur could not speak. Madame sent for a priest; he came and administered Extreme Unction to Monsieur. One hour afterwards he shook hands with his sister, Madame de Surville. Since eleven o'clock he has had a rattling in the throat, and he can no longer see. He won't live through the night. If you wish, sir, I will go and look for Monsieur de Surville, who has not gone to bed yet.'

The woman left me. I waited for a few minutes. The candle scarcely lighted the room, its splendid furniture and the fine paintings by Porbus and Holbein on the walls. The marble bust stood out vaguely against the gloom like the spectre of the man who was dying. A corpse-like smell pervaded the house.

Monsieur de Surville entered and confirmed all that the maidservant had said. I asked to see Monsieur de Balzac.

We went along a corridor, climbed a staircase covered with red carpet, and lined with *objets d'art*—vases, statues, pictures, credence-tables carrying enamels—and then another corridor, and I saw an open door. I heard a loud and sinister rattling noise. I was in Balzac's bedroom.

A bed stood in the middle of the room, a mahogany bedstead with a suspensory arrangement at the head and foot for moving the sick man. Monsieur de Balzac was in his bed, his head propped up on a pile of pillows, to which had been added the red damask cushions from the sofa. His face was purple, almost black, and leaned towards the right, his beard untrimmed, his grey hair cut short, his eyes fixed and open. I saw him in profile, and seen like that he bore a resemblance to the Emperor.

An old woman (the nurse) and a manservant stood at each side of the bed; a candle was burning behind the head of the bed on a table, another on a chest of drawers near the door. There was a silver vase on the night-table. This man and this woman stood silent in fear, and listened to the loud death-rattle of the dying man.

The candle behind the bed threw a bright light over the portrait of a man, young, pink-faced and smiling, hanging near the fireplace.

An unbearable smell was coming from the bed. I lifted the counterpane and took Balzac's hand. It was clammy. I squeezed it. He did not respond to the pressure.

This was the same room in which I had come to see him a month previously. Then he had been cheerful, full of hope, with no doubt about his recovery, showing his swelling and laughing. We had a long conversation and a political argument. He reproached me for my demagogic tendency. He was a Legitimist. He said to me: 'How could you discard so calmly the title of Peer of France, the finest after that of King of France?' He also said: 'I have Monsieur de Beaujon's house without the garden, but with the gallery overlooking the little church at the corner of the street. A door in my staircase opens into this church; one turn of the key and I am at Mass. I think more of the gallery than of the garden.' When I was about to leave him he led me to this staircase, walking with difficulty, and showed me the door, and then he called out to his wife: 'Mind you show Hugo all my pictures.'

The nurse said to me: 'He will die at daybreak.'

I came downstairs seeing in my mind's eye that livid face. Crossing the dining-room I found the bust motionless, impassive, haughty, vaguely radiant, and I compared death with immortality.

It was Sunday, and when I reached home I found several people waiting for me, among others Riza-Bey, the Turkish chargé d'affaires, Navarete, the Spanish poet, and Count Arrivabene, the exiled Italian. I said to them: 'Gentlemen, Europe is on the point of losing a great mind.'

He died in the night. He was fifty-one years of age.

They buried him on the Wednesday. He lay first in the Beaujon Chapel, passing through that door whose key was more precious to him than all the beautiful gardens of the old farmer-general.

Giraud made a portrait of him on the very day of his death. They wanted to take a cast of his face but could not; decomposition was too rapid. The morning after his death the modellers who came found his face deformed and the nose fallen on the cheek. They put him in an oak coffin lined with lead.

The service was held at Saint-Philippe du Roule. As I sat by the coffin I remembered that it was there that my second daughter had been baptized, and I had not been in the church since. In our memories death rubs shoulders with birth.

The Minister of the Interior, Baroche, came to the funeral. He sat beside me in church, near the bier, and from time to time spoke to me. He said: 'He was a distinguished man.' I replied: 'He was a genius.'

The procession crossed Paris and went by way of the boulevards to Père-Lachaise. A few drops of rain fell as we were leaving the church and as we reached the cemetery. It was one of those days on which it seems that the heavens shed a few tears.

I walked in front of the coffin, on the right, holding one of the silver tassels of the pall; Alexandre Dumas was on the opposite side.

When we came to the grave, which was high up on the hill, we found a huge crowd. The road was rough and narrow; the horses had some difficulty in pulling the hearse, which kept rolling back downhill. I was trapped between a wheel and a tomb, and was very nearly crushed. The spectators who were standing on the tomb hoisted me up by my shoulders.

We walked all the way.

The coffin was lowered into the grave, which is close to those of Charles Nodier and Casimir Delavigne. The priest said the last prayer, and I spoke a few words. As I was speaking the sun set. All Paris appeared in the distance enveloped in the splendid haze of the setting orb. A few lumps of earth fell into the grave almost at my feet, and I was interrupted by the dull sound of this earth dropping on the coffin.

THE DEATH OF
MADAME VICTOR HUGO

25 August 1868

TODAY, about three o'clock in the afternoon, my wife had an attack of apoplexy. Whistling breath. Convulsions. Doctor Crocq and Doctor Jettrand were sent for. At midnight the convulsions became less violent, but a hemiplegic condition supervened. The right side was paralysed. Doctor Jettrand summoned Doctor Émile Allix by telegraph.

At three o'clock in the morning the convulsions stopped. Fever has occurred.

26 August 1868

This morning the three leading doctors in Brussels were consulted. Alas, there is little hope.

At midday I sent for a nun to look after my wife. At two o'clock Doctor Émile Allix arrived from Paris. My wife opens her eyes when I speak to her and squeezes my hand. She does the same with her sons. This afternoon she moved her right arm. It seems to me that she is better.

My wife has fewer convulsions. Doctor Allix has sent Doctor Axenfeld this telegram: 'Condition serious, but hope.'

27 August 1868

Died this morning, at half-past six.

I closed her eyes. Alas!

God will receive that great, gentle soul. I render her to Him. May she be blessed!

In accordance with her wishes, we are going to send her coffin to Villequier, to rest beside our sweet dead daughter.

I shall accompany it as far as the frontier.

To send the coffin into France the permission of the French Government is required. Telegram to Paul Foucher to tell him to take the necessary steps.

Vacquerie has arrived. Laussedat has come. Paul Meurice arrived at ten o'clock at night.

Our dear departed has been photographed.

28 August 1868

Tiresome formalities all day. Exchange of telegrams to enable the coffin to cross the frontier.

Four o'clock in the afternoon: The coffin is a double one. She was placed inside it wrapped in a white shroud lined with muslin. Doctor Allix covered her with spices, leaving the face bare. I took some flowers which were there. I surrounded the head with them. Around the head I put a ring of white marguerites, without hiding the face, then I scattered flowers over the whole body and filled the coffin with them. Then I kissed her on the forehead and whispered to her: 'Be thou blessed!' And I remained on my knees near her. Charles came up, then Victor. Weeping, they kissed her and remained standing behind me. Paul Meurice, Vacquerie, and Allix were weeping. I prayed. They bent down one after another and kissed her.

At five o'clock the lead coffin was soldered and the lid of the oak coffin screwed down. Before the lid of the oak coffin was placed in position, I took a little key I had in my pocket and scratched on the lead, over her head, the letters: V.H. When the coffin was closed, I kissed it.

Before leaving, I put on the black clothes which I shall wear for the rest of my life.

At six o'clock we left the house, No. 4, Place des Barricades, for the Gare du Midi. We were in three mourning carriages behind the hearse, together with Messieurs Laussedat, Gustave Frédérix, Gaston Bérardi, Coenaès, Albert Lacroix, and several others. At seven o'clock the coffin was placed in a special carriage and we set off. Charles, Victor, and I were in the same carriage with Auguste Vacquerie, Paul Meurice, Henri Rochefort, Émile Allix, and Camille Berru. At nine o'clock we arrived at Quiévrain. There was a crowd around our carriage. This crowd greeted me with obvious emotion when I got out. The stationmaster took me to the mortuary carriage. It was opened. I climbed into it. The coffin was in a sort of alcove hung with black on a platform, under a mourning sheet, between a pair of curtains strewn with tears, under a pile of green branches, ivy and laurel. I picked up a few leaves and kissed the coffin. I spoke to her a little in a whisper.

Then I got out again. When we were back on the platform the carriage was closed. Vacquerie, Meurice, and Allix, who are going to take her to Villequier, got back into the train. I stayed there watching the train disappear into the darkness.

After a while Charles touched my shoulder. A worthy inhabitant of Quiévrain, Monsieur Pitot, offered us hospitality at his house. We made for the station exit. Rochefort offered me his arm. I said to him:

'You have just seen the carriage in which I shall return to France.'

29 August 1868

The Pitots' house is quite close to the station. Their hospitality was cordial and sympathetic. We spent the night there. In my room there was the illustrated volume of *Les Misérables*. I wrote my name and the date in it, leaving my host this memento.

This morning, at half-past nine, we set off on the return journey to Brussels, where we arrived at midday.

30 August 1868

Proposals by Monsieur Lacroix for my unpublished works. Come now! I must get back to work and return to life. Duty.

1 September 1868

News from Villequier. Paul Meurice made an admirable oration. The burial has taken place. I have given instructions for the following inscription to be carved on the tombstone:

ADÈLE

WIFE OF VICTOR HUGO

5 September 1868

Auguste Vacquerie has sent me three flowers picked on 4 September from the three graves.

THE SIEGE OF PARIS

1870–71

Brussels, 1 September 1870: Charles[1] leaves this morning with Messieurs Claretie, Proust, and Frédérix for Virton. Fighting is going on near there, at Carignan. They will see what they can of the battle, and return tomorrow.

2 September: Charles and his friends did not return today.

[1] V.H.'s elder son.

3 September: Yesterday, after the decisive battle had been lost, Louis Bonaparte, taken prisoner at Sedan, surrendered his sword to the King of Prussia. Just a month ago, on 2 August, at Sarrebrück, he was playing at war.

To save France now would be to save Europe.

Shouting newsboys pass, carrying enormous posters on which are the words: 'Napoleon III a Prisoner'.

Five o'clock. Charles and our friends have returned.

Nine o'clock. Meeting of exiles at which Charles and I are present.

Query. Tricolour flag or red flag?

4 September: The deposition of the Emperor is proclaimed in Paris.

At one o'clock a meeting of exiles is held at my house.

At three o'clock I receive a telegram from Paris in the following terms: 'Bring the children immediately.' Which means 'Come.'

Messieurs Jules, Claretie, and Proust dine with us.

During dinner a telegram signed 'François Hugo' arrived, announcing that a provisional government had been formed: Jules Favre, Gambetta, Thiers.

5 September: At six o'clock in the morning a telegram signed 'Barbieux' and asking the hour of my arrival in Paris is brought to me. I tell Charles to answer that I shall arrive at nine o'clock at night. We shall take the children with us. We shall leave by the 2.35 train.

The Provisional Government (according to the newspapers) is made up of all the Deputies of Paris, with the exception of Thiers.

At noon, as I was about to leave Brussels for Paris, a young man, a Frenchman, stopped me on the Place de la Monnaie and said:

'Monsieur, they tell me that you are Victor Hugo.'

'Yes.'

'Please tell me something. I would like to know whether it is prudent to go to Paris at present.'

'Monsieur,' I replied, 'it is very imprudent, but you should go.'

We entered France at four o'clock.

At Tergnier, at half-past six, we dined on a piece of bread, a little cheese, a pear, and a glass of wine. Claretie insisted on paying, and said: 'I particularly want to treat you to dinner on the day of your return to France.'

On the way I saw in a wood a camp of French soldiers, the men and horses together. I shouted to them: 'Long live the army!' and I wept.

At frequent intervals we came across troop-trains on their way to Paris. Twenty-five of these passed during the day. As one of them went by we gave the soldiers all the provisions we had, some bread, fruit, and wine. The sun shone brightly and in the evening there was clear moonlight.

We arrived in Paris at 9.35. A huge crowd was waiting for me. An indescribable welcome. I spoke four times. Once from the balcony of a café and three times from my carriage.

When I took leave of this constantly growing crowd, which escorted me to Paul Meurice's, in the Avenue Frochot, I said to the people: 'In one hour you have repaid me for twenty years of exile.'

They sang the *Marseillaise* and the *Chant du Départ*. They shouted: 'Long live Victor Hugo!' Every now and then I could hear lines from *Les Châtiments* in the crowd. I gave over 6,000 handshakes. The journey from the Gare du Nord to the Rue de Laval took two hours. They wanted to take me to the Hôtel de Ville. I shouted: 'No, citizens! I have not come to overthrow the Provisional Government of the Republic, but to support it.' They tried to unharness my carriage. I stopped them. All the time a woman held the bridle of one of the horses. A man in a smock recited the verses about little Georges[2] which are in my garden. He shouted:

[2] V.H.'s grandson.

'Long live little Georges!' And the crowd shouted: 'Long live little Georges!'

We arrived at Meurice's, where I am to stay, at midnight. I had supper with my travelling companions and Victor. I went to bed at two o'clock.

At daybreak I was awakened by a tremendous storm. Thunder and lightning.

I shall lunch with Paul Meurice, and we shall dine together at the Hôtel Navarin, No. 8 Rue Navarin, where my family is staying.

Paris, 6 September: Countless visits, countless letters.

Rey came to ask me whether I would agree to join a triumvirate composed as follows: Victor Hugo, Ledru-Rollin, and Schœlcher. I refused. I told him: 'It is almost impossible to amalgamate me.'

I reminded him of experiences we had shared. He said: 'Do you remember that it was I who met you when you arrived at the Baudin barricade?'[3] I replied: 'I remember that very well. Listen to this . . .' And I recited the first lines of my (unpublished) poem on the Baudin barricade.

He burst into tears.

7 September: Louis Blanc, Alton-Shée, Banville, and others came to see me.

The women of the markets brought me a bouquet.

8 September: I am warned that there is a plan to assassinate me. I shrug my shoulders.

This morning I wrote my *Letter to the Germans*. It will be published tomorrow.

A visit from General Cluseret.

[3] Baudin was killed at the barricade in the Faubourg Saint-Antoine on 2 December 1852, during Louis Napoleon's *coup d'état*.

At ten o'clock I went to the office of the *Rappel* to correct the proofs of my *Letter to the Germans*.

9 September: Received a visit from General Montfort. The generals are asking me for commands, others ask me to grant audiences, yet others ask me for places. I reply: 'But I am nobody.'

I saw Captain Féval, the husband of Fanny, Alice's sister.[4] He was a prisoner of war, and was released on parole.

All the newspapers publish my *Appeal to the Germans*.

10 September: Alton-Shée and Louis Ulbach lunched with us. Afterwards we went to the Place de la Concorde. At the foot of the flower-decked statue of Strasbourg there is a register. Everybody comes to sign the resolution of public thanks. I write my name. The crowd promptly surround me. The ovation of the other night was about to begin again. I hurriedly got back into my carriage.

Among the people who called upon me was Cernuschi.

11 September: A visit from Mr. Wickham Hoffman, Secretary of the United States Legation. Mr. Washburne, the American Minister, had requested him to ask me whether I thought that some good might result if he were to intervene officiously and see the King of Prussia. I referred him to Jules Favre.

12 September: Among other callers was Frédérick Lemaître.

13 September: Today there is a review of the army of Paris. I am alone in my room. The battalions march through the streets singing the *Marseillaise* and the *Chant du Départ*. I hear this immense shout:

> *For France a Frenchman must live,*
> *For France a Frenchman must die.*

[4] Alice was Alice Lehaenne, Charles Hugo's wife.

I listen and I weep. On, brave men! I will go where you go.

A visit from the United States Consul-General and Mr. Wickham Hoffman.

Julie[5] writes to me from Guernsey that the acorn I planted on 14 July has sprouted. The oak of the United States of Europe issued from the ground on 5 September, the day of my return to Paris.

14 September: I received a visit from the Committee of the Société des Gens de Lettres, which wants me to be its president; from Monsieur Jules Simon, the Minister of Public Instruction; from Colonel Piré, who commands a corps of volunteers, etc.

16 September: A year ago today I opened the Peace Congress at Lausanne. This morning I wrote the *Appeal to the French* for a war to the bitter end against the invasion. Going out, I saw hovering over Montmartre the captive balloon from which a watch is to be kept on the besiegers.

17 September: All the forests around Paris are burning. Charles toured the fortifications and is perfectly satisfied with them. I deposited at the office of the *Rappel* 2,088 francs 30 centimes, subscribed in Guernsey for the wounded and sent by Monsieur H. Tupper, the French Consul.

At the same time I deposited at the *Rappel* office a gold bracelet and some gold earrings, sent anonymously for the wounded by a woman. With them she had sent me a little gold medal for Jeanne[6] to wear on a necklace.

20 September: Charles and his little family left the Hôtel Navarin yesterday and installed themselves at No. 174 Rue de

[5] Julie Chenay, Madame Victor Hugo's sister.
[6] Hugo's grand-daughter.

Rivoli. Charles and his wife, as well as Victor, will continue to dine with me every day.

The attack on Paris began yesterday.

Louis Blanc, Gambetta, the Minister of the Interior, and Jules Ferry came to see me this morning.

I went to the Institut to sign the declaration about the monuments of Paris.[7] As the secretariat was closed, I took a sheet of paper from the porter's lodge and wrote on it: 'I support the declaration of the Institut de France: Victor Hugo. Paris, 20 September 1870.'

21 September: This evening a crowd, including soldiers and mobiles, was standing at the corner of the Rue des Martyrs, looking at lights which looked like signals moving about on the fifth floor of a tall house. There were angry shouts. The crowd nearly went in and searched the house.

Jules Favre's interview with Bismarck has come to nothing.

25 September: This evening Jules Claretie, accompanied by Emmanuel des Essarts, brought me a gold bee which he had taken from the imperial cloak at the Tuileries. He had written on the envelope the line in *Les Châtiments* in which I urge the bees to fly off that cloak.

27 September: Monsieur Victor Bois, Alice's uncle, one of the most brilliant organizers of the defence of Paris, has just died suddenly. He dined with me three days ago.

2 October: We went round Paris by the ring railway. Our trip round Paris lasted three hours. Nothing could be more interesting: Paris demolishing herself to defend herself is magnificent. She is turning her ruins into her barricades.

Toul and Strasbourg have been taken.

[7] A document protesting against the shelling of monuments.

3 October: Two delegates from the Eleventh Arrondissement came to ask me to accept nomination as a candidate. I refused.

I will not accept any limited candidacy. I would gladly accept the candidacy of the city of Paris. I want the voting to be not by a constituency poll, but for candidates on a single list.

I went to the Ministry of Public Instruction to see Madame Jules Simon, who is in mourning for her old friend Victor Bois. Georges and Jeanne were in the garden. I went and played with them.

Nadar came to see me this evening to ask me for any letters I had for a balloon which he is going to send up the day after tomorrow. It will carry with it my three addresses: *To the Germans, To the French, To the Parisians.*

My address *To the Germans* has been posted up again all over Paris. Nobody knows by whom.

5 October: Nadar's balloon, which is called the *Barbès,* and which is taking my letters, etc., set off this morning, but had to come down again, as there was not enough wind. It will leave tomorrow. It is said that Jules Favre and Gambetta are going to travel in it.

Last night General John Meredith Read, the United States Consul-General, called to see me. He had seen the American General Burnside, who is in the Prussian camp. The Prussians, it appears, have respected Versailles. They are afraid to attack Paris. This is something we can see for ourselves.

7 October: This morning, strolling along the Boulevard de Clichy, I saw a balloon at the end of a street leading to Montmartre. In this space three balloons were being inflated, a large one, a medium-sized one, and a small one. The large one was yellow, the medium one white, and the small one striped yellow and red.

In the crowd it was whispered that Gambetta was leaving.

Sure enough, I saw him in a group near the yellow balloon, wearing a heavy overcoat and sealskin cap. He sat down on a paving-stone and pulled on a pair of fur-lined boots. A leather bag was slung over his shoulder. He took it off and climbed into the car of the balloon, and a young man, the aeronaut, tied the bag to the cords above Gambetta's head.

It was half-past ten. The weather was fine with a light southerly breeze, and a gentle autumn sun. All at once the yellow balloon rose, with three men in it, including Gambetta. Then the white balloon went up with three men, one of whom waved a tricolour flag. Under Gambetta's balloon there hung a long tricolour streamer. 'Long live the Republic!' shouted the crowd.

The two balloons went up for some distance, the white one going higher than the yellow one, then we saw them descending. Ballast was thrown out, but they went on falling. They disappeared behind Montmartre hill. They must have landed on the Saint-Denis plain. They were too heavily weighted, or else the wind was not strong enough.

The departure took place, for the balloons went up again.

We paid a visit to Notre-Dame, which has been admirably restored. To go into the choir, one pays fifty centimes for the wounded.

We also went to see the Tour Saint-Jacques. While our carriage was standing there one of the delegates I saw the other day (from the Eleventh Arrondissement) came up and told me that the Eleventh Arrondissement had come round to my views, considered that I was right in insisting upon a vote on a single list of candidates, begged me to accept nomination on the conditions I had imposed, and wanted to know what ought to be done if the Government refused to allow an election. Ought force to be resorted to? I replied that a civil war would help the enemy and deliver Paris to the Prussians.

T

On the way home I bought some toys for my little ones—a Zouave in his sentry-box for Georges, and for Jeanne a doll that opens and shuts its eyes.

8 October: I have received a letter from Monsieur L. Colet, of Vienna, by way of Normandy. It is the first letter that has reached me from the outside since Paris was surrounded.

There has been no sugar in Paris for six days. Meat rationing began today. We shall get three-quarters of a pound per person, per day.

Some incidents as a result of the postponement of the Commune. Feverish unrest in Paris. Nothing to cause alarm, though. The bass voice of the Prussian cannon thunders continuously. It recommends unity among us.

The Minister of Finance, Monsieur Ernest Picard, through his secretary, Monsieur Pallain, asks me to 'grant him an audience': these are the terms he uses. I make an appointment for Monday morning, 10 October.

9 October: Five delegates from the Ninth Arrondissement came in the name of the arrondissement to *forbid me to get myself killed.*

10 October: Monsieur Ernest Picard came to see me. I asked him to issue at once a decree liberating all articles pawned for less than fifteen francs (the present decree making absurd exceptions, linen, for instance). I told him that the poor could not wait. He promised to issue the decree tomorrow.

There is no news of Gambetta. We are beginning to feel uneasy. The wind carried him to the north-east, which is occupied by the Prussians.

11 October: Good news of Gambetta. He landed at Epineuse, near Amiens.

Last night, after the demonstrations in Paris, passing a group which had gathered under a street lamp, I heard these words: 'It seems that Victor Hugo and the others . . .' I continued on my way, and did not listen to the rest, as I did not wish to be recognized.

After dinner I read to my friends the verses with which the French edition of *Les Châtiments* begins ('When about to return to France'. Brussels, 31 August 1870.).

12 October: It is beginning to get cold. Barbieux, who is in command of a battalion, brought us the helmet of a Prussian soldier who was killed by his men. This helmet greatly astonished little Jeanne. These angels know nothing yet of the earth.

The decree I demanded for the poor was published this morning in the *Journal Officiel*.

Monsieur Pallain, the Minister's secretary, whom I met as I came out of the Carrousel, told me that the decree would cost 800,000 francs.

I replied: 'All right; eight hundred thousand francs. Taken from the rich. Given to the poor.'

13 October: Today I met Théophile Gautier, whom I had not seen for so many years. I embraced him. He was rather nervous. I told him to come and dine with me.

14 October: The Château of Saint-Cloud was burned down yesterday by our shells from Mont-Valérien.

I went to Claye's to correct the final proofs of the French edition of *Les Châtiments* which will appear on Tuesday. Dr. Émile Allix brought me a Prussian cannon-ball which he had picked up behind a barricade, near Montrouge, where it had just killed two horses. This cannon-ball weighs twenty-five pounds. Playing with it, Georges trapped one of his fingers under it, which made him cry a good deal.

Today is the anniversary of Jena.

16 October: There is no more butter. There is no more cheese. There is scarcely any milk or eggs left.

The report that my name has been given to the Boulevard Haussmann is confirmed. I have not been to see it myself.

17 October: Tomorrow a postal balloon called the *Victor Hugo* is to be sent up from the Place de la Concorde. I am sending a letter to London by this balloon.

18 October: As I was walking along the boulevard I was handed a card bearing the address of a firm which manufactures sewing machines: Bienaimé et Cie, No. 46, Boulevard Magenta. On the back of the card is a portrait of me.

I have been to see Les Feuillantines. The house and garden of my childhood have disappeared. A street now passes over them.

19 October: Louis Blanc came to dine with me. He brought a declaration by the former Representatives for me to sign. I said that I would not sign it unless it were drawn up in a different manner.

29 October: Visit from the committee of the Gens de Lettres.

Today the first postage stamps of the Republic of 1870 were put in circulation.

Les Châtiments (French edition) appeared in Paris this morning.

The papers announce that the balloon *Victor Hugo* has

landed in Belgium. It is the first postal balloon to cross the frontier.

21 October: They say that Alexandre Dumas died on 13 October at his son's home at Le Havre. He was a man with a great heart and great talent. His death distresses me deeply.

Louis Blanc and Brives came to speak to me again about the Declaration of the Representatives. My opinion is that it would be better to postpone it.

Nothing could be more charming than the sounding of the reveille in Paris. It is dawn. First one hears, close to, a roll of drums, followed by the blast of a bugle, an exquisite melody, winged and warlike. Then all is still. Twenty seconds later the drums roll again, then the bugle rings out, but farther off. Then silence once more. The next moment, farther off still, the same song of bugle and drum can be heard, more faintly but still distinctly. Then after a pause the roll and blast are repeated very far away. Then they are heard again, at the extremity of the horizon, but indistinctly and like an echo. Day breaks and the shout 'To arms!' is heard. The sun rises and Paris awakes.

22 October: The edition of 5,000 copies of *Les Châtiments* has been sold in two days. I have authorized the printing of another 3,000.

Little Jeanne has imagined a way of puffing out her cheeks and raising her arms in the air which is adorable.

The first 5,000 copies of the Parisian edition of *Les Châtiments* has brought me in 500 francs, which I am sending to *Siècle* as a subscription to the national fund for the cannon which Paris needs.

Mathé and Gambon, the former Representatives, called to ask me to take part in a meeting of which former representatives would form the nucleus. The meeting would be impossible without me, they said. But I see more disadvantages than advantages in such a meeting. I think I shall have to refuse.

We are eating horsemeat in every form. I saw this notice in a pork-butcher's window:

Saucisson chevaleresque

23 October: The 17th Battalion asked me to be the first subscriber of one sou to a fund for purchasing a cannon. They will collect 300,000 sous. This will make 15,000 francs, which will buy a 24-centimetre gun with a range of 8,500 metres—equal to the Krupp guns.

Lieutenant Maréchal brought to collect my sou an Egyptian cup of onyx dating from the Pharaohs, engraved with the moon and the sun, the Great Bear and the Southern Cross (?) and with two cynocephalus demons as handles. The engraving of this cup represented the life-work of one man. I gave my sou. Alton-Shée, who was present, gave his, as did also Monsieur and Madame Meurice, and the two servants, Mariette and Clémence. The 17th Battalion wanted to call the gun the *Victor Hugo*. I told them to call it the *Strasbourg*. In this way the Prussians will go on receiving shots from Strasbourg.

We chatted and laughed with these officers of the 17th Battalion. It was the duty of the two cynocephalus genii of the cup to carry souls off to hell. I said: 'Very well, I confide William and Bismarck to them.'

Visit from Monsieur Édouard Thierry. He came to ask me to allow *Stella* to be read at the Théâtre Français in aid of the wounded. I gave him all the *Châtiments* to choose from. That startled him. And then I asked that the readings should be for a cannon.

Visit from Monsieur Charles Floquet. He has a post at the Hôtel de Ville. I commissioned him to tell the Government to call the Mont Valérien *Mont Strasbourg*.

24 October: Visit from General Le Flô. Various deputations received.

25 October: There is to be a public reading of *Les Châtiments* for a cannon to be called *Le Châtiment*. We are preparing for it.

That good fellow Rostan, whom I upbraided one day, and who likes me because I was right, has been arrested for indiscipline in the National Guard. He has a little motherless boy six years old who has nobody else to take care of him. What was to be done, the father being in prison? I told Rostan to send his boy to me at the Pavillon de Rohan. He sent him today.

26 October: At half-past six Rostan, released from prison, came to fetch his little Henri. Father and son were overjoyed.

28 October: Edgar Quinet came to see me.

Schœlcher and Commander Farcy, who has given his name to his gunboat, dined with me. After dinner at half-past eight, I went with Schœlcher to his home at No. 16, Rue de la Chaise. We found there Quinet, Ledru-Rollin, Mathé, Gambon, Lamarque, and Brives. This was my first meeting with Ledru-Rollin. We had a very courteous argument about the question of founding a club, he being for and I against it. We shook hands. I returned home at midnight.

29 October: Visits from the committee of the Gens de Lettres, Frédérick Lemaître, Messieurs Berton and Lafontaine and Mademoiselle Favart (about a third cannon to be called the *Victor Hugo*). I oppose the name.

I have authorized the third impression of 3,000 copies of *Les Châtiments*, which will make to date 11,000 copies for Paris alone.

30 October: I received the letter from the Société des Gens de Lettres asking me to authorize a public reading of *Les Châtiments*, the proceeds of which will give Paris another cannon to be called the *Victor Hugo*. I gave the authorization. In my reply written this morning I asked for the gun to be called the *Châteaudun* instead of the *Victor Hugo*. The reading will take place at the Porte Saint-Martin.

Monsieur Berton came. I read him *L'Expiation*, which he is to read. Monsieur and Madame Meurice and Alton Shée were present at the reading.

News has arrived that Metz has capitulated and that Bazaine's army has surrendered.

Bills announcing the reading of *Les Châtiments* have been posted. Monsieur Raphaël Félix came to tell me the time of the rehearsal tomorrow. I hired a seven-seat box for this reading, which I placed at the disposal of the ladies.

On my way home this evening, in front of the *mairie,* I met Monsieur Chaudey, who was at the Lausanne Peace Conference and who is Mayor of the Sixth Arrondissement. He was with Monsieur Philibert Audebrand. We talked sadly about the taking of Metz.

31 October: Skirmish at the Hôtel de Ville. Blanqui, Flourens, and Delescluze tried to overthrow the provisional authorities, Trochu and Jules Favre. I refused to associate myself with them.

A huge crowd. My name was on the list of members for the proposed Government. I persisted in my refusal.

Flourens and Blanqui held some of the members of the Government prisoners at the Hôtel de Ville all day.

At midnight some National Guards came from the Hôtel de Ville to fetch me 'to preside', they said, 'over the new Government'. I replied that I strongly disapproved of this attempt to seize power and refused to go to the Hôtel de Ville.

At three o'clock in the morning Flourens and Blanqui left the Hôtel de Ville and Trochu entered it.

The Commune of Paris is to be elected.

1 November: We have postponed for a few days the reading of *Les Châtiments*, which was to have been given at the Porte Saint-Martin today, Tuesday.

Louis Blanc came this morning to ask me what should be done about the Commune.

The newspapers unanimously praise the attitude I took yesterday in rejecting the approaches made to me.

2 November: The Government demands a 'yes' or a 'no'. Louis Blanc and my sons came to talk to me about it. The report that Alexandre Dumas is dead has been denied.

4 November: I was asked to be Mayor of the Third, then of the Eleventh, Arrondissement. I refused.

I went to the rehearsal of *Les Châtiments* at the Porte Saint-Martin. Frédérick Lemaître and Mesdames Laurent, Lia Félix, and Duguéret were present.

5 November: Today the public reading of *Les Châtiments*, for the purchase of a cannon for the defence of Paris, was given.

The Third, Eleventh, and Fifteenth Arrondissements want me to stand for Mayor. I refuse.

Mérimée has died at Cannes. Dumas is not dead, but he is paralysed.

7 November: The 24th Battalion called on me and asked me to give them a cannon.

8 November: Last night, on my way home after paying a return visit to General Le Flô, I crossed for the first time the Pont des Tuileries, which has been built since my departure from France.

9 November: The net receipts from the reading of *Les Châti-*
ments at the Porte Saint-Martin for the gun which I have
named the *Châteaudun* amounted to 7,000 francs, the balance
going to pay for the attendants, firemen, and lighting, the
only expenses charged.

The Cail factory is now producing *mitrailleuses* of a new
model, called the Gattlir model.

Little Jeanne is beginning to chatter.

A second reading of *Les Châtiments* for another cannon is to
be given at the Théâtre-Français.

12 November: Mademoiselle Périga called today to rehearse
Pauline Roland, which she is to read at the second reading of
Les Châtiments, announced for tomorrow at the Porte Saint-
Martin. I took a carriage, dropped Mademoiselle Périga at
her home, and then went to the rehearsal of tomorrow's read-
ing at the theatre. Frédérick Lemaître, Berton, Maubant,
Taillade, Lacressonnière, Charly, Mesdames Laurent, Lia
Félix, Rousseil, Monsieur Raphaël Félix, and the committee of
the Société des Gens de Lettres were there.

After the rehearsal the wounded of the Porte Saint-Martin
ambulance asked me, through Madame Laurent, to go and see
them. I said: 'With all my heart,' and I went.

They are installed in several rooms, the chief of which is the
old green-room of the theatre with its big round mirrors, where
in 1831 I read *Marion de Lorme* to the actors. Crosnier was
the manager then, and Madame Dorval and Bocage were
present at that reading.

On entering, I said to the wounded men: 'You see in me
a man who envies you. I desire nothing more on earth than one
of your wounds. I salute you, children of France, favourite
sons of the Republic, elect who suffer for the Fatherland.'

They seemed to be greatly moved. I shook hands with them
all. One held out his amputated wrist. Another had lost his
nose. One had undergone two painful operations that very
morning. A very young man had been decorated with the

military medal a few hours before. A convalescent said to me: 'I am a Franc-Comtois.' 'Like myself,' I said. And I embraced him. The nurses in their white aprons, who are the actresses of the theatre, burst into tears.

13 November: I had Monsieur and Madame Paul Meurice, Vacquerie and Louis Blanc to dinner this evening. We dined at six o'clock, as the second reading of *Les Châtiments* was due to begin at the Porte Saint-Martin at half-past seven. I offered Madame Paul Meurice a box for the reading.

14 November: Visit from Monsieur Arsène Houssaye, and Henri Houssaye, his son. He is going to have *Stella* read at his house in aid of the wounded.

Monsieur Valois came to tell me that the two readings of *Les Châtiments* brought in 14,000 francs. This sum will buy not two, but three guns. The first having been named by me the *Châteaudun* and the second *Les Châtiments*, the Société des Gens de Lettres wishes the third to be called the *Victor Hugo*. I gave my consent.

Pierre Véron has sent me Daumier's fine drawing representing the Empire annihilated by *Les Châtiments*.

16 November: Baroche is said to have died at Caen. Monsieur Édouard Thierry refuses to allow the fifth act of *Hernani* to be played at the Porte Saint-Martin for the victims of Châteaudun and for the cannon of the 24th Battalion. He is a queer obstacle, this Monsieur Thierry!

17 November: Visit from the committee of the Gens de Lettres. The committee came to ask me to authorize a reading of *Les Châtiments* at the Opéra to raise funds for another cannon.

I declare here once for all that I authorize anyone who wishes to do so to read or perform, in any theatre, whatever he likes that I have written, if it is for cannon, the wounded, ambulances, workshops, orphanages, victims of the war, or the poor, and that I abandon all my royalties on these readings or performances.

I have decided that the third reading of *Les Châtiments* shall be given at the Opéra *gratis* for the people.

19 November: Madame Marie Laurent came to recite to me *Les Pauvres Gens*, which she is to recite at the Porte Saint-Martin tomorrow to raise funds for a cannon.

20 November: Last night there was an aurora borealis.

La Grosse Joséphine is no longer my neighbour. She has just been transported to Bastion No. 41. It took twenty-six horses to draw her. I am sorry they have taken her away. At night I used to hear her deep voice, and it seemed to me that she was speaking to me. I shared my love between *Grosse Joséphine* and Little Jeanne.

Little Jeanne can now say 'papa' and 'mamma' very well.

Today there was a review of the National Guard.

21 November: Madame Jules Simon and Madame Sarah Bernhardt came to see me.

After dinner a great many visitors called, and the drawing-room was crowded. It seems that Veuillot has insulted me.

Little Jeanne is beginning to crawl on her hands and knees very well indeed.

23 November: Jules Simon writes to tell me that the Opéra will be given to me for the people (for a free reading of *Les*

Châtiments any day I wish. I wanted Sunday, but out of consideration for the concert that the actors and staff of the Opéra are giving on Sunday night for their own benefit I have chosen Monday.

Frédérick Lemaître called. He kissed my hands and wept.

It has been raining these last few days. The rain has soaked the plains, the cannon-wheels would sink into the mud, and so the sortie has had to be postponed. For two days Paris has been living on salt meat. A rat costs 8 sous.

24 November: I authorize a performance at the Théâtre-Français tomorrow, Friday the 25th, on behalf of the victims of the war, of the fifth act of *Hernani* by the actors of the Théâtre-Français and of the last act of *Lucrèce Borgia* by the actors of the Porte Saint-Martin, and in addition the recitation, as an interlude, of extracts from *Les Châtiments*, *Les Contemplations*, and La *Légende des Siècles*.

Mademoiselle Favart came this morning to rehearse with me *Booz endormi*. Then we went to the Français together to attend the rehearsal for tomorrow's performance. She acted Dõna Sol very well indeed. Madame Laurent (Lucrèce Borgia) also played well. During the rehearsal Monsieur de Flavigny dropped in. I said to him: 'Good morning, my dear ex-colleague.' He looked at me, then, somewhat moved, exclaimed: 'Good heavens! It's you!' and he added: 'How well preserved you look!' I replied: 'Exile preserves a man.' I returned the ticket for a box which the Théâtre-Français sent to me for tomorrow's performance, and hired a box, which I placed at the disposal of Madame Paul Meurice.

After dinner the new Prefect of Police, Monsieur Cresson, called on me. Monsieur Cresson was a young barrister twenty years ago. He defended the murderers of General Bréa. Those men were sentenced to death. Monsieur Cresson came to see me. I asked for a reprieve for the men from Louis Bonaparte, then President of the Republic. Monsieur Cresson reminded me of all these facts.

Then he spoke to me about the free reading of *Les Châti-ments* to be given on Monday the 28th at the Opéra. It is feared that a huge crowd—all the suburbs—will be attracted. More than 80,000 men and women. 3,000 will be able to get in. What is to be done with the rest? The Government is uneasy. Many are called but few will be chosen, and it is afraid that a crush, a fight, a riot, might result. The Government will refuse me nothing. It wants to know whether I will accept the responsibility. It will do whatever I wish. The Prefect of Police has been instructed to come to an understanding with me.

I said to Monsieur Cresson: 'Let us consult Vacquerie and Meurice and my two sons.' He replied: 'Gladly.' The six of us held a council. We decided that 3,000 tickets should be distributed on Sunday, the day before the reading, at the *mairies* of the twenty arrondissements to the first persons who presented themselves after midday. Each arrondissement will receive a number of tickets in proportion to the number of its population. The next day the 3,000 holders of tickets (to seats anywhere in the Opéra) will wait their turn at the doors without causing any obstruction or trouble. The *Journal Officiel* and special posts are to inform the public of the arrangements made in the interest of public order.

25 November: Mademoiselle Lia Félix came to rehearse *Sacer esto*, which she is to recite to the people on Monday.

Monsieur Tony Révillon, who is to make a speech, came to see me with the Committee of the Gens de Lettres.

A deputation of Americans from the United States came to express their indignation with the Government of the American Republic and with President Grant for abandoning France 'to whom the American Republic owes so much,' I said. 'Owes everything,' declared one of the Americans present.

A good deal of cannonading has been heard for several days. Today it was louder than ever.

Napoleon the Little is going to be published in a Paris edition similar to that of *Les Châtiments*. Hetzel sent me some copies this morning.

Madame Meurice wants some hens and rabbits in order to provide against the coming famine. She is having a hutch made for them in my little garden. The carpenter who is making it came into my room a little while ago and said: 'I would like to touch your hand.' I pressed both his hands in mine.

27 November: The Académie has given a sign of life. I have received official notice that from now on it will hold an extraordinary session every Tuesday.

Rat pies are being made. They are said to be very tasty.

An onion costs a sou. A potato costs a sou.

People have given up asking my authorization to recite my works, which are being recited everywhere without my permission. They are right. What I write is not my own. I am public property.

28 November: Noël Parfait came to ask my help for Châteaudun. Certainly: with all my heart!

Les Châtiments was recited *gratis* at the Opéra. A huge crowd. A gilt wreath was thrown on the stage. I gave it to Georges and Jeanne. The collection taken in Prussian helmets by the actresses produced 1,521 francs and 35 centimes in coppers.

Émile Allix brought us a leg of antelope from the Jardin des Plantes. It is excellent.

The sortie is due to be made tonight.

29 November: All night long I heard the cannon. The hens were installed in my garden today.

The sortie has been delayed. The bridge thrown across the

Marne by Ducrot has been swept away, the Prussians having blown open the locks.

30 November: All night long the cannon thundered. The battle continues.

At midnight last night I was returning home from the Pavillon de Rohan along the Rue de Richelieu, which was deserted, dark, and so to speak asleep at the time. I saw a window open on the sixth floor of a very high house just beyond the Bibliothèque Nationale, and a very bright light, which appeared to be that of an oil-lamp, appear and disappear several times; then the window closed and the street became dark again. Was it a signal?

The cannon can be heard at three points around Paris, to the east, west, and south. A triple attack is, in fact, being made on the ring the Prussians have drawn round us; at Saint-Denis by Laroncière, at Courbevoie by Vinoy, and on the Marne by Ducrot. Laroncière is said to have cleared the peninsula of Gennevilliers and compelled a Saxon regiment to lay down its arms, while Vinoy is said to have destroyed the Prussian works beyond Bougival. As for Ducrot, he has crossed the Marne, taken and retaken Montmesly, and almost holds Villiers-sur-Marne. Hearing the cannon, one feels a great desire to be there.

This evening Pelletan sent his son, Camille Pelletan, to inform me on behalf of the Government that tomorrow's operations will be decisive.

1 December: It seems that Louise Michel has been arrested.[8] I am going to do all that is necessary to have her released immediately. Madame Meurice is seeing to it. She went out this morning for that purpose.

   [8] Louise Michel (1830–1905), a former schoolmistress, was arrested for her inflammatory speeches and writings against the Government. She later took part in the insurrection of the Commune in 1871 and was sentenced to deportation. She returned to France under the amnesty of 1881. [Tr.]

Alton-Shée came to see me.

We ate bear for dinner.

I have written to the Prefect of Police to have Louise Michel released.

There was no fighting today. The positions taken were fortified.

2 December: Louise Michel has been released. She came to thank me.

Last night Monsieur Coquelin called to recite several pieces from *Les Châtiments*.

It is freezing. The basin of the Pigalle fountain is frozen over.

The cannonade started again this morning at dawn.

11.30 a.m. The cannonade is growing louder.

Flourens wrote to me yesterday and Rochefort today. They are coming round to my point of view.

Dorian, the Minister of Public Works, and Pelletan came to dine with me.

Excellent news tonight. The Army of the Loire is at Montargis. The Army of Paris has driven back the Prussians from the Avron plateau. The despatches announcing these successes were read aloud at the doors of the *mairies*. The crowd shouted: 'Long live the Republic!'

Victory! The Second of December has been wiped out.

3 December: General Renault, who was wounded in the foot by a shell splinter, is dead.

I told Schœlcher that I wanted to go out with my sons if the batteries of the National Guard to which they belong were sent to the front. The batteries have drawn lots. Four are to go. One of them is the 10th Battery of which Victor is a member. I will go out with that battery. Charles does not belong to it, which is a good thing; he will stay behind, he has two children. I will order him to stay. Vacquerie and

Meurice are members of the 10th Battery. We shall be together in the fight. I am going to have a cape with a hood
made for me. What I fear is the cold at night.

I made some shadows on the wall for Georges and Jeanne.
Jeanne laughed delightedly at the shadow and the profile's
grimaces, but when she saw that the shadow was me she
cried and screamed. She seemed to be saying: 'I don't want
you to be a ghost!' Poor, sweet angel! Perhaps she has a pre-
sentiment of the coming battle.

Yesterday we ate some stag; the day before, some bear;
and the two previous days some antelope. These were presents
from the Jardin des Plantes.

Tonight at eleven o'clock there was a brief, violent cannonade.

4 December: A notice has been posted on my door indicating
the precautions to be taken *In case of bombardment.* That is
the title of the notice.

There is a pause in the battle. Our army has recrossed the
Marne.

Little Jeanne crawls very well and says 'Papa' very prettily.

5 December: I have just seen a splendid hearse go by empty,
on its way to fetch its load. It was draped with black velvet,
embroidered with a silver H surrounded by silver stars. A
Roman would not scorn it.

Gautier came to dine with me. After dinner Banville and
Coppée called.

Bad news. Orleans has been taken from us again. No
matter. Let us persist.

7 December: I had Gautier, Banville, and François Coppée
to dinner. After dinner Asselineau came. I read *Floréal* and
L'Égout de Rome to them.

8 December: The *Patrie en Danger* has ceased to appear. For want of readers, says Blanqui.

Monsieur Maurice Lachâtre, a publisher, came to make me an offer for my next book. He has sent me his *Dictionary* and the *History of the Revolution* by Louis Blanc. I shall give him *Napoleon the Little* and *Les Châtiments*.

9 December: I woke up in the night and wrote some poetry. At the same time I could hear the cannon.

Monsieur Bowes came to see me. The correspondent of *The Times* at Versailles has written to tell him that the guns for the bombardment of Paris have arrived. They are Krupp guns. They are waiting for their carriages. They are lined up in the Prussian arsenal at Versailles, according to this Englishman, side by side, 'like bottles in a cellar'.

I copy the following item from a newspaper:

Monsieur Victor Hugo has expressed the intention of leaving Paris unarmed, with the artillery battery of the National Guard to which his two sons belong.

The 144th Battalion of the National Guard went in a body to the poet's residence in the Avenue Frochot. Their delegates called on him.

These honourable citizens went to forbid Victor Hugo to carry out his plan, which he had announced a long time ago in his *Address to the Germans.*

'Everybody can fight,' the deputation told him. 'But everybody cannot write *Les Châtiments*. Stay at home and take care of a life which is so precious to France.'

I cannot remember the number of the battalion. It was not the 144th. Here are the terms of the address which was read to me by the major of the battalion:

The National Guard of Paris forbids Victor Hugo to go to the front, inasmuch as everybody can go to the front, whereas Victor Hugo alone can do what Victor Hugo does.

'Forbids' is touching and charming.

11 December: Rostan came to see me. He has his arm in a sling. He was wounded at Créteil. It was at night. A German soldier rushed at him and pierced his arm with a bayonet. Rostan retaliated with a bayonet thrust in the German's shoulder. Both fell and rolled into a ditch. Then they became good friends. Rostan speaks a little broken German.

'Who are you?'

'I am a Wurtemberger. I am twenty-two years old. My father is a Leipzig clockmaker.'

They remained in the ditch for three hours, bleeding, numb with cold, helping each other. Rostan, wounded though he was, brought the man who wounded him back as a prisoner. He goes to see him in hospital. These two men worship each other. They wanted to kill each other, and now they would die for each other.

Eliminate kings from the dispute!

Visit from Monsieur Rey. The Ledru-Rollin group is completely disorganized. No more parties; the Republic. That is good.

I presented some Dutch cheese to Madame Paul Meurice.

Sleet is falling.

12 December: I arrived in Brussels nineteen years ago today.

13 December: Since yesterday Paris has been lighted by petroleum.

A heavy cannonade tonight.

14 December: Thaw. Cannonade.

Tonight we glanced through Goya's *Disasters of War* (brought along by Burty, the art critic). It is beautiful and horrible.

15 December: Emmanuel Arago, the Minister of Justice, came to see me and informed me that there would be fresh meat until 15 February, but that from now on only brown bread would be made in Paris. There will be enough of this to last for five months.

Allix brought me a medal struck to commemorate my return to France. It bears on one side a winged genius and the words 'Liberty, Equality, and Fraternity', and on the other side, round the rim: 'Appeal to Universal Democracy' and in the centre: 'To Victor Hugo, From His Grateful Fatherland. September 1870.'

This medal is sold in the streets and costs 5 centimes. There is a little ring on it by which it can be hung on a chain.

16 December: Pelleport came tonight. I asked him to visit Flourens, in Mazas Prison, on my behalf, and to take him a copy of *Napoleon the Little*.

17 December: The *Électeur Libre* calls on Louis Blanc and me to enter the Government, and declares that it is our duty to do so. My duty is dictated to me by my conscience.

I saw the gunboat *Estoc* pass under the Pont des Arts, going up the Seine. She is a fine boat and her big gun is extremely imposing.

18 December: I worked the magic lantern for little Georges and little Jeanne.

My royalty from Madame Favart's recitation of *Stella* at a performance given by the 14th Battalion amounted to 130 francs. My agent took my royalty in spite of my instructions. I have ordered him to turn the money over to the sick fund of the battalion.

Monsieur Hetzel writes: 'The closing of all the printing works is imminent, for want of coal to keep the presses going.'

I authorize another impression of 3,000 copies of *Les Châtiments*, which will bring the total for Paris up to 22,000.

20 December: Captain Breton, of the Garde Mobile, who has been cashiered on the charge of being a coward, brought by his lieutenant-colonel, demands a court-martial—but first of all to be sent to the front. His company leaves tomorrow morning. He begs me to obtain from the Minister of War permission for him to go and get himself killed. I have written to General Le Flô about him. I think that Captain Breton will be in tomorrow's battle.

21 December: At three o'clock this morning I heard the bugles of the troops marching to battle. When will my turn come?

22 December: Yesterday was a good day. The action continues. The thunder of cannon can be heard all the way from the east to the west.

Little Jeanne is beginning to talk at some length and very expressively. But it is impossible to understand a word she says. She laughs.

Leopold has sent me thirteen fresh eggs, which I will reserve for little Georges and little Jeanne.

Louis Blanc came to dine with me. He came on behalf of Edmond Adam, Louis Jourdan, Cernuschi, and others, to tell me that he and I must go to Trochu and call on him to save Paris or resign. I refused. I should be posing as an arbiter of the situation and at the same time hindering a battle which had begun and which may be successful. Louis Blanc shared my opinion, as did Meurice, Vacquerie, and my sons, who also dined with me.

23 December: Henri Rochefort came to dine with me. I had not seen him since August of last year, when we were in Brussels. Georges did not recognize his godfather. I was very cordial. I like him very much. He has great talent and great courage. The dinner was a very merry one, although we are all in danger of being incarcerated in a Prussian fortress if Paris is captured. After Guernsey, Spandau. So be it.

I bought for 19 francs at the Magasins du Louvre a grey soldier's cape with a hood, to wear at the front.

My house continues to be crowded with visitors every evening. Today a painter called Le Genissel called. He reminded me that I saved him from the galleys in 1848. He was one of the June insurgents.

Heavy cannonade during the night. A battle is in preparation.

24 December: It is freezing. Ice floes are floating down the Seine.

Paris eats only brown bread now.

25 December: Heavy cannonade all night.

An item of news of present-day Paris. A basket of oysters has just reached the city. It sold for 750 francs.

At a bazaar in aid of the poor at which Alice and Madame Meurice acted as vendors, a young turkey fetched 250 francs.

There are ice floes on the Seine.

26 December: Louis Blanc called, then Monsieur Floquet. They urged me to call on the Government to do something or resign. I again refused.

Monsieur Louis Koch paid 25 francs for a copy of the *Rappel* at the Bazaar in aid of the poor. The copy of *Les Châtiments* was bought by Monsieur Cernuschi for 300 francs.

27 December: Violent cannonade this morning.

The firing this morning was an attack by the Prussians. That is a good sign. Waiting bores them. Us too. They fired nineteen shells, which killed nobody, into the Fort of Mon-rouge.

Madame Ugalde dined with us and sang *Patria*. I escorted Madame Ugalde to her home in the Rue Chabannais, then returned home to go to bed.

The concierge said to me:

'Monsieur, they say that shells are going to fall in this neighbourhood tonight.'

'That is all right,' I replied. 'I am expecting one.'

29 December: Heavy firing all night. The Prussian attack continues.

Théophile Gautier has a horse. This horse was requisi-tioned. It was wanted for food. Gautier wrote to me begging me to save the animal. I asked the Minister to grant his re-quest. I saved the horse.

It is unfortunately true that Dumas is dead. This is known through the German newspapers. He died on 5 December at his son's home at Le Puys, near Dieppe.

I am being urged more strongly than ever to enter the Government. The Minister of Justice, Monsieur Emmanuel Arago, called and stayed to dinner. We talked. Louis Blanc dropped in after dinner. I persist in my refusal.

Besides Emmanuel Arago and the friends who usually dine with me on Thursdays, Rochefort came with Blum. I invited them to come every Thursday if we still have a few Thursdays to live. At dessert I drank Rochefort's health.

The cannonade is increasing. The plateau of Avron has had to be evacuated.

30 December: Alton-Shée called on me this morning. It appears that General Ducrot wants to see me.

In the past three days the Prussians have sent us over 12,000 shells.

Yesterday I ate some rat.

As from next week there will be no more laundry washed in Paris, because there is no more coal.

Lieutenant Farcy, the commander of the gunboat, dined with me.

It is bitterly cold. For three days I have worn my cloak and hood whenever I have had to go out.

A doll for little Jeanne. A basketful of toys for Georges.

The shells have started to demolish the Fort of Rosny. The first shell has fallen in the city itself. The Prussians today fired 6,000 shells at us.

In the Fort of Rosny a sailor working at the gabions was carrying a sack of earth on his shoulder. A shell knocked it off. 'Much obliged,' said the sailor, 'but I wasn't tired.'

Alexandre Dumas died on 5 December. Looking through this notebook I see that it was on 5 December that a large hearse with an H on it passed me in the Rue Frochot.

It is no longer even horse that we are eating now. Perhaps it is dog? Maybe it is rat? I am beginning to suffer from pains in the stomach. We are eating the unknown!

Monsieur Valois, representing the Société des Gens de Lettres, came to ask me what was to be done with the 8,000 francs remaining from the proceeds of the three readings of *Les Châtiments*, the guns having been delivered and paid for. I told him to hand the whole amount over to Madame Jules Simon for the fund for the victims of the war.

1 January 1871: Louis Blanc has addressed a letter on the situation to me through the newspapers.

Little Georges and little Jeanne were amazed and dumbfounded at their basketful of New Year presents. The toys, when unpacked from the basket, covered a large table. The children touched all of them and did not know which to take. Georges was nearly mad with happiness. Charles remarked: 'It is the despair of joy!'

I am hhngry. I am cold. So much the better. I suffer what the people are suffering.

U

Decidedly horse is not good for me. Yet I ate some. It gave me the gripes.

The Prussians are bombarding Saint-Denis.

2 January: Daumier and Louis Blanc lunched with us.

Louis Koch gave his aunt as a New Year gift a couple of cabbages and a brace of live partridges!

This morning we lunched on wine soup. The elephant at the Jardin des Plantes has been slaughtered. He wept. He is going to be eaten.

The Prussians go on sending us 6,000 shells.

3 January: Heating two rooms at the Pavillon de Rohan now costs 10 francs a day.

The Montagnard club again demands that Louis Blanc and I be added to the Government in order to direct it. I continue to refuse.

There are at present twelve members of the French Académie in Paris, among them Ségur, Mignet, Dufaure, Haussonville, Legouvé, Cuvillier-Fleury, Barbier, and Vitet.

Bright moonlight. Intense cold. The Prussians bombarded Saint-Denis all night.

From Tuesday to Sunday the Prussians hurled 25,000 projectiles at us. It took 220 railway trucks to carry them. Each shot costs 60 francs; total, 1,500,000 francs. The damage to the forts is estimated at 1,400 francs. About ten men have been killed. Each of our dead costs the Prussians 150,000 francs.

5 January: The bombardment is becoming heavier. Issy and Vanves are being shelled.

There is a shortage of coal. Clothes cannot be washed because they cannot be dried. My washerwoman sent this message to me through Mariette:

'If Monsieur Victor Hugo, who is so powerful, would ask the Government to give me a little coal-dust, I could wash his shirts.'

Besides my usual Thursday guests I had Louis Blanc, Rochefort, and Paul de Saint-Victor to dinner. Madame Jules Simon sent me a Gruyère cheese. An extraordinary luxury, this. We were thirteen at table.

6 January: Out of curiosity the Parisians visit the bombarded districts. They go to see the shells fall as they would go to a firework display. National Guards have to keep the people back. The Prussians are firing on the hospitals. They are shelling Val-de-Grâce. Their shells set fire last night to the wooden booths in the Luxembourg, which were full of sick and wounded men who had to be transported, undressed and wrapped up as well as they could be, to the Charité Hospital. Barbieux saw them arrive there about one o'clock in the morning.

Sixteen streets have already been hit by shells.

7 January: The Rue des Feuillantines, which runs through the place where the garden of my childhood used to be, is under heavy fire. I was nearly struck by a shell there.

My washerwoman, having nothing to make a fire with, and being obliged to refuse work as a result, addressed a demand to Monsieur Clemenceau, the Mayor of the Ninth Arrondissement, for some coal, which she said she was ready to pay for. I endorsed it in these terms:

'I am resigned to everything for the defence of Paris, to die of hunger and cold, and even to forgo changing my shirt. However, I commend my laundress to the Mayor of the Ninth Arrondissement.'

And I signed my name. The Mayor gave her the coal.

8 January: Camille Pelletan brought us good news from the Government. Rouen and Dijon retaken, Garibaldi victorious at Nuits, and Faidherbe at Bapaume. All goes well.

We had brown bread, now we have black bread. Everybody fares alike. That is good.

Yesterday's news was brought by two pigeons.

A shell has killed five children in a school in the Rue de Vaugirard.

The performance and readings of *Les Châtiments* have had to be stopped, the theatres having no more gas for lighting or coal for heating.

Prim is dead. He was shot in Madrid the day the King after his own heart, Amedeus, Duke of Genoa, entered Spain.[9]

The bombardment was a furious one today. A shell fell in the chapel of the Virgin at Saint-Sulpice, where my mother's funeral took place and where I was married.

10 January: Shells on the Odéon Theatre.

Chifflard sent me a piece of a shell. This shell, which fell at Auteuil, is marked with an H. I am going to have an inkstand made out of it.

12 January: As from today the Pavillon de Rohan asks me to pay 8 francs a head for dinner, which wit hwine, coffee, fire, etc., brings the cost of dinner up to 13 francs for each person.

We had elephant steak for luncheon today.

Schœlcher, Rochefort, Blum, and all the usual Thursday guests dined with us. After dinner Louis Blanc and Pelletan dropped in.

[9] Juan Prim Y Prats (1814–1870) was one of the Spanish generals who brought about the overthrow of Isabella II in 1868. His search for a king for Spain was one of the contributory causes of the Franco-Prussian War. [Tr.]

13 January: An egg costs 2 francs 75 centimes. Elephant meat costs 40 francs a pound. A sack of onions costs 800 francs.

The Société des Gens de Lettres asked me to attend the presentation of the cannon to the city at the Hôtel de Ville. I begged to be excused. I will not go.

We spent the day looking for another hotel. Nothing suitable. All are closed. Expenses for the week at the Pavillon de Rohan (including the cost of a broken window-pane), 701 francs 50 centimes.

Remark by a poor woman about some newly felled wood. 'I feel sorry for this poor green wood; it didn't expect to be put on the fire, and it weeps all the time!'

15 January: A furious bombardment is in progress. I have written a poem entitled *Dans le Cirque*. After dinner I read it to my Sunday guests. They want me to publish it. I will give it to the newspapers.

17 January: The bombardment has been going on for three nights and three days without pause.

Little Jeanne was cross with me because I would not let her play with the works of my watch.

All the newspapers publish my poem *Dans le Cirque*. It may do some good.

Louis Blanc called this morning. He urged me to join with Quinet and himself in bringing pressure to bear upon the Government. I replied: 'I see more danger in overthrowing the Government than in supporting it.'

18 January: Monsieur Krupp is making guns for use against balloons.

There is a cock in my little garden. Yesterday Louis Blanc lunched with us. The cock crowed. Louis Blanc stopped and said:

'Listen!'

'What is it?'

'The cock is crowing.'

'Well, what of it?'

'Don't you hear what it is saying?'

'No.'

'It is crowing: "Victor Hugo!"'

We listened and laughed. Louis Blanc was right. It did sound as if the cock were crowing my name.

I gave the hens some crumbs from our black bread. They would not eat them.

This morning a sortie against Montretout was made. Montretout was taken. This evening the Prussians recaptured it from us.

20 January: The attack on Montretout has interrupted the bombardment.

A child of fourteen has been suffocated in a crowd outside a baker's shop.

21 January: Louis Blanc came to see me. We held a council. The situation is becoming urgent and desperate. The *mairie* of Paris wants my advice.

Louis Blanc dined with us. After dinner we held a sort of council at which Colonel Laussedat was present.

22 January: The Prussians are bombarding Saint-Denis.

Stormy demonstrations at the Hôtel de Ville. Trochu withdraws. Rostan comes to tell me that the Breton mobiles are firing on the people. I doubt it. I will go myself, if necessary.

I have just returned. There was a simultaneous attack by both sides. To the combatants who consulted me I said: 'In

the hands of Frenchmen I recognize only those rifles which
are aimed at the Prussians.'

Rostan said to me:

'I have come to place my battalion at your disposal. We are
500 men. Where do you want us to go?'

'Where are you now?' I asked.

'We were massed near Saint-Denis, which is being shelled,'
he replied. 'Now we are at La Villette.'

'Then stay there,' I said. 'It is there that I would have sent
you. Do not march against the Hôtel de Ville, march against
Prussia.'

23 January: Last night there was a conference in my rooms.
In addition to my Sunday guests, Rochefort and his secretary, Mourot, dined with us. Rey and Gambon came in the
evening. They brought me, each with a request for support,
the former Ledru-Rollin's poster-programme (an assembly of
200 members) and the latter the programme of the Republican
Union (50 members). I declared that I approved of neither the
one nor the other.

Chanzy has been beaten. Bourbaki is making headway.
But he is not marching on Paris. This is a puzzle of which I
fancy I can half guess the secret.

There seems to be an interruption in the bombardment.

24 January: Flourens called this morning. He asked for my
advice. I replied: 'No violent pressure on the situation.'

25 January: Flourens is reported to have been arrested as he
was leaving the house after calling on me.

I had a couple of fresh eggs cooked for Georges and Jeanne.

Monsieur Dorian came to the Pavillon de Rohan this morning to see my sons. He announced that capitulation is
imminent. Frightful news from outside. Chanzy defeated,
Faidherbe defeated, Bourbaki driven pack.

27 January: Schœlcher came to tell me that he was resigning as colonel of the artillery legion.

Again I have been asked to head a demonstration against the Hôtel de Ville. All sorts of rumours are in the air. To everybody I counsel calmness and unity.

28 January: In the course of the negotiations at Versailles Bismarck said to Jules Favre: 'What do you think of that fool of an Empress proposing peace to me!'

It has turned cold again.

Ledru-Rollin (through Brives) says he wants to come to an understanding with me.

Jeanne, the sweet little thing, is poorly.

Leopold told me this evening that I was the subject of a dialogue between Pope Pius IX and Jules Hugo, my nephew, the brother of Leopold, who died a *camerico* of the Pope. The Pope, seeing Jules, said to him:

'Your name is Hugo, is it not?'

'Yes, Holy Father.'

'Are you a relative of Victor Hugo?'

'His nephew, Holy Father.'

'How old is he?' (This was in 1857.)

'Fifty-five.'

'Alas! He is too old to return to the Church!'

Charles tells me that Jules Simon and his two sons spent the night drawing up lists of possible candidates for the National Assembly.

Cernuschi is having himself naturalized a French citizen!

29 January: The armistice was signed yesterday. It was published this morning. The National Assembly will be elected between February 5 and 18, and will meet on the 12th at Bordeaux.

Little Jeanne is a trifle better. She almost smiled at me.

No more balloons. The post. But the letters unsealed. It is snowing. It is freezing.

30 January: Little Jeanne is still poorly and does not play. Mademoiselle Périga brought me a fresh egg for Jeanne.

31 January: Little Jeanne is still ill. She is suffering from a slight attack of catarrh of the stomach. Doctor Allix says it will last another four or five days.

My nephew Leopold came to dine with us. He brought us some pickled oysters.

1 February: Little Jeanne is better. She smiled at me.

2 February: The Paris elections have been postponed to 8 February.

Horsemeat continues to disagree with me. Pains in the stomach.

Little Jeanne's improvement continues.

4 February: The weather is becoming milder.

A crowd of visitors this evening. Proclamation by Gambetta.

5 February: The list of candidates of the Republican newspapers appeared this morning. I am at the head of the list.

Bancel is dead.

Little Jeanne has recovered from her cold this evening.

I entertained my usual Sunday guests. We had fish, butter, and white bread for dinner.

6 February: Bourbaki, defeated, has killed himself. A noble death.

Ledru-Rollin is drawing back from the Assembly. Louis Blanc came and read this news to me tonight.

7 February: We had three or four cans of preserves which we ate today.

8 February: Today the elections were held for the National Assembly. Paul Meurice and I went to vote together in the Rue Clauzel.

After the capitulation had been signed, Bismarck, leaving Jules Favre, went into the room where his two secretaries were waiting for him and said: 'The animal is dead.'

I have put my papers in order in readiness for my departure.

Little Jeanne is very merry.

11 February: The counting of the votes is going very slowly.

Our departure for Bordeaux has been put off to Monday the 13th.

12 February: Yesterday, for the first time, I saw *my* boulevard. It is a fairly long stretch of the old Boulevard Haussmann. *Boulevard Victor Hugo* is placarded on the Boulevard Haussmann at the corners of four or five streets giving on to this boulevard.

The National Assembly opens today at Bordeaux. The result of the elections in Paris has not yet been determined and proclaimed.

Although I have not yet been elected, time presses, and I expect to leave for Bordeaux tomorrow. There will be nine of us, five masters and four servants, plus the two children. Louis

Blanc wants to leave with us. We shall make the journey together.

In my bag I shall take various important manuscripts and
works that I have begun, including *Paris Besieged* and the
poem *Grand-Père*.

13 February: Yesterday, before dinner, I read two poems
which will form part of *Paris Besieged* ('To Little Jeanne' and
'No, You will not take Alsace and Lorraine') to my guests,
Monsieur and Madame Paul Meurice, Vacquerie, Lockroy
and Monsieur and Madame Ernest Lefèvre, Louis Koch and
Villain (Rochefort and Victor did not arrive until the dinner
hour).

Pelleport brought me our nine passes. Not having yet been
proclaimed a Representative, I wrote on mine: 'Victor Hugo,
Landowner', as the Prussians require the quality or profession
of the holder of the pass to be stated.

It was with a heavy heart that I left this morning the
Avenue Frochot, and the pleasant hospitality that Paul
Meurice has extended to me since my arrival in Paris on 5
September.

THIERS AND ROCHEFORT

1 October 1871

I WENT to see Monsieur Thiers for Rochefort. At half-past
twelve departure for Versailles. In the train a man wearing
yellow gloves seemed to recognize me and scowled at me.

Arrival at Versailles at half-past one. Rain and sunshine.
At two o'clock I entered the Prefecture, where Monsieur
Thiers is living. I was shown into a room hung with crimson
silk.

A moment afterwards, Thiers entered. He held out his

hand, and I took it. He led me along some corridors and stair-cases to a secluded apartment where he had a small fire lit. We chatted together. The interview was a long one and reasonably cordial. I congratulated him on what he had done for the liberation of the territory, and added: 'But there is a great gulf between my opinions and yours. Between us there are dissensions in which you stand firm, and so do I; but an encounter in the sphere of conscience is possible. The so-called Commission for Pardons is so ferocious that we cannot hope for any official commutation for Rochefort, but in default of that there can be a commutation in fact.'

This is what I obtained from Thiers for Rochefort:

Rochefort will not be transported. He will serve his sentence in a French fortress. I objected to a fortress, to Belle Isle, to Mont Saint-Michel.

Thiers said to me: 'I will bear your wishes in mind; I will do more.' I declared in favour of Nice. Rochefort will be able to see his family as much as he pleases. As he has to live, he will be able to write the history of Napoleon III, as he wishes to do, and then in six or seven months the amnesty will come and he will be free.

I should add that Thiers went into details a good deal. Notably, he described to me private scenes in the Assembly and in the councils of war, and his conversations with the Emperor of Austria about the Emperor of Germany, whom the Emperor of Austria calls 'my uncle'. Suddenly Thiers stopped and remarked: 'I am saying too much.' Then he went on: 'No, I know that I am dealing with an honest man.' I said to him: 'Set your mind at rest.' For this reason I cannot relate this conversation in greater detail.

He said: 'I am like you, a conquered man who looks like a conqueror. I, like yourself, walk through a whirlwind of abuse. A hundred journals drag my name in the gutter every morning. I ignore them.'

I replied: 'That is exactly what I do. Your method is the same as mine.' And I added: 'To read diatribes is to breathe the decomposition of one's reputation.'

He laughed and shook hands with me.

I called his attention to the atrocities already committed, and I urged him not to allow any of the condemned to be executed. I begged him to muzzle the men in epaulets. I insisted on an amnesty, and he replied: 'I am only a poor devil of a dictator in a black coat.'

The interview began at quarter-past two and lasted until half-past three.

At four o'clock I set off on the return journey to Paris.

In my compartment there were two young officers fresh from Saint-Cyr, and a young woman with a young man, probably her husband. She was reading a paper, the *Éclipse*, in which there was a caricature of Henri V by Gill. I was looking at Sèvres and the woods of Meudon. Suddenly the young woman pointed to a line in the paper, and said:

'Ah! Look—Victor Hugo.'

'Careful!' said the young man. 'He is there.'

And he pointed me out discreetly.

The young woman took my hat, which was lying on the seat, and kissed the crape on it; then she said to me:

'You have suffered greatly, sir. Go on defending the vanquished.' And she wept.

I kissed her hand. She was a charming creature, and had beautiful eyes.

I gave her my hand to help her down from the carriage at Paris, and after exchanging greetings, we went our opposite ways and mixed with the crowd.

A RETROSPECT

I HAVE had as friends and allies, I have seen successively pass before me, and according to the changes and chances of destiny I have received in my house, sometimes in my private

life, chancellors, peers, dukes, Pasquier, Pontécoulant, Montalembert, Bellune; and great men, Lamennais, Lamartine,
Chateaubriand; a President of the Republic, Manin; revolutionary leaders, Louis Blanc, Montanelli, Arago, Héliade;
popular generals, Garibaldi, Mazzini, Kossuth, Mieroslawski;
and artists, Rossini, David d'Angers, Pradier, Meyerbeer,
Eugène Delacroix; marshals, Soult, Mackau; and sergeants,
Boni, Heurtebise; bishops, the Cardinal of Besançon, Monsieur de Rohan, the Cardinal of Bordeaux, Monsieur Donnet;
and actors and actresses, Frédérick Lemaître, Mademoiselle
Rachel, Mademoiselle Mars, Madame Dorval, Macready;
ministers and ambassadors, Moli, Guizot, Thiers, Lord
Palmerston, Lord Normanby, Monsieur de Ligne; and a
peasant, Charles Durand; princes, Imperial and Royal Highnesses and plain Highnesses, the Duc d'Orléans, Ernest of
Saxe-Coburg, the Princess of Canino, Louis, Charles, Pierre,
and Napoleon Bonaparte; and a shoemaker, Guay; kings and
emperors, Jerome of Westphalia, Max of Bavaria, the Emperor of Brazil; and a street conjuror, Bourillon. I have
sometimes had at one and the same time in my two hands the
gloved and white hand of the upper class, and the clumsy,
black hand of the lower class, and have recognized that there
is only one man. After all these have passed before me, I say
that humanity has a synonym—Equality; and that under
Heaven there is only one thing that one should bow to—
Genius; and only one thing that one should kneel to—
Goodness.